Praise for *Mississippi in Africa*:

"A superior historical and journalistic investigation. . . . [Huffman's] reports from the field are full of smart observations on the history of a nation that, although closely linked to the U.S., has too long been ignored. . . . Thought-provoking and expertly told."
—*Kirkus Reviews* (starred review)

"Part U.S. history, part African history, part genealogy, part investigative reporting, part travelogue, part biography, part memoir, part mea culpa. Huffman has tried to accomplish a great deal in slightly more than 300 pages. . . . Compelling."
—Steve Weinberg, *Atlanta Journal-Constitution*

"[Huffman] creates a deeply empathetic portrait of a country that usually gets nothing but bad headlines. . . . A great story. In the journey from Mississippi to Liberia, Huffman has uncovered a fascinating tale that's spent too long in obscurity."
—Dave Gilson, *San Francisco Chronicle*

"*Mississippi in Africa* tells of heroism too often deprecated and of depravity too painful to contemplate. . . . Considering the narrative from both historical and contemporary perspectives provides extraordinary insight in the matter of race in the modern world. . . . Well-meaning and generous."
—Ira Berlin, *The New York Times Book Review*

"A fascinating explanation of what he acknowledges is a 'long, contentious, and unevenly documented' story . . . Huffman tells a provocative story in an evenhanded manner, and in the process we learn little-known facts about slavery, Liberian history, and U.S.-Liberian relations." —Elizabeth Bennett, *Houston Chronicle*

"An amazing tale, and Huffman is a capable writer, sensitive to its troubling contradictions. . . . The book is a page-turner, illuminating a history little discussed in the United States and deserving of our attention."
—Liza Featherstone, *Newsday*

"*Mississippi in Africa* reads almost like two separate books: one about what happened here, the other about how what happened here affected what's now happening in Liberia. Each story is interesting in its own right. Taken together, they illustrate the bitter irony of slaves who would kill to leave America, and Liberians who are dying to return." —Dan Danbom, *Rocky Mountain News*

"Alan Huffman engagingly illuminates that history by recounting how a place came to be called 'Mississippi in Africa'. . . . A compelling storyteller, Huffman illustrates the utter futility of colonialism and of any impulse to dominate others." —Anne Grant, *Providence Journal*

"Huffman's *Mississippi in Africa: The Saga of the Slaves of Prospect Hill Plantation and Their Legacy in Liberia Today* pieces together history, descendants' stories, and current observations for a provocative read. An eye and ear for telling details sweep the story along, from crumbling Jefferson County records to the 'post-apocalyptic' streets of Liberian capital Monrovia." —Sherry Lucas, *Clarion-Ledger* (Mississippi)

"*Mississippi in Africa* will be a work of enduring interest because of Huffman's skill in doing two things—telling the personal and individual stories in a humane and compelling fashion and setting the entire story in a broad historical and national context. Few writers handle both of these items well." —Scott Naugle, *Biloxi Sun Herald*

"[Huffman] tells this stranger-than-fiction story in compelling style, capturing the hope, conflict, and tragedy of the endeavor. . . . Events move swiftly in this complex and turbulent tale, but with the skill of a Southern storyteller, Huffman weaves the threads together in a clear and readable narrative. Piecing together a story he first heard about during his own Mississippi childhood, he has produced a well researched account that illuminates a distant event and its lasting legacy." —Glenn Townes, *Book Page*

"A captivating true story that spans cultures on two continents, and calls into question American colonialism and the good intentions that have paved the road to the deprivation and strife in modern West Africa. . . . In Huffman's hands, the real story behind the slaves of Prospect Hill and the tumultuous history of the colonization effort in Liberia is brought to life. It is a lost chapter of American history that illuminates the legacy of slavery."

—*Northside Sun* (Mississippi)

"An engaging meditation on tangled race relations in the American South." —Curtis Wilkie, author of *Dixie: A Personal Odyssey Through Events That Shaped the Modern South*

"Alan Huffman has pulled from the dust bin of history a saga of immense present-day significance."

—William Winter, former governor of Mississippi

"An absolute must-read for everyone who is interested in the tangled history of the American South and of colonialism in Africa."

—Ellen Douglas, author of the novels *A Lifetime Burning; Can't Quit You, Baby;* and *Truth: Four Stories I Am Finally Old Enough to Tell*

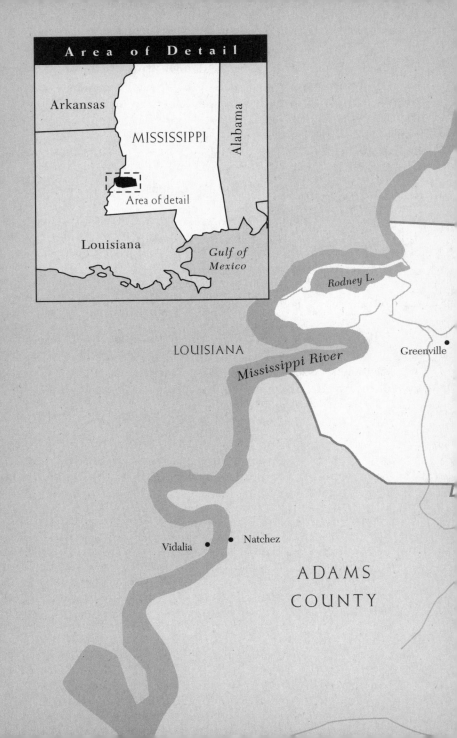

Area of Detail

Arkansas

MISSISSIPPI

Alabama

Area of detail

Louisiana

Gulf of Mexico

Rodney L.

LOUISIANA

Greenville

Mississippi River

Vidalia   Natchez

ADAMS
COUNTY

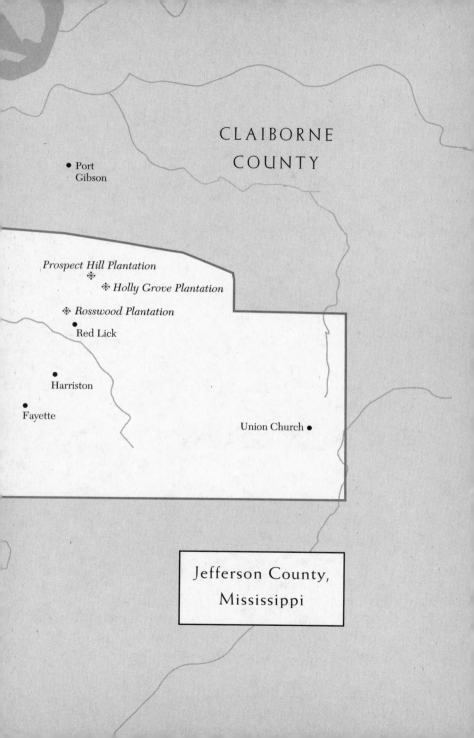

CLAIBORNE
COUNTY

● Port
Gibson

Prospect Hill Plantation
✳
✳ *Holly Grove Plantation*

✳ *Rosswood Plantation*
● Red Lick

●
Harriston
●
Fayette

Union Church ●

Jefferson County,
Mississippi

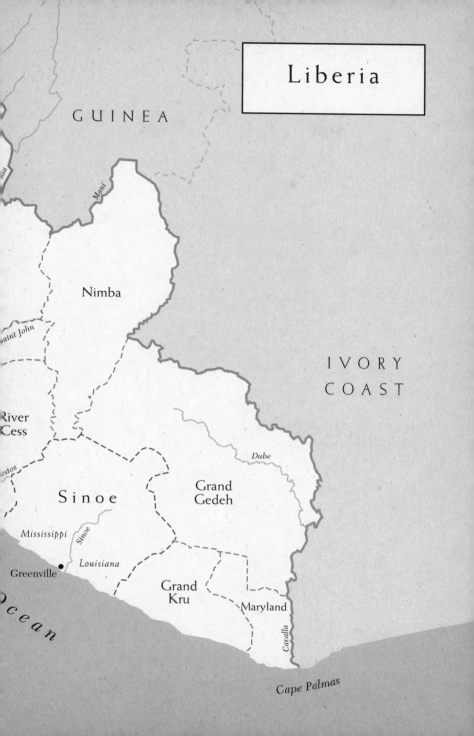

MISSISSIPPI IN AFRICA

Alan Huffman

GOTHAM BOOKS

For my parents

GOTHAM BOOKS
Published by Penguin Group (USA) Inc.
375 Hudson Street, New York, New York 10014, U.S.A.
Penguin Group (Canada), 10 Alcorn Avenue, Toronto, Ontario, Canada   M4V 3B2
(a division of Pearson Penguin Canada Inc.); Penguin Books Ltd, 80 Strand, London WC2R
0RL, England; Penguin Ireland, 25 St Stephen's Green, Dublin 2, Ireland (a division of
Penguin Books Ltd); Penguin Group (Australia), 250 Camberwell Road, Camberwell, Victoria
3124, Australia (a division of Pearson Australia Group Pty Ltd); Penguin Books India Pvt Ltd,
11 Community Centre, Panchsheel Park, New Delhi - 110 017, India; Penguin Group (NZ),
Cnr Airborne and Rosedale Roads, Albany, Auckland, New Zealand (a division of Pearson
New Zealand Ltd); Penguin Books (South Africa) (Pty) Ltd, 24 Sturdee Avenue, Rosebank,
Johannesburg 2196, South Africa

Penguin Books Ltd, Registered Offices: 80 Strand, London WC2R 0RL, England

Published by Gotham Books, a division of Penguin Group (USA) Inc.
Previously published as a Gotham Books hardcover edition.

First printing, January 2005
10   9   8   7   6   5   4   3   2   1

Gotham Books and the skyscraper logo are trademarks of Penguin Group (USA) Inc.

THE LIBRARY OF CONGRESS HAS CATALOGED THE GOTHAM BOOKS
HARDCOVER EDITION AS FOLLOWS:

Huffman, Alan.
    Mississippi in Africa : the saga of the slaves of Prospect Hill Plantation and their legacy
in Liberia today / by Alan Huffman.
       p.   cm.
    ISBN 1-592-40044-2 (acid-free paper)
    1-592-40100-7 (pbk.)
1. Slave insurrections—Mississippi—Jefferson County—History—19th century.   2. Plantation
life—Mississippi—Jefferson County—History—19th century.   3. Jefferson County (Miss.)—
Race relations.   4. Ross family.   5. Wills—Mississippi—Jefferson County—History—19th
century.   6. Plantation owners—Mississippi—Jefferson County—Biography.   7. Slaves—
Mississippi—Jefferson County—Biography.   8. Freedmen—Mississippi—Jefferson County—
Biography.   9. Jefferson County (Miss.)—Biography   10. Liberia—Biography.   I. Title.

F332.J4H835   2004   976.2'28300496073—dc21   2003013458

Printed in the United States of America
Set in New Caledonia

INTRODUCTION

LONG SLATS OF MOONLIGHT fall through the shuttered window, across the floor, and up the legs of the massive old grand piano that commands a corner of my living room. It is the middle of the night and the room is still and quiet, which is odd, considering that a few moments before, I was awakened by the sound of random banging on the piano keys. I had pictured my dog Jack with his paws on the ivory, chasing a moth, but in the dim light I see that the piano's keyboard is closed, and that Jack is nowhere to be found. There is no moth fluttering dumbly against the windowpanes.

When I later recount the story to friends, their first reaction is to blame the noise on ghosts, but that is not what comes to mind as I stand scratching my head at three A.M. I think instead of the discord unleashed upon the world by one of the piano's former owners, Isaac Ross Wade, who has been consuming my thoughts lately and, from all appearances, is now entering my dreams.

I first saw the old square grand piano in my friend Gwen Shipp's home in Slate Springs, Mississippi, in the late 1970s, when her son, Tinker Miller, and I stopped by to visit during a duck-hunting trip. Gwen was particularly proud of the piano because it had originally belonged to a Revolutionary War veteran named Isaac Ross, who was Wade's grandfather and from whom Gwen is descended. It is a beautiful piece of furniture, crafted of rosewood and ebony, made for the sort of pleasant, restless melodies that once resonated through the hushed parlors of the Old South. But after too many long, hot summers in houses without air-conditioning, its soundboard is warped and most of its notes are false. It has not played music for a very long time.

The piano had previously occupied a prominent spot in the parlor of Gwen's old family home, Holly Grove, which is now my house, and prior to that it had narrowly missed destruction at two family homes that burned. The first fire, at Ross's plantation mansion, Prospect Hill, occurred in 1845, midway through a decade of litigation over his controversial will, allegedly as a result of a slave uprising. The uprising and fire, as well as their preamble and aftermath, were defining moments for many people in Jefferson County, Mississippi, at the time, and would remain so for certain of their descendants for the next century and a half. The piano was my portal into the story.

You hear a lot of interesting stories growing up in the South, and if you listen closely, you can't help wondering how much of what you're told is true. The story of Prospect Hill was the most intriguing I had come across, and had one of the widest margins for error, if only because so much was at stake and the cast of characters was so diverse. Before I knew what I was getting into, I was committed to finding out what really happened, and now, after devoting several years to researching and unraveling it, I am finally able to tell the story in full.

Holly Grove was an early kit house, manufactured in Cincinnati and brought down the Mississippi River and overland to Jefferson County, where it was assembled on the Killingsworth family's cotton plantation in 1832. When I first visited the house in 1971, it had been empty for decades and was used only for family reunions, but it still contained furnishings dating from the frontier era to the 1940s. It was isolated and had never been repainted, and had no electricity or running water. It felt frozen in time. When we were in high school, Tinker and I and a group of our friends sometimes camped in Holly Grove's musty parlor, in sleeping bags stretched out atop faded, tattered Oriental rugs. It was on one of those trips that Tinker first told me the story of Prospect Hill, which stood a few miles down the road. As we sat on the rotting gallery of Holly Grove, he told me about the vast cotton plantation that Ross had established, how he had planned to free his slaves after his death to emigrate to a new nation called Liberia, in West Africa, and how a dispute over his will instigated a legal conflict that spawned a slave uprising in which the house was burned. The idea of American slaves settling an African colony was particularly intriguing to us then, because there had recently been a fatal shootout in Jackson, Mississippi, near where we lived, between a group known as the Republic of New Africa and police and FBI agents at the group's heavily armed headquarters. The RNA had issued a manifesto demanding that the U.S. government cede to them the states of Mississippi, Louisiana, Alabama, Georgia, and South Carolina to form a black separatist nation, and pay $400 billion in slave reparations. Clearly, the conflict at the core of the story of Prospect Hill was far from over, and even in the 1970s it was far from dry, old history for us. For Tinker, it also had personal meaning.

Over the next few years, most of the original furnishings were stolen from Holly Grove, after which the house began an inexorable decline. Our camp-outs became fewer and farther between, until finally we stopped going, aside from rare day trips. Gwen had earlier moved Isaac Ross's piano to her home in Slate Springs, but with the family dispersed from Jefferson County and no one around to maintain it, Holly Grove's poignant, evocative decay began lurching toward certain doom. By the late 1980s it was going down fast.

I had grown to love the house and had been badgering Tinker for years to do something to preserve it, so when it became apparent that no one in the family would return to live there, Gwen decided to give it to me, if I would move it to my own property and restore it. It was not an easy matter to convince the elderly ladies who shared ownership, and lived mostly in other states, because they remembered the house the way it once had been, with no leaks in the roof and no rats or snakes roaming freely through its empty rooms. In their mind's eye it was filled with family members gathered around the long dining table or dancing with friends to tunes by minstrel groups at locally famous parties. To force the familial hand, I took a series of graphic photos—of walls that had given way from rot, sunlight visible through holes in the roof, gang graffiti on the doors, and the ground exposed through gaping cracks in the floor, and eventually they agreed to let it go. In 1990 my friends and I took the house apart, board by board, and hauled it sixty miles to my property, where we put it all back together again and replaced the rotten lumber.

Moving and restoring Holly Grove was not so different from the challenge that grew from it—reconstructing the story of Prospect Hill, which became increasingly important to me the more I learned about the Ross family and the slaves who "returned" to Africa before the

Civil War. Holly Grove today is restored, but it is my reconstruction, and though it has been saved, it now stands at a new location, facing a different way. It is, essentially, a new interpretation that I hope will last.

I had heard bits and pieces of the story of Prospect Hill over the years, but my interest grew after Gwen presented me with Ross's piano on permanent loan. No one knew how the piano had survived the fire that consumed the Prospect Hill mansion and took the life of a young girl, but Gwen knew that it had also been spared from a second conflagration, at another family home, Oak Hill, because it had been moved to Holly Grove. With Holly Grove now secure, she felt it was time for the piano to return. After she filled me in on the details of the alleged slave uprising at Prospect Hill and all that led up to it and came after, the sounds of the piano evoked for me less the echoes of sonatas than the cries of lynched slaves and of a doomed girl being burned alive. Eventually, it would also invoke an endless series of calls for help over the phone from Africa.

Ross was a slaveholder in the Wateree River region of South Carolina, and had the piano made in Philadelphia soon after the end of the Revolutionary War. Whether he played it himself has been lost in the telling, as has been a great deal more. But according to family accounts, in 1808 he hauled it with his other possessions, his family and his slaves to the Mississippi Territory, where he established Prospect Hill. Gwen, who is a member of the Isaac Ross Chapter of Colonial Dames of the 17th Century, inherited the piano a century and a half later, after it had been passed down the family line.

At first the piano seemed a dubious gift to me. In addition to its uselessness as a musical instrument, it was extremely heavy. Gwen could not bear to watch as Tinker and I wrestled it down the stairs from her balcony, accompanied by alternately discordant and sonorous protests from the strings. We had trouble holding on to its smooth surfaces, and broke off a piece of the veneer as we awkwardly rounded the bend and collided with the wall. I would later discover that these were the least of the transgressions it had endured during its years of wandering.

The difficulty in moving the piano left me wondering how it could possibly have been rescued from a burning mansion. The odds seemed long that anyone could have gotten it out in a hurry, particularly when they were unable to save the girl. I wondered if something had been left out of the story of the uprising—and even if it was entirely true. As it turned out, I would begin to question a great deal more, for the fire was part of a larger maelstrom unleashed by Ross's will that would ultimately span two centuries and two continents—the unintended result of his effort to do what he believed was the right thing.

There were legions of wealthy planters in Jefferson County before the Civil War, but what set Ross apart was that he ordained, from his deathbed, the destruction of the very thing that he had spent his life building up—his prosperous, 5,000-acre plantation. Ross's will, which was probated in 1836, described a radical plan to ensure that his life did not end as might have been expected, its sum total reduced to an embarrassment of riches for his heirs, and a hopeless fate for the slaves on whose backs his fortune was made. Ross stipulated that at the time of his daughter Margaret Reed's death, Prospect Hill would be sold and the money used to pay the way for his slaves who wanted to emigrate to Liberia, where a colony of freed slaves had been established by a group called the American Colonization Society. There was already a community there called Mississippi in Africa, founded by a Mississippi chapter of the Colonization Society a decade before.

Margaret Reed would remain faithful to her father's wishes, but some of his heirs did not cotton to the idea of handing the bounty of his estate over to the slaves, and then setting them free. Those heirs filed a contest of the will with the Jefferson County probate court soon after Reed's death in 1838, and pursued the litigation to the state supreme court. They also attempted an end-run around the courts in the state legislature. They had many supporters, because some area planters and state elected officials were convinced that the colonization plan smacked of abolitionism. The fight dragged on for a decade, and during that contentious time, according to the family account, the slaves grew restless and set fire to the mansion, hoping to take out the offenders.

The heirs ultimately lost the contest of the will. By 1849 approximately 200 of the 225 slaves had been given their freedom and had emigrated to Mississippi in Africa, where they were joined by approximately 200 slaves freed by other, more sympathetic Ross family members. The rest of the Prospect Hill slaves chose to remain behind, enslaved. According to the provisions of the will, the remaining slaves were sold at public auction, in family units, so that close relations were not separated. Some of the freed slaves for a time wrote letters to their former masters at Prospect Hill, but when I began my research no one knew what had become of them.

Once I began reading about the colonization movement, I found that it stirred controversy far beyond Prospect Hill. Opponents, including many abolitionists, saw the effort as essentially a deportation of free blacks, while supporters—who also included abolitionists—were embarrassed by reports that some of the freed-slave immigrants had resorted to enslaving members of Liberia's indigenous tribes. Many of the new settlers, including some of the Prospect Hill immigrants, established large plantations and built grand mansions in the same Greek Revival style they had known back home, and some of the native tribes had a name for them, which is still occasionally used to refer to blacks of American ancestry: white. This may have been because they occupied the master's role in this African version of a Southern plantation society, or because they tended to have complexions that were considerably lighter than the native groups. The settlers were also referred to as "kwi," which means "western" or "civilized."

So it turns out that the story of Prospect Hill is more complicated than it first appeared, and covers a lot of ground. Over a span of 175 years or so, in fact, it has managed to touch just about every hot button in the histories of the American South and colonial Africa—slavery and exploitation, conflict and greed—while encompassing almost every imaginable human predicament. And as I probed deeper into the details, I detected what I believed were a few flaws in the narrative thread that had long been accepted by local tradition.

Old stories in the South tend to get a lot of grooming, often to within an inch of their lives, but inevitably they start mixing with other narrative lines. Sometimes the stories are ephemeral and, as a result, endlessly malleable. With no documentation to support or refute, the details blossom fantastically, in ways that are unlikely to be corroborated by any written record. Other times there is ample documentation, which helps if it says what you expect it to, but there is always the question of who did the documenting and why. For the most part, in the Southern storytelling tradition, big things happen, people talk about them, hone a few ideas, revise the story and delete here and there, add entertaining details from other sources, then take the finished product out for a test drive. This goes on for generations, and sometimes myth and reality are blended seamlessly into what passes for fact. This is how you end up with something like the minié ball pregnancy, which was the tale told by a Vicksburg, Mississippi, family whose daughter had hastily married a Yankee soldier during the Civil War, after which it was said that a sniper's bullet had passed through his testicles and into her womb. (If anyone needed proof, of course, there was the actual child.)

The story of Prospect Hill was a natural target for this honing instinct, and the more people I talked with, the less sure I was of the veracity of the official account, which until now had been firmly rooted in the slaveholders' vantage point, because they alone had the power to document history at the time. Yet even the versions told by otherwise attuned slaveholder descendants vary to some degree, depending largely upon whether the person traces his lineage to Isaac Ross or to his grandson, the contester of the will. As the piano stared back at me in my living room, I began to wonder about the circumstances of the infamous fire, including whether the uprising itself may have actually been a fabrication, designed to discredit the slaves. Notably, the threat of insubordination had been a key component of the opponents' legal argument against the will. I wondered if, upon closer scrutiny, the familiar parlor story of Prospect Hill would still play after so many decades, or if, like the piano, it was hopelessly warped. I also wanted to know what had become of everyone involved, from the divided slaveholding family to the slaves who chose to remain behind and those who emigrated to Africa. What might their descendants know about the story? And what revelations might come from a more thorough review of the written record?

Tinker Miller and I mulled over the possibilities one summer evening as we sat on the porch of the newly relocated Holly Grove. We had spent many hours deconstructing history there over the past twenty-five years, and none of the stories intrigued us more than how there came to be a place called Mississippi in Africa, and what the saga meant for all the key players on both sides of the Atlantic.

On this particular evening, fireflies drifted randomly across the lawn and the air was soft and sweet with the scent of Japanese honey-suckle. The songs of crickets, cicadas, and frogs rose to such loud crescendoes that now and then we had to raise our own voices to be heard.

We are of a generation and bent that once dissected Civil War bat-tles as we might a football game, but when it came to the story of Prospect Hill our knowledge had until now been mostly hearsay. We knew what we had been told, and we have had no real reason to ques-tion it until now, when I had decided to try to piece the story together in detail. Tinker was to be my first official interview.

For Tinker, our conversation probed a very personal history, and I was gently challenging him to reconsider the comfortable, accepted truths that were told to him by people he loved and respected. He had no trepidation about digging deeper, because we know each other well and it was unlikely that either of us would go anywhere with the story that the other could not follow—or, if we did, there would be no acri-mony in pointing it out. It was just that we were dragging the memory of people like his late Uncle Anon into the twilight, critiquing what he said when he was not there to answer.

We talked about Uncle Anon for a while, and when the conversa-tion found its way back to Prospect Hill, Tinker glanced disapprovingly at my tape recorder. "That thing," as he called it, made him overly aware of his words, because he knew he could not retract any of them. There were a lot of long silences.

I said I had no pretenses about being able to uncover the all-encompassing, indisputable truth of Prospect Hill, mainly because I knew from reading Faulkner that with a story as complicated and sweeping as this one, where the characters are so diverse, the likeli-hood was that everyone claimed only a piece of the truth and the pieces did not necessarily jibe. I wanted only to isolate the narrative thread, find out what became of the people involved, and see what hand history had dealt their descendants.

He nodded, noncommittally.

What Tinker thinks matters a great deal to me, particularly because he first told me the tale one afternoon as we sat on this same porch with our friends, drinking beer and watching the sun set. It was still a favorite story of his because he loves history, it concerns his own fam-ily, the whole premise is so unexpected, so oversized and dramatic, and after 165 years its effects still reverberate in both Mississippi and in Liberia. He was also aware that my version had the potential to trump the others, and I had to admit that the family lore had already started to seem a bit stylized.

There is no question that Prospect Hill burned on April 15, 1845, and that a family member, Martha Richardson, died in the fire. But once I started to dig, I became increasingly dubious about the slave uprising, which so many descendants point to as the cause of the fire, because every account of the incident harks back to a single source—Thomas Wade, the son of the man who contested the will. Like many local histories, this one has been honed to a narrow focus over time, told by people with their own agendas, and there is a lot that the more recent narrators simply did not know.

As we talked about the alleged uprising, Tinker allowed that "It's possible that the whole thing was a fabrication, but why? What would anyone have to gain? My perception of the family tale was that these blacks were not mean; they were misguided or confused by the situation. There were no harsh feelings from the ancestors of my family toward the ancestors of the blacks. These families were close, have always been close, and this whole episode with Isaac Ross Wade trying to nullify the will is just contrary to everything they were about."

This disclaimer was not an effort to further distance himself from a man whose character had been called into question. He had told me many times before that his family falls squarely on the side that supported the will.

I watched the red dot of his cigarette dancing in the gathering darkness as he repeated the family lore—the story of the slaves growing restless prior to the uprising, the cook drugging the slaveholders' coffee, the slave at the door with the axe to kill the man who stood in their way of emigrating to Africa. "That's just the story," he said. "It was part of the family history. There was no variation of the story when I was growing up . . . it wasn't questioned."

Tinker is open-minded, and I knew that if he is not willing to budge from the family line, it was unlikely that other descendants of the slaveholding family would. That would leave only the slave descendants to test my theory that there was more at work than a simple conflict involving irrational slaves. Perhaps the descendants of the Prospect Hill slaves, if I could find any, would have something to add

to all of this. The same is true for the descendants of the emigrants to
Liberia, although the nation has been in turmoil since 1980, and at this
point I was not at all inclined to travel to a war zone to find out.

He shrugged when I suggested this.

"Growing up, you couldn't help but be proud of what Isaac Ross
did," he said. "Everybody in the family was proud that he freed his
slaves. The fact that the will was contested by his grandson . . . the family didn't really play that aspect of it up much. We didn't see Isaac Ross
Wade as representing our family. We were proud that our family wasn't
the malevolent, mean, make-a-dollar-off-the-slave-industry type people, that they had a history of compassion for people. They didn't voice
it like that, but that was the primary story. Then again, Isaac Ross was
still a slaveowner, and my family were still slaveowners and that's a horrible thing."

He said his own views have been influenced by contemporary history, which include his having lived through the Civil Rights era and
having attended racially integrated schools. "The Mississippi we grew
up in was a segregated place, but we saw that change," he said. "Our
parents grew up in a different world. You hear all this stuff, and it's
confusing. You know your ancestors owned people, you kind of have
this paternalistic moonlight-and-magnolias mentality, then you read
about people that you grew up admiring, like [Confederate General]
Nathan Bedford Forrest and his involvement with the Klan, and you
know it was a bad, bad thing. And deep down, no matter what gloss you
put on it, it was always a bad thing. It never got good. . . .

"I can't pass judgment on them because that was the culture, that's
the way life was. But the fact that some of the freed slaves or their
descendants, whatever, enslaved the indigenous people in Liberia—
that just shows what a terrible thing it is. . . .

"I guess it's just human nature to try to dominate other people.
Which is why you have to give someone like Isaac Ross credit for trying, even if it was late in the game, to basically do the right thing."

With that, he thumped his spent cigarette over the rail.

"Now turn that thing off," he said, motioning toward the tape
recorder.

But I have one more question: How did the piano make its way
from Prospect Hill to Oak Hill?

He shook his head and shrugged.

The piano is one of the few surviving items that was contested during the litigation, and one of the last heirlooms of the original Prospect Hill mansion. The irony is that had Wade not removed it from the house, however he did, it would have burned in the fire. But then, had he not contested the will, there would have been no fire.

In a region beset by racial divisions and economic disparities, sorting through numerous differing accounts can get complicated, with key roles reversed in different sources' tellings—heroes transformed into villains, and vice versa. This may be true all over, but it is especially so in the South, where major conflicts from the past are routinely distilled to very personal encounters today. The backdrop of history looms constantly, and sometimes its weight can be overwhelming, and you just have to let it go, and move on. Other times the story is too compelling and too provocative to ignore. That was the case with Prospect Hill, which is why I began digging through moldering records that had not seen the light of day for perhaps a hundred years, and eventually, found myself on my way to war-torn Liberia, where Mississippi means something altogether different, and where the conflicts of the old American South not only still matter, they are matters of life and death.

Part I

MISSISSIPPI

CHAPTER ONE

NEKISHA ELLIS WATCHES AS I hoist the massive old record book onto the Xerox machine, unable to prevent it from pulling apart at the seams. With each turn of a page, bits of parchment break away and rain down upon the floor. I look up at her and wince.

"Don't worry," she says, and smiles apologetically. "It's just old."

Nekisha is a deputy court clerk in Jefferson County, where the surviving documents chronicling the Prospect Hill litigation are housed. A smile comes naturally to her face. She watches brightly as one irreplaceable record after another crumbles in my hands.

This particular book, which contains county probate records for the 1840s, has been sheltered at the back of a dusty, unopened box for decades, and represents one of our first major finds. Nekisha is happy to have unearthed it, although this is more due to her desire to help than her interest in what the book contains. Irreplaceable though it may be, the book is just one more piece of moldering detritus in one of the poorest counties in the poorest state in America.

The lack of funds may partly explain why there seems to be almost no official interest in maintaining records from the time before the Civil War, but there also seems to be some deep-seated inertia at work—the kind that keeps things from being done, and the kind that ensures that what is already happening continues (which in this case is the steady decay of the county's oldest records). Day-to-day life here is harder in many ways than in most parts of the country, while the literal burden of history is heavier, which is why I did not expect much when I arrived. It turns out I am lucky.

When I explain to Nekisha why I am searching for the records, she tells me that she recalls hearing the name of Prospect Hill before, although there is little left of the community that the plantation once anchored. This is not unusual—in a county as historic as this one, many residents remember things for which there is little or nothing to show. I am hoping this communal memory will improve the chances of finding descendants, but it is a big haystack that I am probing for a handful of needles. Nekisha, in fact, was at first skeptical that any of the documentation existed, because the county's oldest records have been in serious disarray for years. I had been told that prior to the disastrous fire in the 1980s that consumed the former, Gothic-style courthouse, which had stood since around 1900, one local resident had taken to carting off historic records after finding that they were being ruined by leaks in the roof, and that no one seemed to care. So began a systematic, surreptitious looting in the name of preservation. I have also heard of less noble inroads. One woman recalled finding purloined pages torn from deed books and Spanish land grants for sale at a flea market in nearby Natchez, which she bought but did not return. Instead she donated them to the state Department of Archives and History, in Jackson, saying she had little hope for their preservation in Jefferson County. All of this was discouraging, because the corresponding records in Liberia were reportedly lost in the burning of that nation's archives at the height of the country's civil war in the 1990s— a conflict precipitated by long-running animosity between the descendants of the freed slaves and the indigenous tribes. So I was undertaking my research with a certain urgency. I needed to pull together what was left, or, in cases where nothing was left, glean the details from a diverse array of people.

Nekisha tells me that some of the county's older records were removed to an annex prior to the fire, and because she is energized by the discovery of the probate book in a rusty filing cabinet, she begins probing every decaying cardboard box she can find. Along the way she inspires others in the research room to join in, and before long discovers the mother lode of records relating to the litigation over Isaac Ross's will.

As we plunder cabinets and the dark recesses of closets, one man whom Nekisha has pressed into service, who is doing his own African-American genealogy, listens to my fledgling account of the story with a slightly bewildered look on his face, then repeats the words "Mississippi in Africa" aloud, nodding, with a furrowed brow. I have seen this response before, and will see it again many times before my research is over. He is not sure what to make of this. The story seems implausible, defies conventional wisdom, and lends itself to opposing stereotypes. Several people have asked, "How come I've never heard of this?"

From all appearances, Jefferson County is an unlikely launching pad for a saga of such bafflingly broad proportions. The county, which borders the Mississippi River between Vicksburg and Natchez, is barely even flyover country, and what's worse, it seems to be in the throes of an extraordinarily long death scene. Piles of bricks, a few old storm-battered trees and the occasional roadside display of daffodils in spring are all that remain of a hundred former plantation homes, while at isolated crossroads, junked cars surround clusters of small houses and trailers that look more like encampments than permanent settlements. Telltale slave quarters have quietly vanished from the landscape, abandoned roads have degenerated into unofficial dumps, historical markers have been stolen for scrap metal, and marble angels and filigreed cast-iron fences sprawl across forgotten cemeteries, toppled by vandals and falling trees. By the standards of twenty-first-century America, the county has, essentially, nothing—no factories, no significant retail business, no evidence of any real production or commerce. Even the cotton gins closed down years ago.

The county's population has been declining for years, and now stands at just under 10,000 people, most of whom are supported by government programs or commute to distant jobs. Some get by on interest on old money, the sale of timber, or income from hunting leases or the sale of discarded aluminum cans picked up from the side of the road. Others benefit from more unpredictable windfalls—drug deals or multimillion-dollar class-action legal verdicts. Jefferson County's poverty today has contributed to a national reputation as an attractive venue for personal-injury lawsuits—it is essentially a victim-based economy. In 2001, the Jackson *Clarion-Ledger* newspaper noted that asbestos manufacturer Owens-Corning had been slapped with a landmark $48 million judgment by a Jefferson County jury in June 1998, and that the company had subsequently filed its own suit in the county against tobacco companies that it claimed were partly responsible for the injuries cited. An attorney for R.J. Reynolds Tobacco told the newspaper that Jefferson County has a particularly bad reputation for corporate defendants.

Aside from legal cases, much that is important to the community happened long ago, and old stories still spark debate, but for the most part the physical evidence is fast fading away.

Jefferson County was the second county chartered in the Mississippi Territory, in 1799, and its history spans the frontier, the boom of the South's plantation economy, the bust that followed the Civil War, the tumult of Reconstruction, and the inevitable upheaval of the Civil Rights era. The region, which was originally known as the Natchez District, was first settled by the French and later occupied by Spain and Great Britain, but did not reach its full flower until it became part of the United States in 1798. By the outbreak of the Civil War in 1861, it stood at the forefront of the antebellum cotton empire, an aspect of local history that is often misconstrued as a sort of "white phase" by people of both races, although it was also the formative era of local black culture and political power. Back then, slaves far outnumbered slaveholders, and nearby Natchez boasted more millionaires per capita than any other city in the United States. Money transformed a remote wilderness into a region of wealthy fiefdoms anchored by Greek Revival, Federal, and Italianate mansions filled with imported furnishings, the most elaborate of which were surrounded by landscaped gardens, sometimes stepping down toward the river on terraces, while just out of sight were the rude dwellings of the slave quarters, with dirt yards. These were the sets upon which Jefferson County's high dramas were acted out, which is something no one seems to have forgotten.

Despite its contentious history and pervasive poverty, there is an odd romance about Jefferson County's decline, with its abandoned gardens overgrown with flowering vines, its silent churches redolent of incense and mildew, its scores of ruined houses with tattered curtains twisting on the breeze through broken windows. For sheer historical weight, none of the sites can compare with the cemetery at Prospect Hill, which lies a short distance from the second house on the site, built by Ross's grandson after the first was burned. The cemetery was wrecked a few years back by a falling cedar tree that narrowly missed a marble monument to Ross, which was erected by the Mississippi branch of the American Colonization Society and bears this hopeful inscription:

"His last will is graced with as magnificent provisions as any over
which philanthropy has ever rejoiced and by it will be erected
on the shores of Africa a monument more glorious than marble
and more enduring than Time."

That the inscription is written in stone does not mean that its conclusions are indisputable, yet there is no question that Ross was destined
to leave an enduring wake.

Although his family in South Carolina was at the time comparatively
wealthy, Ross must have found the availability of good, cheap cotton
land in the Mississippi Territory an irresistible lure. White settlers from
Europe and the eastern United States were pouring into the region in
wagon trains, on horseback, and aboard steamboats in search of opportunity. The boom is evident in the cemetery at the now abandoned river
town of Grand Gulf, which includes numerous graves of young men
from France, Scotland, and the eastern United States, some killed in duels
or by yellow fever, who were drawn to the area by the promise of the
new, and by stories of fortunes made from the fertile soil. To many people at the time, the burgeoning cotton empire meant very much the same
thing that the dot-com economy of California would mean to men and
women in the late twentieth century, and its crash would be equally sudden and profound. The slave-based boom ended in 1865, after passage
of the Emancipation Proclamation and the Confederacy's defeat in the
Civil War. For those who reaped the largess of the cotton empire, fewer
than thirty years separated the highest peak from the deepest valley.

During the war, army and naval battles swept across the region, and
the local economy and social order fractured. Jefferson County, like
much of the rural South, began losing population soon after, with the
first wave of emigration led by newly freed blacks and by whites who
had seen their way of life collapse. Simultaneously, the area's fertile
topsoil began to wash away, with erosion sending huge, hungry chasms
creeping into the hills. For the next 150 years the population and tax
base spiraled downward, taking with it much of the infrastructure that
had supported the one-crop economy—railroads, farms, ports, ferries,
bridges, roads, countless communities, and more than a few towns.
Since nothing came along to take cotton's place as an economic
engine, the county foundered. Today the county seat of Fayette is a

study in small-town desolation. Even the parking meters in front of the courthouse don't work, and in many cases the meter itself is gone—there's only the rusted pole.

The status of the black majority changed dramatically in the second half of the twentieth century, but they inherited a dying commonwealth. Jefferson County now has the highest percentage of African-American elected officials in the United States, but with a population that is largely undereducated and poor, and with few resources to exploit, it has increasingly come to rely upon the federal government for support. Less than half the residents have a high school education and only 10 percent have a college degree, while 20 percent are on Social Security and about a third live on income that is below the poverty level. The per capita annual income at the turn of the twenty-first century was around $10,000.

Because the county is poor and 90 percent black, stories of innovative slaveholders and the colossal homes they built with slave labor do not inspire the kind of ancestral pride that drives the narratives at mansion tours in nearby Natchez and Vicksburg. For the average resident of Jefferson County, those days are long gone, and many have bidden them good-bye and good riddance. It is not so surprising, though it is distressing, that the written record of the county's tumultuous history has been consigned to what amounts to a communal attic, the recesses of the courthouse. Yet Ross's story is not easily dismissed as a relic of a dead era. For one thing, none of the descendants—black or white—can claim exclusive ownership of the tale.

While Nekisha and company are busy plundering the record room, I notice a woman watching me curiously from another table. When she catches my eye, she rises and approaches my table. She does not introduce herself, but asks, rather officiously, "What are you here to do?"

I am a bit put off by her tone, and say, simply, "Research." It is not a satisfactory answer, but she backs off.

When she goes to lunch I ask Nekisha who she is.

"That's Ann Brown," she says. "You need to know her."

When she returns, Nekisha introduces us. It turns out that Ann Brown is actually quite friendly, and helpful. She is a transplanted Canadian whose husband was descended from a local slaveholding family, and who, in recent years, has undertaken a wholesale genealogical survey of Jefferson and Claiborne counties, including the lineages of African-American families, which are notoriously poorly documented. Ann is interested in everyone's family line, which is why she might be seen as a busybody were she not on an inspired public mission.

I tell Ann what I am looking for and why, and she fills me in on her own genealogical efforts with the explanation, "There's just no one else doing it." She asks a few questions about Isaac Ross and Prospect Hill, takes my name, number, and e-mail address, and says I will be hearing from her. With that, she returns to her own work.

I now have numerous boxes scattered before me on a massive, old wooden table. So far I have primarily scanned the probate and land records books, deciding it would be best to make copies and decipher the baroque handwriting of the other documents later. As soon as I open the first of the new boxes, though, the scanning ends. It becomes clear that the box's contents will encompass far more than simple legal arguments. All of the stories that I have so far heard refer primarily to the slaveholding Rosses, with few detailed references to the slaves themselves, but the first item I come to is a ledger, written in what will soon be a familiar style of florid, archaic hand, with a title that speaks volumes: "Births of the Negros on Prospect Hill Place." In it are the names of more than a hundred slaves born at Prospect Hill, beginning in the early 1800s, including many whose names I will come to recognize from the letters they wrote home to Prospect Hill from Mississippi in Africa.

CHAPTER TWO

ISAAC ROSS WAS BORN in Charlotte, North Carolina, in 1760, moved with his family as a child to near Camden, South Carolina, and then, as a young man, enlisted in the revolutionary army. By war's end he had been promoted to the rank of captain and commanded a company of South Carolina dragoons who fought in the battles of Kings Mountain, North Carolina, in 1780, and Cowpens, South Carolina, in 1781, both of which were patriot victories. In the latter battle, he lost his right eye. He wore a glass replacement for the rest of his life.

By his early forties, Ross no doubt had heard tales of Mississippi's productive climate from his brother, Arthur, who had immigrated to the territory a few years before. In 1808 he joined the exodus of planters from the East who were being crowded out by other heirs or whose comparatively old farmlands had declined in productivity.

The soil of Jefferson County was among the most fertile in North America, but for ambitious men like Ross it held little value without the addition of slaves. Cotton was a labor-intensive crop, and no one could have grown as wealthy as many of the region's planters did, as quickly as they did, through their own labor. The fertility, which carried southwest Mississippi's slave-based cotton economy to new heights, was the result of two ancient geologic forces—dust storms that had borne down continually across the plains of North America at the end of the last ice age, and scouring torrents from melting glaciers through what is today the basin of the Mississippi River. Over time, the channel of the river carved a chasm deep into a bed of limestone that was once the bottom of a sea, and the exposed cliff on the eastern bank caught deposits of wind-blown dust the way a beached log captures sand. The result was a series of undulating hills with fine, deep topsoil that in some places ran a hundred feet deep, bordered by broad bottom lands where fertile silt had been deposited by successive floods over thousands of years. Atop these rich foundations had been laid several feet of fecund humus from decaying trees and leaves, which left the soil so soft and malleable that in the early years, it was said, farmers could plant their crops without the need for plows. Until the richest organic matter was depleted (which took only a few decades), seeds were simply scattered on the surface and walked into the ground by the feet of men and women.

The combination of rich soil and subtropical climate proved both a boon and a bane to the early settlers. All vegetative growth was prolific—not just the crops selected for cultivation—and there were plagues of insects and other pests. French settlers who arrived in the early eighteenth century encountered dense jungles of towering beech and magnolia trees festooned with long falls of moss, great brakes of cane on the open ridge tops, and lakes brimming with fish that were cast in perpetual shadow by primeval cypress trees. Much of the terrain was impenetrable. From all appearances the French were wholly unprepared for the task they faced, and because they were never fully supported by their government, their attempts at colonial settlement failed. Their contributions to the history of the region were nonetheless profound: the annihilation of the Natchez Indians in retaliation for an attack at Fort Rosalie in 1729, and the introduction of African slaves to replace Native American slaves who had proved both susceptible to European diseases and adept at escape. The occupation of the new lands by transplanted Africans would be entwined with the region's history from that day forward.

The French reign ended with the conclusion of the French and Indian War in 1760, after which the district came under British rule. Britain's tenure was also short-lived, but it brought the first permanent settlements, in the 1780s, peopled by immigrants who had largely sided with the crown during the Revolution. Afterward, the region briefly fell into the hands of Spain, and the first serious attempts were made to clear the land for agriculture, mostly for tobacco and indigo. These efforts were only sporadically successful. It would take another change of regime, and the invention of the cotton gin, to transform the Natchez District into the venue for one of the most lucrative and controversial enterprises in the history of American agriculture. Nearly all of the great houses that tourists come to Mississippi to see today were built during that era, from roughly the 1820s to 1860.

It was just prior to the great boom, ten years after Spain had ceded the region to the United States, that Isaac Ross arrived. For white settlers like Ross and his brother, the region was just opening up, but for blacks and people of mixed race it was about to begin closing in. Under newly imposed U.S. laws, free mulattoes, who had previously inhabited a cultural and political gray area of society, were officially classified as black, which made them subject to more rigid legal restrictions that were also being imposed on free blacks. Greater prohibitions were also placed on slaves. Notably, Ross counted a large cadre of mulattoes among the slaves he brought with him from South Carolina, along with a core group of free blacks.

One of Ross's descendants, Thomas Wade, noted that during the Revolution Ross had fought alongside "several free negroes, who made good soldiers," and that "when he moved to Mississippi they followed him and settled near him on land he helped them to buy. Drew Harris, one of these old soldiers, who drew a pension from the government, was buried near the Drew Spring on Prospect Hill Plantation, the home of Captain Ross. Some of his descendants were living in Claiborne County a few years since and some of them may be there now."

Aside from the more restrictive laws, Ross and company arrived at a fortuitous time, when refinements to the cotton gin, which had been invented in 1793, were changing the economic landscape. Small subsistence farms of tobacco, indigo, and corn were being supplanted by large plantations devoted primarily to cotton, which greatly increased in value after Europe's most readily available supply was interrupted by a slave uprising on the Caribbean island of Saint-Domingue (now Haiti). With the Caribbean supply cut off, cotton prices skyrocketed, and after a Natchez slave fabricated an improved cotton gin based upon a description by his owner, who had seen Eli Whitney's invention, many planters began converting all of their fields to cotton. Some no longer grew corn to feed their horses, mules, cows, oxen, and slaves, but instead bought it from other markets so as to devote all of their acreage to the more valuable crop. With so much incentive, and the only limitation the availability of labor, the value of slaves escalated. Because the U.S. Constitution banned the importation of slaves after 1808—the year Ross arrived—most of the new slaves came from established plantations back East.

A large part of the acreage that Ross bought upon his arrival in Jefferson County would have certainly been classified as "unimproved," meaning stands of timber would have to be cleared before it could be converted to arable land. On the Mississippi frontier, this usually involved deadening trees—girdling the trunks with an axe to cut off the flow of nutrient-laden sap. Because deadened trees take a few years to finally die, and even longer to fall, crops were routinely planted in the soils of a ghost forest, nurtured by sunlight falling through ominous snags. Most planters occupied crude log structures until they made their fortune and a more lavish dwelling could be built, but Ross appears to have made his splash upon arrival. The best description of his house comes from Ross's great-grandson, Thomas Wade, who described Prospect Hill as a monument to style and substance, built of poplar milled on the plantation, with wainscoting throughout the downstairs, bookcases that rose to the ceiling of the parlor, and a finely executed stair rail, all crafted of cherry wood.

"The book cases in the parlor were filled with the best books obtainable at that time and among them was a complete file of the *National Intelligencer*, a weekly paper, published at Philadelphia," Thomas Wade wrote. "On the walls of this parlor, along with other fine pictures, there hung the picture of the sloop of war *Bonhomme Richard*, and the frigate *Constitution* of the War of 1812. Captain Ross prized those two pictures highly and often spoke of the daring exploits of John Paul Jones."

According to Wade, Ross designed the house himself and supervised its construction by his slaves. The lumber was milled in a pit, with one man below and one above operating a long ripsaw. "During wet or excessively dry weather the poplar lumber expanded and contracted and at night often worried those not accustomed to the noise," Wade observed.

At the time Ross began work on Prospect Hill, the methods of farming had changed little since the medieval era, but advancements came quickly, in improved gins, plows, cotton presses, and strains of seeds. The effects of these technological advances were far-reaching.

Slavery, which had been practiced throughout recorded time, was soon transformed from a comparatively small-scale system of feudal bondage to a rapidly expanding, fully institutionalized and widespread engine of economic growth. The advent of the steamboat, meanwhile, meant that commodities could be moved in volume over long distances, and shipped wherever they were needed in response to world markets, which was particularly important to the lower Mississippi Valley, where a network of rivers, lakes, and bayous meant that even remote plantations were seldom far from a navigable waterway.

The era brought unprecedented development to the Natchez District, though there were downturns. Historian John Hebron Moore noted that the price of ginned cotton dropped dramatically from a high of thirty-two cents per pound in 1801 to fourteen cents per pound in 1809, the result of a federal tariff on European trade. During the War of 1812, the price further dropped to twelve cents per pound, and continued to fluctuate for the next decade. In 1811 a particularly aggressive fungus began attacking the crop, which prompted local planters to experiment with new varieties of seed. One, a strain known as Petit Gulf developed by Dr. Rush Nutt, a Jefferson County planter and amateur scientist, proved a godsend. Petit Gulf was resistant to the fungus and more productive than previous strains, and as a result, by the 1820s field slaves were picking significantly larger volumes of cotton than they had in previous years. With the availability of abundant raw material, the textile industries in England and the northern United States also experienced unprecedented growth, which in turn increased the demand for cotton and yet again for slaves.

Ross's fortune and the number of his slaves grew significantly during the boom, but what should have been a happy time of flush finances and a growing family was marred by a succession of deaths. Some descendants say the series of tragedies caused Ross to diverge from the path of a typical Mississippi slaveholder and planter toward the role that he would become most famous for—as the man responsible for sending the largest group of freed-slave emigrants to the colony of Liberia, and in so doing, for dividing his family, his community, the courts, and the state legislature.

Ross and his wife, Jane, who was also from South Carolina, had two sons, Isaac Jr. and Arthur, and three daughters, Jane, Martha, and Margaret. The 1820 census for Jefferson County also includes two

unnamed young men living in the house at Prospect Hill, along with
158 slaves on the plantation. Among his offspring, only Isaac Jr. and
Jane would have children—he, a son, Isaac Allison Ross; and she, several by two husbands, including Isaac Ross Wade, who would later join
her in the contest of her father's will.

From all appearances Ross's children ascended easily through local
society and were poised to make their way in the world when the series
of tragedies began unfolding. Descendant Annie Mims Wright wrote
that the first was the death of the fiancé of Ross's daughter Martha, in
a duel in 1813. According to family accounts, a messenger galloped up
the drive to Prospect Hill on the day of the couple's intended marriage
to deliver the news that the young man was preparing to fight a duel in
nearby Rodney. The reason for the duel is unclear, and the timing is
debatable, because there seems to be an inordinate number of tales
circulating through Mississippi history of young belles whose intended
grooms were killed on the day they were to be married. Still, having
her fiancé killed at any time near the planned wedding would have
been shock enough. As father and daughter raced to the scene to intervene, they reportedly encountered a second messenger who told them
that her betrothed was already dead.

The next tragedy came five years later, in 1818, when Martha herself died of yellow fever, at age twenty-five. She had been helping care
for her second fiancé, who preceded her in death, and who had contracted the disease while caring for his mother, another victim. Two
years later, the husband of Ross's daughter Jane also succumbed to
fever, and Ross became legal guardian of the couple's son, Isaac Ross
Wade, his grandson and later the executor (and would-be nemesis) of
his will. In 1829, at the age of sixty-four, Ross's wife died, and she was
followed the next year by another son-in-law, U.S. senator Thomas
Reed, who had married Margaret. In 1832, Isaac Jr. died, and two
years after that, Ross's son Arthur died. All of these losses, in such
close succession, must have taken a heavy toll, but, according to
Wright, it was Martha's death that shook Ross to his foundation.

Wright contended that after Martha died, "Captain Ross was so
overcome with grief, he left the familiar scenes and went with his
nephew, John B. Conger, through the then wild Indian country to
Mobile, where he took a boat for the North. He visited Princeton,
where his son [Isaac Jr.] was at school, but not wishing to burden him

with grief, did not even call on him. On his return, by way of the West, he was taken ill in the Indian country and was found by some hunters, who took care of him and sent word to his family." Members of his family traveled to the western frontier to escort Ross home.

There is no mention of where in the West (which at the time encompassed today's midwestern states) Ross's sojourn took him, and there is some disagreement over exactly when and why he went, but there seems no question that he returned a changed man. Thomas Wade noted that Ross's nephew had left him upon their arrival in Mobile, and that once up North, "Ross came in close contact with the people of wealth and culture as well as the masses, and talked with some of them interested in the American Colonization Society. From these men he learned of the growing sentiment in the North relative to the ultimate abolition of slavery in America. It was from this contact in the North that he learned that the institution of slavery could not last." When he returned home, Wade wrote, Ross had been gone for more than a year, "and this was the first word his family had that he was still alive. They feared that he had been killed by Indians or lost at sea."

Although Wright attributed Ross's wanderings to grief over Martha's death, historian Harnett Kane speculated in the 1940s that the sojourn followed the death of his wife, Jane Allison Ross. According to Kane, when Jane Ross died in the summer of 1829, Ross was so aggrieved that he could barely attend the funeral, and when he managed to rise to the occasion his slaves crowded around and cried with him. Kane believed it was daughter Margaret's idea for Ross to travel as an antidote to the depression that afterward gripped him.

Kane described Ross as "an individual of stringent honesty, proud that he had won his place in the world, who scorned pettifoggers, people who put on airs or tried to cut corners," and a man who shared the responsibility for operating the plantation with his wife. Jane Ross, he noted, "was modest, but talked over the plantation management with him, helped him in dealings with men and women in the fields," while Margaret, his favorite surviving child, inherited both her mother's reticence and her father's stubbornness.

Kane's account had Ross returning from his travels with an obsession about slavery, which had always been a favorite topic of conversation. He described Ross questioning his slaves about their ideas of freedom—what it would mean to them, and what they would do if they were freed. Ross reportedly had never allowed any of his slaves to be sold, had sequestered them away from slaves on other plantations, and had allowed many of them to be taught to read and write. It seems safe to assume that he was concerned not only about the future of slavery but that his carefully constructed slave world might not outlast his daughter Margaret, who shared his desire to keep the community intact and under the family's comparatively benign rule.

Either way, Kane wrote, after Ross returned from the wilderness and broached the subject of freedom, "In the flickering of the cabin lamps, excitement spread."

CHAPTER THREE

IT IS A HALCYON day, the sun high and warm but the ground still cool in the shadows, and in Jefferson County's remaining fields the last of its farmers are breaking ground. It is mostly the bottom lands that they plow now, for soybeans rather than cotton, using great John Deere tractors that belch diesel smoke as they groan against the earth. The plowing still brings the scent of fresh earth to the countryside, but the field cabins are mostly gone, and one man can do in a day what took weeks for more than a hundred men in 1825.

Before the Civil War these fields would have been crowded with men and horses, and on any given spring day, the ground would have been laid bare by a hundred plows, with earthworms clamoring in the raw sunlight, attracting great flocks of red-winged blackbirds to swoop down and feast. The birds would rise and fall above the already sweating brows of men for whom another year, another crop of cotton, had just begun. Now and then the breeze might carry a whiff of desire, of catfish and bream spawning in the ponds and creeks, or of wood smoke curling in thin tendrils from distant cabin chimneys from the remains of last night's fires, on which the morning's meals of biscuits with cane syrup and fatback were cooked and quickly consumed in darkness. Each day the ringing of the plantation's great cast-iron bells heralded the rising sun.

Then, as now, the crop year would begin as soon as the land dried out in spring, interrupted only when periodic rains fell in torrents upon the exposed ground, making it too wet to plow. Soon summer would roll inexorably over everything, and it would seem to last forever. It would be hot when the sun came up, hot in the fields all day, hot in the houses at night. There would be no relief—no air-conditioning, no electric fans, no screens on the windows, or insect repellant. Horses and plowmen would travel in their own personal clouds of dust, bucking and weaving between the narrow rows, cultivating the young crop up and down the sun-drenched hillsides.

By midsummer the fields would be filled with women, too, chopping the weeds from the cotton rows when the crop grew too tall and lush to plow through. Afterward, pink and white cotton blossoms would unfurl beneath the broad leaves, the bolls at their base slowly maturing before finally bursting open, making the fields beautiful, white with cotton. In the fall the awful, backbreaking, finger-slitting picking would commence, the world smelling of cotton, a smell like nothing else, the smallest children smelling of it from playing in the piles, lint in their hair. Cotton was everywhere, and for the people working in the fields, it was someone else's cotton.

The ritual was repeated, year after year. When slavery ended, sharecropping took its place, and then in the mid-twentieth century the tractors came, along with mechanical cotton pickers, and just when things were getting easier came the onslaught of full-scale erosion. As late as the 1970s, a few old men in Jefferson County were still working small patches of ground with horses, the jangle of trace chains and the whoosh of the plow an echo of the old world, but they—and eventually, cotton itself—slowly passed from the scene. Today only a few isolated fields remain. What is left is a careworn landscape, and fading memories.

Not surprisingly, descendants of slaveholders tend to harbor happier memories of the old days than the descendants of slaves. People like Laverne McPhate, a descendant of Isaac Ross who now lives across the river in Ferriday, Louisiana, can envision scenes from the old days with fondness.

"When you stood on the old galleries at Prospect Hill, you could see just beyond that old brick wall the fields of indigo and cotton, and I could just imagine sitting on the porch, watching them work," she says, over the phone. "They had a good relationship. To know how well they got along and then to look at the situation today, well . . . hostility is just rampant now. I'm sure there were many hotheads and rebellious

ones in that day and time, but from all that I understand Isaac Ross
helped all that he could."

A large percentage—some say more than half—of white Mississippians before the Civil War owned no slaves, and a handful of free
blacks did, but the line of demarcation between slave owners and their
descendants and slaves and their descendants is abundantly clear. The
plantation and its cotton belonged to Isaac Ross, and when Laverne
pictures the gangs of slaves toiling in the fields, it is with pride over the
plantation legacy that encompasses the Rosses and another prominent
local family, the Davenports.

"I remember my grandmother talking about a slave man who
helped them when she was a child," she says. "He helped around the
farm. He chose this woman to marry and he took the Davenport
name. He always kept the property up. He farmed with them. They
killed hogs together. There was no big deal, they were just happy. This
girl that works for me now, my aunt named her. We just all grew up
together.

"But then comes the change of times. If I had my druthers I would
have rather lived in the 1800s, because it would've proved interesting.
Jefferson County was one of the most prosperous counties around. To
me it was just fascinating. We all had to get along, and everyone was
provided for. Isaac Ross provided everything for his slaves."

Laverne's pride is not universally shared, but the fact that Ross
freed his slaves makes the story of Prospect Hill more palatable in a
racially charged place and time. She is buoyed by the belief that Ross
was driven by a sense of noblesse oblige, that in the case of Prospect
Hill, nothing was simply black and white. It is an attractive idea, but a
hard sell.

Scant information about the daily lives of Prospect Hill slaves can
be found today, aside from those birth records found in plantation
ledgers, random entries in area planters' journals, court-ordered
inventories associated with the contest of Ross's will, and family lore.
Slaves were chattel, utterly subject to their owners' desires, and had no
role in drafting the written record. The dearth of records to corrobo-
rate, clarify, or contradict hearsay has robbed their descendants of
many of the details of their ancestors' world, but by the same token, it
has given them, and their descendants, free rein to create an oral
record of their own choosing.

From existing records, it seems clear that one of the Prospect Hill slaves, Grace Ross, held a place of some importance in the household, because for many years she cooked for the entire family and spent most of her waking hours in close proximity to them. Described in Isaac Ross's will as "my negro woman cook," she would also have lived close by, perhaps just across the yard. We have no way of knowing other details, though, and some of them are crucial. Grace seems to have been cast as a villain in many accounts of the alleged slave uprising at Prospect Hill, without ever actually being named. According to Ross and Wade family tradition, when the slaves revolted during the long period of litigation over Ross's will, they set fire to the house in an effort to kill Isaac Ross Wade. To ensure that no one escaped the fire, the story goes, the cook had laced the family's coffee with an herb that was supposed to induce deep sleep. Although she would likely have had help in the kitchen, Grace is the only slave who is specifically identified in the record as a cook, and while it is possible that Isaac Ross Wade replaced her when he took over the management of Prospect Hill during the litigation, there is no reference to his having done so. In the record, Grace is never given an opportunity to refute the charge.

We also know that Ross provided in his will that upon his daughter Margaret Reed's death, Grace and her children were to be inherited by his granddaughter Adelaide, unless Grace chose to emigrate to Liberia (she did, which also seems to indicate that she was not held accountable for the uprising). Grace's husband Jim appears to have been inherited by Ross's daughter Margaret Reed, because her estate is the provenance listed on his registration on the barque *Laura*, on which the couple and three of their four children set sail for Africa.

Grace is listed in the 1836 inventory of Ross's estate, age thirty-five, with a value of $1,000. Her children Paris, fifteen, Levy, thirteen, Julia, nine, Peggy, five, and Virginia, three, ranged in value from $200 to $700. Judging from the inventory, very young slaves were valued low, owing to their comparative lack of utility and the possibility that they would not reach a productive age, while older slaves declined in value simply because they could not do much and often required special care. As a result an infant and a sixty-year-old might both be valued at $100, while slaves in between often ran as high as $1,500. A few who had specialized skills or were for other reasons considered indispensable could go as high as $2,000. All of which means that, from a financial perspective, Grace was highly valued but not considered utterly irreplaceable.

Grace's kitchen would have occupied a structure separate from the big house to isolate the heat of cooking and the danger of fire, and would certainly have been well-stocked, because this was not a household where any expense was spared. From the receipts of the Ross estate, we know that the family was fond of peppermint and brandied cherries, fine china, and Irish linen, and that in addition to wild game and fish from the surrounding fields, forests, and streams and vegetable and herb gardens tended by the slaves, there was plenty of domestic meat on the table. Included in one inventory of the estate were 198 hogs, 193 sheep, 109 cows, and thirty young steers. The bulk of the meat would have been destined to feed the slaves, although certainly not as filets with Bernaise sauce, and in comparison with the big house, the cupboards of the slaves' cabins would have been spartan. Similarly, while the women in the big house were ordering up bolts of velvet, lace, and silk, the master of the plantation was buying calico and gingham in bulk to be fashioned into dresses for the female slaves—483 yards total in one order, along with a dozen palm-leaf hats, scores of shoes, and 172 packages of tobacco.

Most of Ross's descendants, and published accounts by the American Colonization Society, stress that the Prospect Hill slaves fared better than most, and house servants such as Grace would have had it better still. Cooks typically consumed much the same food as their masters, became more intimate with them, and over time, perhaps, picked up some of their speech patterns and mannerisms. They were also more likely to be educated. This was true of house help on most plantations, and as a result, a dichotomy often developed between them and the field hands, which sometimes led to mistrust. Wash Ingram, a former slave in the Tidewater South who was quoted in a series of narratives compiled by the Federal Works Progress Administration in the 1930s, noted that house servants were envied because they "et at tables with plates," while field hands were "fed jus' like hosses at a big, long wooden trough."

Judging from the slave narratives, the relationship between slave and master was complicated for both, regardless of the strata of slave society one occupied. Some former slaves recalled feeling a kinship with their masters, and many chose to remain on their home plantations after emancipation, though it is impossible to say whether this was a result of affection, necessity, or simple inertia.

Among the narratives is an interview with Charlie Davenport of Natchez, who was owned by Laverne McPhate's forebears. Davenport was of mixed blood, part African-American and part Native American, the result of a union between a slave and a member of the Choctaw tribe, some of whom still lived in the area in the early nineteenth century. His memories were certainly mellowed by time, but it is telling that much of what Davenport had to say concerned the status of his former master, whom he described in the vernacular dialect transcribed by the WPA interviewers as "one o'de riches' and highes' quality gent'men in de whole country. I'm tellin' you de trufe, us didn' b'long to no white trash." Davenport could have fallen prey to a sort of postbellum Stockholm syndrome, identifying with his captors, but he may also have been using the memories at his disposal to elevate his own status, a natural human urge.

The tone of the narratives was certainly influenced by the fact that the subjects were reacting to white interviewers, but they provide some of the only recorded personal recollections of the lives of slaves, and it is evident that those lives were more variable than one might expect, despite being framed by the inevitability of forced servitude. Historian Christopher Morris wrote that one slave owner in the Mississippi Delta, Basil Kiger, enjoyed indulging his slaves now and then, perhaps as much for his own entertainment as theirs. Kiger went so far as to provide elaborate clothes for slave weddings in the big house at his Buena Vista plantation, near Vicksburg. In describing the festivities of one slave wedding in a letter to his wife (who was notably absent), Kiger joked that the table was "quite bountifully supplied the variety however was not very great consisting principally of Hog, Shoat, pork, & Pig, with any quantity of cakes & whiskey." He recounted a slave dance in the mansion's wide central hall, complete with a fiddle player, and said he attended the party but fell asleep around two A.M., "leaving them still at it in high glee."

"It does my heart good to see them so cheerful & happy," he wrote, vowing that he would not sell his slaves "for 10000 dollars."

Other accounts mention slaveholders allowing their slaves small stipends, which they spent on shopping sprees in nearby towns, and in his will, Isaac Ross provided for some of his slaves to receive up to $1,000 should they not choose to emigrate to Liberia. But drawing from the WPA narratives, historian Paul Escott pointed out that this generosity, familiarity, and even intimacy was nonetheless based upon an immovable barrier: the fact, for the vast majority, of permanent enslavement.

Northerner Joseph Holt Ingraham recalled observing the raw deal at the famous Forks of the Road slave market on the outskirts of Natchez. "A line of negroes, commencing at the entrance with the tallest . . . down to a little fellow of about ten years of age, extended in a semicircle around the right side of the yard," Ingraham recalled. "Each was dressed in the usual uniform of slaves, when in market, consisting of a fashionably shaped, black fur hat, roundabout and trousers of coarse corduroy velvet . . . good vests, strong shoes, and white cotton shirts, completed their equipment. This dress they lay aside after they are sold, or wear out as soon as may be; for the negro dislikes to retain the indication of his having recently been in the market."

Ingraham described a transaction in which his companion bought a carriage driver for $975, which included having the slave show his teeth for inspection. "The entrance of a stranger into a mart is by no means an unimportant event to the slave," he wrote, "for every stranger may soon become his master and command his future destinies." How would one react to such a situation—by fading into the background, or by making eye contact with the most attractive prospective owner? And what kind of man would you want to own you?

In this case, the coachman, who was twenty-three, seemed eager to be sold, because he apparently had concluded that the man would be a fair master. When the transaction was complete, the slave "smiled upon his companions apparently quite pleased, then entreated his new owner to also buy his wife, which the man did, contingent upon the approval of his own wife, for $750. The poor girl was as much delighted as though already purchased," Ingraham wrote.

Slavery in the United States traced its origins to a small enterprise in the early colonies, when about twenty black indentured servants arrived in Jamestown, Virginia, in 1619. Many of the indentured who followed were white, and like their black counterparts, could buy their way out of servitude, but eventually nearly all blacks were subject to lifelong enslavement.

According to Escott, the consensus among former slaves was that a good owner was one "who did not whip you too much," while a bad owner "whipped you till he'd bloodied you and blistered you." Those who were fortunate enough to have good owners could expect to have most of their physical needs met but still faced a life of hard work with almost no hope of freedom. The less fortunate faced the potential for hunger, illness, separation from family members, and whatever abuse an angry, disturbed, or bad-tempered owner might inflict.

Escott quoted a Louisiana slave who said that when his masters lamented the departure of their two sons to fight in the Civil War, "It made us glad to see dem cry. Dey made us cry so much." Another slave, interviewed by researchers at Fisk University, told of her effort to get back at a particularly cruel mistress. When the elderly woman suffered a stroke, the young slave was assigned the task of fanning her and keeping the flies away. Taking advantage of the time when the two were alone, the slave would strike the woman across the face with the fan, knowing that she could not tell anyone. "I done that woman bad," the slave admitted. "She was so mean to me." After the mistress died, "all the slaves come in the house just a hollering and crying and holding their hands over their eyes, just hollering for all they could," she said. "Soon as they got outside of the house they would say, 'Old God damn son-of-a-bitch, she gone on down to hell.'"

Even slaves who were treated relatively well by their owners faced the threat of white "patrols" that roamed the countryside at night looking for slaves who were at large without a pass. A slave could, under Mississippi law, venture eight miles from his plantation and be gone for up to two days without being considered a runaway, but it is unlikely that such legal details mattered to some of the patrols. According to many accounts, capturing a lone slave was sometimes a source of entertainment for the men on the patrol, and often ended with whippings.

Among the other indignities of slave life was the appearance of the "breedin' nigger," as former slaves called him, who would be rented by the master to improve the genetic stock of his slaves. One slave said his master's interest in slave husbandry went so far as to include castration of what he called "little runty niggers . . . dey operate on dem lak dey does de male hog so's dat dey can't have no little runty chilluns." Sexual incursions by the master were also common, sometimes as a result of affection but at other times by force.

In an 1852 article in *The New York Times*, Frederick Law Olmsted wrote of a visit to an unnamed Mississippi plantation during which he observed that the slaves were predominately "thorough-bred Africans"—what his host labeled "real black niggers"—but that there were also numerous mulattoes, including one girl who was "pure white with straight, sandy-colored hair." It was not uncommon, Olmsted wrote, citing comments from his host, to find slaves "so white that they could not be easily distinguished from pure-blooded whites." His host, he wrote, "had never been on a plantation before, that had not more than one on it.

"'Now,' said I, 'if that girl should dress herself well, and run away, would she be suspected of being a slave?'"

His host replied, "Oh yes; you might not know her if she got to the North, but any of us would know her."

"How?" Olmsted asked.

"By her language and manners."

"But if she had been brought up as a house-servant?"

"Perhaps not in that case."

Sexual intermingling was common enough both before and after the Civil War that the Mississippi legislature passed a law imposing stiff penalties on whites who engaged in the practice. In what was known as the Black Code, which was instituted after the war, the legislature ordained that white men who had sexual relations with freed slave women could be fined $200 plus up to six months in jail. The penalties were worse for whites than for the blacks involved.

According to Escott, some slave women acquiesced to sexual relations with their masters in order to improve their status. One former slave in the upper South recalled that one reason this was done was because "They had a horror of going to Mississippi and they would do anything to keep from it." Mississippi represented the most frightening aspects of slavery because so many of the plantations were isolated and large, which meant that slaves often had less personal identity to shield them from abuse. In addition, laboring in the vast, steamy fields, which had recently been carved from the hostile wilderness, was reportedly more brutal than having to work the older, smaller, and more established plantations back East. Escott wrote that there were "fabulously wealthy and tastefully cultured families who could afford to treat their slaves with the indulgence that comes from unquestioned security. But most planters were not of that stripe." The latter was particularly true in developing plantation regions, he wrote.

Some planters recognized the importance of keeping their slaves comparatively content, providing them with their own vegetable plots, access to smokehouses, and even opportunities for occasional parties and repasts. These relative indulgences and freedoms may have had their basis in humanitarianism, or they may have been simply a part of the proper maintenance of the human machinery that produced the crop. No doubt the horses, too, were well shod, got their vaccinations, and enjoyed an occasional treat of sweet feed. It is evident, though, that Isaac Ross was among the more progressive planters in the treatment of his slaves. Thomas Wade noted with obvious pride that the Prospect Hill slaves "were taught to be self reliant in many ways as he would give each family a certain number of corn fed hogs for their year's supply and each one had smokehouses and cared for their own meat. His large herd of fine cattle was used for the most part in supplying his slaves with fresh beef during the summer and fall as it was his custom to have two fine beeves slaughtered each week for their benefit." While it is tempting to think that Wade, as a proud descendant, may have embellished his portrait of antebellum Prospect Hill, the record shows that a large number of Ross's slaves were taught to read and write, in clear defiance of state law, that he never sold any of them or allowed families to be broken up, and that he provided them posthumously with the option of freedom, albeit with strings attached.

During Ross's years at Prospect Hill more than 100 slaves were born, and like many planters of the era, he often bestowed upon them lofty names that belied their status, such as Alexander the Great, and Plato. According to Wade, the slaves represented much more than interest on an investment. In Wade's view, Ross treated his slaves more like an extended family. An 1848 report by the New York Colonization Society seems to confirm Ross's paternalistic leanings, as well as his practice of keeping his slave community sequestered and intact. According to the report, "To render them happy appears to have been a principal object of their owner. He was an excellent planter; yet for many years, instead of endeavoring to increase his estate, he developed and applied its great resources to comforts of his people." Furthermore, the slaves "enjoyed almost parental care and kindness."

The possibility exists, of course, that some of the slaves were actually related to Ross. A researcher for a 1996 public television documentary on prominent mixed-race families in America claimed that Isaac Ross's mother was black or of mixed race. Family accounts and genealogical records cite Ross as the offspring of Isaac and Jean Brown Ross, but historian Mario Valdes disagreed in a memo to the producers of the Public Broadcasting Service's *Frontline* report, "Claiming Place: Bi-Racial American Portraits." Valdes wrote that Ross was a "prominent descendent of those Gibsons of colour" in South Carolina who later emigrated to Mississippi, adding that historical references that cite the elder Isaac Ross and Jane Brown as his parents have "conveniently glossed over the fact that Captain Isaac was in fact the son of a Gibson woman (Mary Gibson who was married to Isaac)."

Valdes is not alone in making that assertion. Ed Adams, a retired Chicago police detective who responded to one of my Internet postings about the family, said he believed that Ross was the son of the elder Isaac Ross and a woman of African descent named Mary Gibson. Ed wrote that Mary Gibson "was married to Isaac Ross (the elder) in a wedding performed by a Reverend Randall Gibson, who was believed to be of African descent," and added that he traces his own lineage to a mixture of slaves and slave owners, and calls himself an indirect descendant of Prospect Hill.

Thomas Wade noted that the marriage of Ross's daughter, Jane, to John I. W. Ross (her first cousin) was performed by Rev. Randle Gibson, and while it seems unlikely that Gibson was of obvious African descent—he served in the U.S. embassy in Madrid and later as a Confederate general, a U.S. congressman, and a U.S. senator, he was also among the prominent Americans mentioned in the Public Broadcasting Service report.

Laverne McPhate seems unperturbed when I throw out this provocative tidbit, and allows that history and family lore are notoriously inexact. It is sometimes difficult just to keep the branches of the family tree straight, she says, because so many names are repeated over time. Records of births and deaths in family Bibles and the tombstones at Prospect Hill seem fairly reliable, but even they must be closely scrutinized. In the cemetery are the graves of three Isaac Ross Wades, all brothers, grandsons of Isaac Ross. The first two died as toddlers, only a year apart, while the third grew up to become the executor and contestor of Ross's will.

As for Valdes' claim, Laverne says, "I haven't heard that, but it's highly possible. When they left the Carolinas and came down here, so many things changed. But that's the sort of thing . . . well, they always leave that part out."

CHAPTER FOUR

AS A SLAVEHOLDER IN 1830s Mississippi, Isaac Ross's motives for seeking to repatriate his slaves were no doubt questioned by his Northern peers in the American Colonization Society, and likewise his devotion to the Southern way of life was likely questioned by neighboring planters who considered him a closet abolitionist. One can't help wondering, too, if his slaves wondered whether he would ever make good on the deal.

Slaveholders who supported African colonization were caught in the crossfire of a burning issue of the era: how best to deal with free blacks, whether for humanitarian reasons or out of fear. Many in the colonization society saw free blacks as potential emissaries, who would use their freedom to help educate and Christianize native Africans, while others saw colonization simply as a mechanism for deporting free blacks from America. Free blacks were a source of great concern for the white power structure in the South because they had the potential to upset the status quo. As historian Mary Louise Clifford noted, "the free Negro posed a threat to the economic system of the American South, for he was an example to cause discontent and rebellion among the slave labor upon which the system rested."

At the time Ross drafted his will, the memory was comparatively fresh of the Nat Turner slave revolt in Virginia, in 1831, in which fifty to sixty whites had been killed. During the revolt, which effectively ended the fledgling abolitionist movement in the South, Turner's approximately seventy followers moved from farm to farm in Southampton County, murdering whites and taking on new followers among the slaves they freed. In the aftermath, new laws controlling the activities of slaves were passed across the South, and the Maryland general assembly joined in the colonization effort in Liberia, providing an annual appropriation to the Maryland Colonization Society. Maryland already had a statute forbidding free blacks from other states from settling there, but in 1831 the penalties were stiffened. The assembly also forbade free blacks from buying liquor, owning guns, selling food without a license, and even attending religious meetings if no whites were present. State law required that slaves who were freed following passage of the act be transported out of state.

Fear of the potential dangers posed by slaves and free blacks was not limited to the South. Indiana enacted restrictive laws in 1831, including a requirement that free blacks entering the state post a $500 personal bond, while the District of Columbia enforced a ten P.M. "colored curfew" which carried penalties of arrest, fine, and flogging. When slavery was eventually abolished in Washington by an act of Congress in 1862, $100,000 was set aside to pay the transportation costs of D.C. slaves who chose to emigrate to Haiti, Liberia, or any other country outside the United States.

The idea of removing free blacks had first been seriously considered in 1800, when whites managed to prevent a Virginia slave uprising and subsequently hanged thirty-five slaves. The Virginia house of delegates had called upon the governor to speak with President Thomas Jefferson "on the subject of purchasing lands without the limits of this state, where persons obnoxious to the laws or dangerous to the peace of society may be removed." The legislators considered removal to the "vacant western territory of the United States," but Jefferson subsequently began talks through the American ambassador in London for a joint effort with Great Britain, which was repatriating freed slaves in what would become the West African nation of Sierra Leone. The talks apparently went nowhere. Then, in 1810, slaves revolted in two Louisiana parishes, and following another uprising in Virginia in 1816, the American Colonization Society came into being.

Although Jefferson owned slaves and made no secret of his belief that blacks were inferior to whites, he was also on record as saying he considered slavery wrong. He was ambivalent—or hypocritical—in other ways, supporting colonization in part as a way of preventing the mixing of the races, while fathering children by his own slaves. If the president and author of the Declaration of Independence personally held conflicting views, however, he was forthright in his support for repatriation, arguing that "Deep rooted prejudices entertained by whites; ten thousand recollections, by the blacks, of injuries they have sustained . . . will divide us into two parties and produce convulsions which will probably never end but in the extermination of one or the other race."

In creating its Liberian colony in 1820, the American Colonization Society used as a template the colony of Sierra Leone, immediately to the west on the coast of West Africa. Freetown, the capital of Sierra Leone, had been founded thirty years earlier by English philanthropists as a home for freed British slaves, many of whom had originated in America but had won their freedom by fighting for the crown during the American Revolution. West Africa was chosen for the colonies for several reasons, but primarily because it was known as the "slave coast" and was the general area of origin of large numbers of slaves, including the majority of those who ended up in the Americas. Historians estimate that approximately sixty million Africans were captured as slaves in West Africa from the first recorded slave sale in 1503 to the end of the trade in the mid-nineteenth century. Of those, an estimated forty million died before arriving at their destinations.

Until the establishment of the two colonies, the territory that would become Liberia had been held by indigenous tribes, many of which were (and in some cases continued to be) active in the slave trade. In hindsight, it was a recipe for disaster.

The society claimed significant support on the national scene, including presidents Jefferson, Andrew Jackson, and James Monroe (for whom Liberia's capital, Monrovia, was named), as well as Henry Clay, Daniel Webster, Francis Scott Key, and Robert E. Lee. Its first president was George Washington's nephew, Supreme Court Justice Bushrod Washington.

Although most of the big names belonged to Southerners, the society's membership also included prominent Northern clergymen and abolitionists. All they agreed upon, apparently, was that "returning" freed slaves to Africa was a good idea. Henry Clay, to whom Isaac Ross's daughter Margaret Reed would leave some of her slaves for repatriation, based his argument on the premise that slaves would never be treated as equals in the United States, that because of "unconquerable prejudice resulting from their color, they never could amalgamate with the free whites of this country." Clay was among a group that reportedly included Monroe, Jackson, Key, and Webster that convened in the Davis Hotel in Washington, D.C., on December 21, 1816, to form the American Colonization Society.

The society's plans were clothed in a garment of philanthropy, and designed to encourage the repatriation of emancipated slaves, rather than only blacks who were already free. Another of its stated purposes was to enlighten the tribes of West Africa through Christian missions and leadership by comparatively educated freed-slave emigrants. For three years beginning in 1816, the society raised funds by selling memberships, and in 1819 the U.S. government granted $100,000 to aid the effort. Congress also authorized President Monroe to use U.S. Navy vessels to seize slaves from American ships at sea that were caught smuggling them to Cuba, Puerto Rico, and Brazil, the primary markets after the slave trade was abolished in the United States by constitutional provision. The slaves liberated from the ships were known as "recaptures," and ultimately, they added another variable to what would be an already volatile cultural mix in the Liberian colony.

In January 1820 the society's first chartered ship, the *Elizabeth*, set sail from New York for West Africa with three society agents and eighty-eight emigrants aboard. The ship first landed in Freetown, then made its way along the coast to the future Liberia, where the colonization effort got off to an inauspicious start. Within three weeks all of the society's agents and twenty-two of the immigrants had died of fever. The survivors were evacuated to Freetown. Undeterred, the society organized two more voyages and began buying additional land, sometimes under threat of force, from tribal chiefs along the coast. According to historian Clifford, U.S. officials struck a deal with indigenous tribes that allowed the emigrants to disembark in exchange for official tolerance of the tribes' active slave trade, which would have meant that as freed slaves were arriving to settle in Liberia, new slaves would have been setting sail. The colonization society board rejected the deal, however. A compromise that gave the coastal region only to the immigrants, and apparently made no mention of the slave trade, was accepted, but when the immigrants actually landed they met armed resistance and so moved farther down the coast, where they were again attacked. Some escaped to Freetown while others remained trapped within crude, hastily built fortifications. Only a small group persevered.

The colonization society received a significant public relations setback in November 1822, when a concerted attack was mounted by the tribes on those settlers who had remained. Although the immigrants were armed with cannons and guns, they were besieged until a British warship came to their aid. According to Clifford, one female emigrant, Matilda Newport, became a folk hero for her role in thwarting the attack. Upon seeing that all the cannoneers were dead or wounded, Newport reportedly lit the fuse of a cannon with the ember from her pipe and thereby repulsed the approaching tribesmen. Matilda Newport Day afterward became a national holiday in Liberia.

By the end of 1822 a tenuous peace was negotiated between the settlers and the tribes. Soon after, colonization society officials rebuked the immigrants for what they considered to be a poor effort at self-sufficiency. Clifford wrote that the settlers considered farming too closely akin to the slavery they had known in the United States, yet they had few other economic options aside from trade, which was dominated by the tribes.

To engender a sense of purpose, and because the colonization society was having difficulty finding leaders who would remain in place, the group named the colony Liberia and sought to regiment its government on the local level. The colonists began bartering for more coastal land and eventually took control of most of the valuable slave trading ports. By 1830 more than 2,500 immigrants had arrived in Liberia from the United States, and the next year the state of Maryland incorporated its colonization society, distinct from the American Colonization Society, and appropriated money for its own colony.

Even as the colonization effort was getting on its feet, opposition in the United States grew. The concept of colonization was challenged by both white abolitionists and free blacks who argued that African-Americans had earned a stake in the United States, and that repatriation was tantamount to deportation. Those concerns would still be echoed in 1851, when Frederick Douglass, in a speech to the Convention of Colored Citizens, attacked colonization, saying, "But we claim no affinity with Africa. This is our home . . . The land of our forefathers." African-Americans, he said, "do not trace our ancestry to Africa alone. We trace it to Englishmen, Irishmen, Scotchmen, to Frenchmen, to the German, to the Asiatic as well as to Africa. The best blood of Virginia courses through our veins." New York University linguist John Singler, who spent several years studying and teaching in Liberia, noted that "In general African-Americans viewed the ACS with profound mistrust."

The colonization effort was meanwhile denigrated in the South as a tool of abolitionists, despite protests from supporters that the potential for slave uprisings would be lessened by the removal of freedmen and slaves. The fact that the latter argument fell on so many deaf ears illustrates just how polarized the slaveholding and anti-slave camps had become. Yet there was support for the effort in Mississippi. In addition to Isaac Ross, state supporters included Stephen Duncan, a prominent Natchez planter who owned approximately 1,000 slaves; Jefferson County Judge James Green, who was among the first to send a group of his slaves to Liberia and for whom Greenville, Liberia, was named; and state Senator John Ker, who helped found the Mississippi Colonization Society, was a close friend of Ross's, and would successfully defend the legality of his will in the Mississippi legislature.

Ross's death came just two years after the founding of the colony Mississippi in Africa, which, like the Maryland settlement, was initially distinct from the greater colony of Liberia. According to a report published in 1848 by the New York Colonization Society (which included an appeal for funds to help repatriate the Prospect Hill slaves), "In 1834 the friends of colonization in Mississippi sent out two worthy and very reputable colored men by the names of Moore and Simpson to examine Liberia and return with their Report. They were highly gratified, and not only made a most favorable report, but actually emigrated the next year, and are still among the most honorable and prosperous citizens of Liberia.

"This gave such an impulse to the spirit of Colonization, that within a short time several large Estates were emancipated in the vicinity of Natchez, among these, the large Estate of Capt. Ross."

The first documented arrival of Mississippi settlers had been in 1835, when sixty-nine freed slaves, most of them emancipated by Judge Green, arrived aboard the *Rover*.

In 1838 the commonwealth of Liberia was founded under a constitution drawn up by the president of the Massachusetts Colonization Society, with the curious provision that citizenship was to be granted only to "persons of colour"—an effort, some say, to exclude white slave traders—and another that limited the right to vote to slave immigrants, excluding members of indigenous tribes. All government officials continued to be white agents of the American Colonization Society until 1842, when the first African-American was appointed governor. That year also saw the incorporation of Mississippi in Africa, at the mouth of the Sinoe River, into the greater colony of Liberia.

In 1846, in response to growing interest among the immigrants in self-government, the ACS officially severed its ties with the colony, and the next year Liberia declared itself an independent nation, the first in Africa, under the motto, "The Love of Liberty Brought Us Here." The U.S. government did not immediately recognize the new nation, however. Some say this was as a result of misgivings in Congress over the idea of black diplomats in Washington.

The colonization effort was the vehicle for the repatriation of one man who would become Mississippi's most famous slave—Prince Abdul Rahman Ibrahima, whose efforts to return to Africa became a cause célèbre during the nineteenth century. Ibrahima's story was chronicled in numerous newspaper accounts and books in the early nineteenth century, and in a later book by historian Terry Alford.

Ibrahima was a West African prince who had been sold into slavery at age twenty-six, in 1788, after his army was defeated in battle. He was subsequently transported to the United States, and eventually found himself at Foster Mound plantation, near Natchez, struggling to convince his owners and anyone else who would listen that he was a nobleman. He was said to have promised Thomas Foster, who had bought him, a ransom of gold in exchange for his freedom, but Foster had scoffed at the offer. Alford suggested that Foster had heard similar stories before. "Whites were suspicious of pretensions of royal birth," he wrote. "They caused dissension in the quarters and were an annoying source of extra-institutional authority."

Apparently most people recognized that Ibrahima was different. Part of a larger group of African prisoners of war brought to Natchez to be sold as slaves in 1788, he reportedly carried himself in a regal manner and at first refused to perform manual labor. He also tried to escape several times, but returned when it became evident that he had no place to go. Although the accounts of others eventually confirmed that his father was the king of a nation known as Timbo, which is now part of Guinea, Ibrahima had no choice but to settle into the life of a common slave, marrying a slave woman named Isabella, with whom he had nine children.

Ibrahima's story took its second major turn with a wildly coincidental meeting in 1807. An Irish ship surgeon, John Coates Cox, who had been rescued by Ibrahima's father in Africa many years before, recognized Ibrahima in Natchez, and confirmed what the prince had been saying all along. Cox had gone ashore on the West African coast in 1781 to hunt, and had become lost and eventually left behind. Ill with fever, ravaged by insect bites, with one leg lame from the bite of a poisonous worm, Cox was near death when Ibrahima's family found him and nursed him back to health. Cox later immigrated to Natchez and spotted Ibrahima in a market where Foster allowed him to sell vegetables from his personal garden, as well as Spanish moss, which he pulled from the trees and used as stuffing for mattresses. Cox offered to buy Ibrahima's freedom but Foster refused, saying he valued his services as an accountant. It is apparent that by then even Foster recognized Ibrahima's noble birth. In addition to his dignified bearing, education, and refined knowledge of Islam, Ibrahima was a master equestrian, and so also became a groom at Foster Mound. Thomas Foster was an avid horse racer and according to local lore once won a race against Andrew Jackson, who owned a trading post in the area, but when Jackson also offered to buy the groomsman, he again refused.

Andrew Marschalk, a local newspaperman, took an interest in Ibrahima and wrote numerous articles and pleas on his behalf, and eventually the story made its way to Secretary of State Henry Clay, who petitioned President Adams to intervene. Adams persuaded Foster to free Ibrahima twenty-five years after Cox had confirmed his identity and forty years after the prince had been enslaved.

Few people seemed clear on where Ibrahima's kingdom lay, a fact that Ibrahima used to his advantage. Marschalk was convinced that Ibrahima was a Moor from Morocco, and, according to Alford, Ibrahima wisely assumed the role, perhaps hoping that a North African identity would improve his chances of release. The ruse seems to have worked. On July 10, 1827, President Adams wrote in his diary that he had been approached about coming to Ibrahima's aid, describing him as "an African, who appears to be a subject of the Emperor of Morocco. . . ." Adams authorized the purchase of Ibrahima, if the price was right. The sale was negotiated with Foster's stipulation that Ibrahima's passage to Africa be guaranteed, and that his offspring remain behind as slaves. The mechanism for the emigration would be the American Colonization Society, which proposed sending Ibrahima to its colony in Liberia.

In a January 12, 1828, letter to the society, Clay cinched the deal, and in February Ibrahima was freed in Natchez. The question then presented itself: what to do about Ibrahima's wife, Isabella? Eventually Thomas agreed to sell her, too, and the necessary funds were raised among the local citizens. The couple then set out on a long tour that ended in Washington, D.C., during which they hoped to raise enough money to buy their children. Prior to the trip, Clay had authorized the expenditure of $200 to outfit Ibrahima in "handsome Moorish dress appropriate to his rank prior to his captivity."

Once he reached Washington, Ibrahima met with the president and told him that he would rather go to Liberia than Morocco. Then he asked that his five sons and eight grandchildren be allowed to accompany him. The latter request was denied.

Before his ship set sail, the colonization society had Ibrahima appear in public, in his Moorish costume, before a panoramic painting of Niagara Falls, and charged an admission of twenty-five cents per head, with half of the proceeds going to him. Ibrahima, whose health was by then declining, finally left for Africa in 1829. Upon his arrival in Liberia, he wrote back to family members at Foster Mound, saying he hoped to raise money for their emancipation and emigration. "I shall try to bring my country men to the Colony and try to open the trade," he wrote. He died five months later, before a caravan from Timbo bearing gold could reach him. Hearing of his death, the caravan turned back.

Ibrahima apparently had a bad feeling about Liberia. According to Alford, he "was appalled with the succession of funerals and asked a man who was fluent in English to draft a letter to a New York minister who had helped him immigrate and was considering joining him there. 'I beg you not mention to come to Africa,' Ibrahima wrote. 'You must stay where you are for the place is not fit for such people as you.'" By the time of Ibrahima's death, $3,500 had been raised in the United

States to pay for the purchase and emigration of his children, but the
intractable Foster refused to sell. Among Ibrahima's five sons and four
daughters, only three are now known by name: Simon, Prince, and
Levi. When Foster died shortly after, his heirs received his slaves, and
all except Prince and his wife and children were sold to sympathizers
and departed Natchez for Liberia in 1830.

In the summer of 2000, while researching the story of Prospect Hill, I
encounter two of Ibrahima's descendants following the same path I am
on, but going the other way. They have arrived in Natchez from Liberia
in hopes of finding their Mississippi kin, and their visit has created a
minor stir in the local news media. Natchez is known for its lavish
mansions, and not surprisingly, most visitors come with white antebellum culture on their minds. The city is a mecca for those interested in
the romanticized lifestyles of the Old South—the grand balls, the Vic-
torian empire furniture, the formal gardens of camellias, azaleas, jasmine, and wisteria. In recent years, however, tourism officials and
historic preservation groups have begun to recognize the importance
of African-American culture in the city's history, and among the relevant stories, Prince Ibrahima's is the most remarkable.

The descendants, Youjay Innis and Artemus Gaye, are descended
from his son Simon. Growing up in Monrovia, Liberia, Innis tells me
over the phone, he heard a lot about Mississippi—about the cotton
fields in which his ancestors had toiled as slaves and about Ibrahima's
efforts to win his freedom. Youjay, who is attending the University of
Evansville, in Indiana, was curious about what Mississippi looked like,
about the people who had owned Ibrahima, and about what had
become of the family members who remained behind when the prince
succeeded in emigrating to Liberia in 1829. He also wanted to see how
his ancestors had lived here before they emigrated. So he set out for
Natchez with Artemus, his cousin, to see what they could find. In
Natchez they talked with anyone who was knowledgeable about
Ibrahima's story or about Foster Mound, and when they met Ann
Brown, she called me. The slaves of Foster Mound, she said, were distant relatives of the Rosses.

Innis told the *Natchez Democrat* that he had long wanted to return
to Mississippi to get a greater understanding of Ibrahima's experience

there, and their arrival in the city coincided with the anniversary of Ibrahima's sale as a slave on August 18, 1788. Gaye told the newspaper that they did not see the timing as a simple coincidence. "The spirits of our ancestors are guiding us," he said. "Everything was leading to Mississippi."

Innis and Gaye visited the site of Foster Mound and strolled nearby cotton fields, and Gaye said he was moved by the experience, and felt "no bit of anger. But a sense of healing and reconciling the past with the present." After meeting one of Foster's descendants in Natchez, they moved on.

Few of the immigrants to Liberia shared the sort of notoriety enjoyed by Ibrahima, but his emigration brought attention to the repatriation effort. During the height of colonization, between 1820 and 1870, the American Colonization Society sent an estimated 13,000 emigrants to the colony, the majority of whom were sponsored by societies in Georgia, Louisiana, Maryland, Massachusetts, Mississippi, New York, Pennsylvania, and Virginia. The largest group came from Prospect Hill.

How Ross decided to repatriate his slaves is still subject to debate, even among his descendants. Some attribute his interest to philanthropy, others to something close to a filial love for his slaves, and still others to fear—either of the fate that would befall his slaves after he died, or of what would become of the South once they and hundreds of thousands of others were inevitably freed.

That Ross shared the society's missionary zeal appears doubtful. Although descendant Annie Mims Wright described him as "of a deeply religious nature," Harnett Kane, citing testimony from the litigation of his will, concluded that "far from being minister-ridden, Ike Ross had a good natured tolerance toward all faiths." John Ker, who alone among them had firsthand knowledge, went a giant step further, arguing that Ross was not a religious man in the traditional sense at all.

"To those who enjoyed his acquaintance, it would be superfluous of me to say that no man could sustain a higher character for unsullied probity and honor; or for vigor, energy and independence," the senator wrote in a published defense of Ross's will. He added that he felt it necessary to stress those points "inasmuch as great pains have been taken to make the impression, that the Will was made in the immediate prospect of death, and under the influence of 'priests and fanatics.' The truth is, he counseled with no priest or clergyman, and no man was ever more free from the influence of that class of men, or of any description of fanaticism." On the contrary, Ross "was rather hostile, than otherwise, to religion, or at least to the creeds taught by any of the prevailing Christian denominations; and although kind and hospitable to clergymen, and all others, who visited his house, he was far from being influenced by any one. Even the Reverend Mr. Butler, who, from having been a classmate in college with a son of Captain Ross, had visited and become intimate in the family, had never been in any way consulted by him relative to the Will."

While Ker was unwavering in his fidelity to Ross's dying wish, his support for repatriation was rooted more in pragmatism than benevolence. In a July 25, 1831, letter to Isaac Thomas, a Louisiana planter who was trying to organize a colonization society in his own state, Ker wrote, "You avow your willingness 'to see every colored person moved from the United States' and I agree with you in thinking the first introduction of them the greatest curse that was or perhaps will be inflicted on the country. The free colored people are more injurious to society than the same number of slaves, and their removal would therefore confer a greater benefit.

"Already," he continued, "an extensive and fertile region in Africa the land of their forefathers but a few generations removed, holds out to the free men of color in the United States the tempting allurements, of a *Home and a country of their own, of freedom, and self government, of a rich reward of industry in plenty and even in wealth.* It certainly would not be contended that there are not inducements which ought to decide Him, to abandon the country where He has experienced only degradation, and the almost necessary consequences, *poverty, vice and misery.*"

Regarding Ross's motivation, Ker argued that the will "was no death-bed alarm of conscience from the abolitionists' sin of slaveholding; on the contrary, if that had been the case, he would have required all of his slaves to immigrate rather than giving each of them a choice." As for a perceived link between colonization and abolition, he wrote that "the most *deadly hostility* exists, on the part of the abolitionists, to the Colonization Society."

Thomas Wade postulated that Ross's motives were rooted in concern over abolition and a desire to reward his slaves, "rather than a deep religious conviction concerning the moral issues of slavery. While he was religious, I am sure, he stated that it was his firm belief that the institution of slavery could not last more than twenty-five years. Subsequent momentous events confirm the fact that he visioned the future well."

Another descendant, Robert Wade, now a retired civil engineer in Port Gibson, says he was always told that Ross had "mixed emotions about slavery," and that "he realized they were going to be more of a liability than an asset in the long run.

"The intent of the Colonization Society was good," Robert says, then adds, rather sardonically, "like so many other intents over the years."

The closest to a consensus among the descendants is that Ross cared about his slaves and that he was both concerned about what would happen after he was gone and convinced that the eventual emancipation would spell trouble for everyone. Although the succession of deaths among his own family members had no doubt shown him that his ability to maintain the balance of life at Prospect Hill was fleeting, freeing his slaves outright was not a viable option. It would have required the approval of the state legislature, which was not likely to grant it. And even if it had been granted—then what? There were few opportunities available to the average free black in the United States at the time.

Ultimately, Ross wanted his slaves to have an opportunity to make their own way, and for whatever reasons, he decided that their best chance was in Africa.

CHAPTER FIVE

BY MID-JANUARY 1836, everyone would have known that Isaac Ross was dying—the family, the neighbors, and the slaves, including Enoch, his manservant, with whom Ross had had a close but tumultuous relationship during the last few years. Ross's dying meant very different things to his grandson, Isaac Ross Wade, who was to be the executor of his estate, and to his daughter Margaret Reed, who was about to lose her father and face the consequences of carrying out the directives outlined in his will.

The scene must have been awkward when Ross called his remaining family to his side, a few days before he died, to reiterate those plans. It is easy to imagine Wade and Reed exchanging a cool glance as the old man lay prostrate on a couch in his salon, finally succumbing to a long and painful illness.

The fallow winter fields of Prospect Hill would have been visible beyond the wavy glass of the windows, with row after row of bare cotton stalks marching away to the horizon, flecked with lint hanging from empty bolls. In earlier days, Ross might have been reading on this very couch, or sitting at his desk reckoning accounts, or hunting in the woods, or making sure there was enough firewood in store and enough food for his family and his slaves and his livestock. But the unnamed sickness had triumphed over everything. In four or five days he would be dead, and everything would be in Wade's and Reed's hands, until her death, which would be the true moment of reckoning.

Wade and Reed were the two people whom Ross had decided he could trust to carry out his plan. If she did not know it then, Reed would find out soon enough that her father had made a crucial, disastrous mistake.

The two would later recount the substance of Ross's words on the day he called them to his side, in an affidavit filed in Jefferson County Probate Court—a document that, it seems safe to assume, marked the last time they agreed upon anything pertaining to Prospect Hill. In the affidavit, Wade and Reed verified that Ross had restated his plans for the repatriation of the slaves, which was to take place after Reed herself had died. Soon, however, Wade reportedly told Reed that he had no intentions of abiding by his grandfather's wishes, which prompted her to draft her own will, mirroring her father's, and to spend the remaining two years of her life doing everything in her power to see that his plan was carried out. Wade would spend the next decade, and most of the funds of the estate, doing everything he could to prevent it.

As he lay dying, Ross apparently knew nothing about the rift. He had no reason to believe his plan would not prevail, for it must have seemed as well-laid and manageable as a fire burning in the hearth. He had succeeded at almost everything he had undertaken in life, sometimes at great peril. He was an honored veteran, respected in the community, and owned 5,000 acres of fertile land in the wealthiest cotton district in Mississippi, perhaps the world. In his house were portraits painted by skilled artists, cases of leather-bound books, carpets from the Orient, massive looking-glasses in gilded frames and other elaborate furnishings, including one of his prized possessions, the rosewood and ebony piano. In his stables were fine horses and expensive, well-sprung carriages. Scattered across his holdings were nearly 200 people whom he owned. All of it was his to do with as he saw fit. Still, even a fire in the hearth must be tended lest it burn itself out or rage out of control, so Ross left nothing to chance.

He had refined the will on several occasions, but the thrust was always the same regarding the repatriation plan. He also provided for contingencies. Should the slaves choose not to go to Liberia, they were to be sold along with the plantation, and the proceeds used to found an institution of learning in Liberia. If the colonization effort failed, the money was to be used to found a school in Mississippi. In any event, his own heirs would receive a comparatively small inheritance. Notably, Isaac Ross Wade was to receive only his secretary desk and a case of books.

Ross directed that the plantation be cultivated under the supervision of the executors for one year after Reed's death, with the profits from the sale of the crop applied to an account for the repatriation of the slaves. Another of his plantations, Rosswood, was to go to Jane B. Ross, the mother of Isaac Ross Wade. From the sale of Prospect Hill, prior to applying the funds to the repatriation, his granddaughter Adelaide Richardson was to receive a bequest of $10,000, along with several slaves—Grace and all of her children; Daphne, Dinah, and Rebecca (unless they chose to go to Liberia, which they did); and Hannabal, who was to receive an annual stipend of $1,000 during the remainder of his life (again, unless he chose to emigrate, which he did). The executors were to carefully explain the repatriation option to the slaves, who would decide whether to stay or go, ten days after the cotton crop was picked.

A few of the slaves were excluded, including those identified as Tom, William, Joe, Aleck, and Henrietta, whom Ross had bought in 1833 and 1834 and so were not part of the cohesive slave community, and another identified only as Jeffers, the son of Harry, whose reasons for being denied were not given. These six were to be sold at public auction. Ross also made it clear that if any of the slaves chose not to go to Liberia the families were not to be divided by their eventual sale.

Ross was apparently most concerned with the fate of Enoch, who seems to have disappointed him once and in retaliation had initially been denied the option of emigrating. According to a coda that Ross attached to his will, Enoch was to have been "absolutely sold" at public auction, to remain enslaved while the rest, including Enoch's wife and children, were given the option of freedom in Liberia. Ross later relented, instructing Reed and Wade while lying on his deathbed to restore to Enoch the option of freedom in Africa as well as to provide for another, unique alternative—emancipation, along with his family, with passage to a free state in the North, and 500 silver dollars to help him on his way. It was the most generous offer any of the slaves received, and Enoch took it.

During what would be their last years together, Ross and Reed had laid careful plans not only for Prospect Hill but for other family plantations, including her own, which was known as Ridges. In addition, although it is not mentioned in later court documents or in family accounts, Isaac Ross Jr. appears to have preceded them in leaving his slaves the option of repatriation. It is possible that Ross Jr.'s slaves were absorbed by his father's or sister's estates, or that his widow or son followed through with his plan, but the colonization society's 1848 report notes that he provided for the repatriation of slaves at his St. Albans plantation in his own will, drafted in 1830, two years before he died.

Reed's life must have taken a particularly difficult turn after Ross Sr. died on January 19, 1836. She faced overwhelming responsibility, declining health, and unsympathetic family members and neighbors. Reed had already endured more than her share of travails, losing her parents, one sister, both brothers, and two husbands. Her first husband had died soon after they were married, leaving her childless, at which point she had moved back into the house at Prospect Hill. Eventually, at a party, she had met Thomas Reed, who had moved down from Kentucky, and they began to court in her family home. They married and in 1818 bought an old house in the area and enlarged and modernized it, adding a columned front gallery nearly a hundred feet long, and named it Linden plantation. The honeymoon proved short-lived. Thomas Reed, who had served as Mississippi's attorney general and had recently become the state's first U.S. senator, was suddenly stricken with a "hopeless illness" and died. She sold Linden to John Ker, her father's close friend, and again moved back to Prospect Hill.

Once her father was gone, some of Reed's neighbors reportedly discouraged her from following through with his plan, saying that it was unladylike and foolhardy, and that the will would not hold up in court. She responded by hiring a lawyer, consulting with others whom she knew would be sympathetic to the cause, and drafting her own will stipulating that Ridges plantation and Prospect Hill be sold and that her own 123 slaves be given the same option of emigrating to Liberia under the direction of the American Colonization Society. She also added a coda in September 1838, a short time before she died: "Having information that an effort will be made to invalidate or annul the last will & testament of my late beloved, venerated father," and "in the event of said will and testament being legally pronounced null & void and his Christian and benevolent plan of colonizing his slaves in Liberia in Africa thereby be frustrated," she wrote, her property should go to Rev. Zebulon Butler and Stephen Duncan, both members of the colonization society.

According to Ker, Reed had initially planned to name one of her nephews as executor of her will, but changed her mind after learning that one of them, Wade, was hostile to the cause and planned to contest it. Ker wrote that, "the course of action taken with regard to his Will had changed that determination, and embittered her feelings towards her relations. She was still further exasperated, by declarations made to her, that a learned lawyer had given his opinion, that she could not make a will, to effect her known wishes, that he could not break." Ker wrote that Reed did not ask Butler or Duncan for permission to leave them her estate. Butler, in fact, "regretted, as he has done ever since, that his dying friend would not release him from the duty of serving her in that capacity," he wrote. More determined than ever, she simply drafted the will along the lines of her father's, and included a letter addressed to her slaves explaining what she had done.

Soon after adding the coda, Reed, whom the 1848 colonization society report described as "a lady of large fortune, cultivated intellect and a heart full of noble and elevated sentiments," died. Wade and his mother Jane Ross then filed his contest of her and Ross's wills.

To Wade and other like-minded family members, it all came down to property, and in particular, the Prospect Hill mansion, the 5,000 acres of prime cotton land, and the slaves, who, by the time of Reed's death, had grown in number to nearly 225. In Thomas Wade's view, which he outlined in an August 21, 1902, letter to the Port Gibson *Reveille*, "It was not expected that the heirs of Captain Ross would quietly permit this valuable estate to pass out of their possession."

After Reed's death, Isaac Ross Wade moved into his grandfather's mansion and set himself up as master of Prospect Hill. He was only twenty, but he was ambitious and determined. He saw himself as the heir apparent. His mother, Jane Ross, was his staunchest ally, and perhaps his inspiration. Working in tandem with her, he was clearly willing to do just about anything to hold on to Prospect Hill.

In the litigation over the wills, Wade initially deferred to his mother, who filed the first lawsuit in Jefferson County Probate Court in 1840, but before it was over, there could be no question that it was his fight. Both Jane Ross and the brother of her late husband, Walter Wade, eventually granted him the power to file appeal bonds in their names, of which there would be several. Isaac Ross Wade, meanwhile, assumed the reins of the plantation and the control of its slaves, earning a commission from the estate as its chief executor and submitting invoices to the probate court for his expenses, which the estate paid even as he sought to undermine the very will that had put him there.

His own legal argument was straightforward: Ross's and Reed's wills violated state law governing the manumission of slaves, which required legislative approval, and were designed "for the benefit of negro slaves and therefore void." But if he expected to sail smoothly through the judicial system, he was wrong.

Almost immediately, the co-executors of his grandfather's will came after him. Soon after the contest was filed, in September 1840, Ellett Payson, attorney for co-executors Daniel Vertner, James Parker, Elias Ogden, and John Coleman, filed a petition in Jefferson County Probate Court asking that Wade be removed as executor. In the petition, Payson explained that the four had agreed to pay Wade a $1,500 annual salary from the estate for operating the plantation, but that on June 13, 1840, he had been cited for "appropriating to his own use about twelve thousand dollars of the funds of the estate which he was unable to refund. . . ." The court prohibited the removal of the current crop of cotton from the plantation "except by the direction of the majority of the Executors," and suggested that after the crop was harvested, the executors "might dispense with the services of a superintendent and thereafter give their personal attention to the management of the Estate."

According to the order, Wade had, "in violation of the resolution, shipped some fifty or a hundred bales of cotton of the present crop . . . in his own name, and refused to obey the wishes of the majority of the Executors. . . ." The petition sought reimbursement from Wade and the authority to disburse $10,000 to Sargent S. Prentiss, a locally famous lawyer known as "the silver-tongued orator," no doubt to come after Wade in court. In addition, the co-executors asked for approximately $2,000 from the estate in balance due for a monument to be erected in tribute to Ross by the Mississippi Colonization Society in the Prospect Hill cemetery, a short distance from the house where Wade now lived, as well as for other outstanding debts that Wade had refused to pay. In the coming months the court would twice enjoin Wade from selling or removing the Prospect Hill cotton crop, under penalty of $1,000. Court records also reflect a February 1844 payment from Ross's estate to Wade's chief attorney, Henry Ellett, of $500 for representation in his case against the American Colonization Society—evidence that Wade was using the profits of the plantation to pay for his legal fight to retain control of the estate.

Wade clearly saw Prospect Hill and everything it encompassed as rightfully belonging to him, and must have been extremely frustrated by having to share the management of the estate with his legal opponents, who were forever looking over his shoulder, second-guessing his management, disputing his claims, and waiting for him to make a mistake for which they could drag him back into court. It must have seemed a godsend to him when that impediment was suddenly eliminated, through a technicality.

According to the New York Colonization Society's 1848 report, three of the executors "by some omission were disqualified and removed." In the words of the report, "the Estate fell into the entire care of the only remaining Executor, of the name of Wade, who has, with other heirs at law, left no plan unassayed to defeat the Will." The fourth co-executor had already stepped down, for unexplained reasons, and the technicality is not described in existing court records. Certainly a lot was going on. When the American Colonization Society filed a complaint against Jane Ross in the Superior Chancery Court for attempting to enjoin them from removing the slaves and for attempting to claim the estate in court, included among the defendants were three of the co-executors, Parker, Ogden, and Coleman. The court responded by enjoining Wade, under penalty of $5,000, from distributing the proceeds of the estate to his mother or anyone else. When the colonization society won its case, Wade and company appealed.

Parker, Ogden, and Coleman may have been caught in the middle. They were sued alongside Wade because they had allegedly shirked their responsibility to see to the transfer of the slaves to the colonization society, yet they argued that they had been prevented from doing so by Wade, and would have, had they been ordered to do so by the court. Ultimately the state's High Court of Errors and Appeals upheld the ruling in favor of the colonization society.

If it galled Wade that the courts continued to rule against him and his mother, and to undermine his attempts at unilateral rule over Prospect Hill, he appears to have been undaunted by these legal episodes. Even had he lost the contest in court, its significance transcended local politics, and if Wade managed to ultimately triumph, none of the rest would matter. So when the probate court ruled against him, finding the wills valid, he sought relief in the chancery court, and when it ruled against him, he turned to the court of appeals. When that court also ruled against him, he filed follow-up suits. He had no intention of stopping until he won, or until he ran out of options.

Jane Ross's attempted end-run around the colonization society was multifaceted, but her primary interest in the suit she filed in Jefferson County Probate Court was to have the bulk of the estate awarded to her and her nephew, Isaac Allison Ross. It is not clear why she did not name her son, Isaac Ross Wade, but perhaps the separate suits were designed as a safety net for a group effort. It is also possible that she and her son did not trust each other. Her own familial status was complicated; after being widowed she had married her first cousin, which made her Jane Brown Ross Wade Ross, but as she explained to the court, she was the sole surviving offspring of Isaac Ross. Her nephew, as the son of Isaac Ross Jr., was her father's sole surviving direct male heir.

As with most lawsuits, hers was all about technicalities. Although she questioned her father's legal right to provide for the repatriation of his slaves, and indirectly, his prudence in doing so, her main contention was that the whole affair was moot, because during the two years that Reed had lived after her father, and the two years since her death, nothing had prevented the executors (which, of course, included her son, Isaac Ross Wade) from polling the slaves on their interest in emigrating, as stipulated by the will. Likewise, there had been no court order during the time to remove the slaves from the state. She argued that the provisions of her father's will had essentially lapsed. As she and her attorney interpreted the will, there was a deadline of ten days after Ross's death for polling the slaves about going to Africa, and no provisions for what to do with them if the deadline was not met. With the supposed deadline passed, and in the absence of further directive under the will, state law required that the estate pass to the nearest heirs, which meant her and her nephew. She asked the court to appoint a "disinterested commission" to divvy things up between the two of them, although she was willing to forego the $10,000 and the slaves (including Grace) who were earmarked in the will for her niece, Adelaide Wade Richardson, as well as "some small pecuniary legacies left to some of the slaves." Also exempt were "said slaves named Enoch and Marilla and her children who have been removed from this state." Otherwise, she asked the court to order her son to distribute the proceeds, which was obviously something he would have been happy to do.

As for Reed's will, Jane Ross contended that it had been more or less a product of conspiracy, of a "secret trust" among Reed, Butler, and Duncan. One of her attorneys, identified only as D. Mays, asked the court, "Is it not part of the policy of Mississippi, to protect her citizens against fanaticism in religion, and a morbid sensibility on the subject of slave holding?" He argued that emancipating slaves by will amounted to nothing less than disinheriting the next generation, and if it were allowed, the court would have "thrown open the doors to the abolitionists and invited them to . . . revel in the destruction of the slave property of the state."

Apparently the court was as unimpressed by these arguments as it had been by Wade's. On March 22, 1843, the Superior Chancery Court enjoined Jane Ross from filing further claims until the court had ruled on the matter at hand, which was the suit brought against her by the American Colonization Society. She must have been particularly bothersome to the court, for the injunction carried a penalty for violation of $5,000. She lost the suit the following year. On June 25, 1844, she, Walter Wade, and a man whose name is illegible in the court record turned to the High Court of Errors and Appeals in Jackson, posting a $500 bond payable to the colonization society in the event the courts again ruled against them. Clearly, they were also in it for the long haul.

Jane Ross and her son had some important allies in the state legislature, for as the lower courts were initially deliberating the case, lawmakers passed an act requiring that slaves freed by will be transported to their destination within one year. This forced the colonization society to file suit claiming that they had been prevented from removing the Prospect Hill slaves, although the court of appeals later ruled that the law did not apply to the case, because the ACS had attempted the removal and been thwarted by the heirs even after a ruling in their favor by the courts.

In arguing before the appellate court, Jane Ross's attorneys cast slavery as the paramount concern. "Slaves constitute a portion of the vested wealth and taxable property of the state," they noted in their legal argument. "Without them her lands are worthless. Would it not therefore be contrary to the policy of the state, to part with this vested wealth, this source of revenue, with that which alone renders her soil valuable . . . would it not be productive of mischief, and would it not be spreading a dangerous influence among the slave population of the country, for the slaves of the whole plantations to acquire their freedom, take leave of the country and make their departure, proclaiming liberty for themselves and their posterity? Would this not render the other slaves of the country dissatisfied, refractory, and rebellious? Would it not lead to insubordination and insurrection? And if so, would it not be contrary to the policy of the law? So certain as the heavens afford indications of a coming storm, so certain will scenes of blood be the concomitants of such testamentary dispositions in this state."

The suit questioned the credibility of the colonization society and its right, under its charter, to actually assume ownership of slaves, even temporarily. Ross's attorney referred to the opponents' conviction that "the colony of Liberia is an object worthy of all philanthropic encouragement," and with self-righteous disdain, responded, "What! That institution from which *reverend agents*, thrust themselves among the slave population of the country, and proclaim the advantages and blessings of Liberia: for it is charged in the bill, that some such persons visited Mrs. Reed. Such a colony may indeed be an object worthy of all commendation and encouragement to some persons, but it can never be so, to the peaceable citizens of a slave holding state."

In what proved to be a series of landmark cases, the high court concluded, among other things, that the state's manumission laws did not apply to slaves removed from the state. The justices cited Mississippi's constitutional prohibition, enacted in 1833, against the commercial importation of slaves (although slaves brought in for private use by their owners were allowed until 1845). There was disagreement over the purpose of the prohibition—some argued that it was designed to prevent the "dumping" of sometimes inferior slaves from eastern states where abolitionist sentiments were then taking hold, but the justices attributed the measure to a general need to reduce the state's population of slaves, a purpose the Ross and Reed wills served.

Regarding Jane Ross's suit against the co-executors, the high court upheld a Superior Chancery Court ruling that stated that "Mississippi has no concern with the question of manumitting slaves elsewhere than within her own limits."

Despite the early rulings against him, Wade refused to release the slaves or any other part of the estate. As a result, the colonization society filed its 1842 suit to force him to abide by the court's decree. The ACS won, Wade appealed, and the high court again ruled against him, noting that although the slaves "are not now free, they have an inchoate right to freedom." It is hard to imagine how such a proclamation, recognizing even an incomplete right to freedom by slaves, could go unnoticed, and it did not. According to the high court's Justice Harris, after the announcement of the opinion, and in express reference to it, the legislature passed a law making it illegal to free slaves by will for any purpose without state approval. But if the court upheld the right to free slaves in Africa, Harris also used the occasion to lament the practice of sending freed slaves to Ohio, a state that he described as beset by "negro-mania."

In upholding the ruling in favor of the American colonization society, Justice Clayton noted that the slaves—whom he described as "the bounty" of Ross's estate—"have been detained against the will, against the will of society, and that of all the executors except one. . . ." He called the suits "a fraud"—borrowing a term Wade had used in describing the American colonization society's effort. The heirs' attempts to thwart the will, Clayton wrote, were "a breach of trust and perversion of power," adding, "Rights acquired by fraud cannot be sustained . . . We need not determine the validity of the law. It has nothing to do with the case; the fraud of the party has placed him beyond the pale."

Those were remarkably strong words for an antebellum Mississippi judge to direct at a powerful slaveholder, which gives an indication of the degree of animosity that the Prospect Hill case had engendered.

During and after the Prospect Hill litigation, several other cases made their way to the high court involving the contests of wills that provided for the freeing of slaves through emigration, including one by the heirs of James Leech, of Wilkinson County, south of Natchez, who died the same year as Isaac Ross. His will stipulated that "his negro woman . . . and her four children" should be freed and sent to "Indiana or Liberia, whichever they might choose." In delivering the opinion that Leech's will was valid, Justice Clayton noted, "This will bears a strong resemblance to that of Isaac Ross, which has been the subject of so much controversy in the courts of this state." In that and every other case involving granting freedom to slaves for the purpose of emigration, the court upheld the wills.

During the long period of Prospect Hill litigation, it appears that nearly all of the slaves remained on the Ross and Reed plantations, including those who were to go to Richardson, because the assets were, ostensibly, frozen by the courts. Wade was under court order to keep detailed records of all transactions involving Prospect Hill, including property taxes paid, expenses, sales of cotton, and scheduled payments to Richardson. Perhaps because Richardson was his sister, he chose to honor the portion of the will affecting her bequest while vigorously repudiating the rest. The receipts and annual inventories covered everything from pantaloons and silver and candy to farm implements, livestock, carriages, wagons, stored cotton, tools, and hundreds of shoes. Most importantly, they listed all of the Prospect Hill slaves, together with their offspring, throughout the litigation.

News of the legal proceedings no doubt made its way to the Prospect Hill slaves, and although Wade and his allies were clearly losing every battle, nine years after Ross died their status had not changed. If the highest court in the state had granted them their freedom, why were they still enslaved? Why was Isaac Ross Wade still their master? Notably, Enoch and his family had at some point been freed, according to the stipulations of Ross's will. Enoch had appeared in the first inventory, twenty-five years old with a value of $1,200, along with his wife Marilla, twenty-six and valued at $900, and their children Anna, seven, and Mathilda, five, valued at $300 and $250, respectively. The family was missing from later inventories, with no reference as to where they had gone.

To forestall any effort to claim the slaves, Wade's attorney, Henry Ellett, sought an injunction in Jefferson County Probate Court in July 1844 against John Chambliss, who had been appointed as receiver for the society by the Superior Chancery Court, to prohibit him from seizing the slaves. After Ellett failed in that effort, he successfully sought an injunction in April 1845 against Jefferson County Sheriff Samuel Laughman to prevent him from seizing the slaves from Wade and

delivering them to Chambliss, who had posted a $100,000 bond. The next month Ellett sought another injunction against Chambliss and an order to have Laughman arrested. "We have no desire to hold the Sheriff in close confinement if he will consider himself in custody and not at liberty to proceed further without additional authority . . ." Ellett wrote in his request to the court.

The Superior Chancery Court, meanwhile, authorized Chambliss to take control of the Prospect Hill slaves and plantation in the name of the American colonization society. According to the New York colonization society report, Chambliss, who was a neighbor and friend of Ross's, was undeterred by the possibility of 500 vigilantes united to oppose him, as was rumored, when he agreed to act as receiver for the slaves. Wade again responded by asking the probate court to restrain Sheriff Laughman from seizing the property and to place him under arrest. According to the report, "The Sheriff, evidently did not know how to act; in the double fear of offending the Chancellor on the one hand, or those on whose favor he and the Probate Judge depended for their offices on the other."

Ultimately Laughman chose to obey the Chancellor. He notified Chambliss to prepare to receive the slaves, then failed to show up on the appointed day. The court had issued the order Wade asked for and Laughman had been arrested by the county coroner. Clearly, the rule of law was teetering under the weight of Wade's political influence.

With the sheriff out of commission, there was no one to force Wade to turn over the slaves to Chambliss, and as late as June 7, 1848, Ellett wrote Wade to say that he had no objection to Sheriff Laughman being discharged from his duties through habeas corpus, with the warning that, "if he becomes rebellious afterward we can attach him again."

Some of the slaves had managed to get out before that point. Notably, a large group had been secretly seized by sympathetic whites and marched at night to a steamboat waiting on the Mississippi River, which transported them to New Orleans, and from which they sailed to Liberia. Those who remained at Prospect Hill still had a long row to hoe, however. With lawmakers who had never known Ross having entered the fray, pounding their fists on the podium at the capitol in Jackson and railing against his will, Wade and his mother had other avenues to explore. Before the conflict was over, Ross's Prospect Hill mansion would become his belated funeral pyre, lighting the sky with its flames and taking with it the life of a young girl, and before the ashes were cold, men whom Ross had owned, and for whom he'd laid careful plans, would be hanging from the nearby trees.

CHAPTER SIX

TURNER ASHBY ROSS is a glib man with a deep, gravelly voice who speaks slowly, as if he has all the time in the world. He lives in Vicksburg, Mississippi, and is the uncle of Laverne McPhate. Like her, he is proud of his ancestry—proud both that Isaac Ross voluntarily freed his slaves, and that one of his grandfathers fought for the Confederacy in the Civil War.

"My name come from the general he fought under in the war—Turner Ashby," he says. Ashby was an icon of the lost cause, known as the Black Knight of the Confederacy, because of his dark complexion and eyes, black hair and beard, and what most accounts describe as his regal bearing while mounted on a horse. He was killed in a skirmish in Virginia early in the war, in 1862.

Proud as he is of his Confederate heritage, Turner is not a stereotypical, unreconstructed Southerner. He clearly sympathizes with the freed slaves of Prospect Hill when it comes to the trials they faced after emigrating to Liberia. "You think of what they went through," he says. "Some of 'em was writin' back wantin' more money, 'cause I'm sure they got a little money and a little education, and then they found out right quick there was always gonna be somebody waitin' by the side of the road to blink 'em out of it."

Still, if he can empathize with them as individuals, he views the collective slaves of Prospect Hill in the oldest sense, as chattel. The way he sees it, if Isaac Ross wanted to free his slaves, it was nobody else's business. He doesn't like the idea of neighboring planters voicing objections, much less forming vigilante squads to prevent the will's provisions from being carried out.

"They say all the plantation owners figured this would start a new trend," he says. "This was way before the Civil War, but there was already a lot of talk about antislavery. But what Isaac Ross did was his business. That was his money he paid for those slaves, and he had every right in the world to set 'em free or to do whatever he wanted with 'em."

Offensive as the concept may be to modern sensibilities, the right to ownership did, in fact, drive the contest of the will, and was at issue during the remarkably vitriolic debate in the state legislature, which was later recounted in Ker's published account. Although Ker was a biased participant, he seems to have had a high regard for facts and made no secret of his opinions. He drafted his narrative in response to a December 10, 1841, letter from eleven men who supported Ross's will and wrote to express their gratitude for his efforts to defeat a bill that would have made emancipation and repatriation by will retroactively illegal. Ker, they wrote, had precluded "a gross and dangerous violation of private rights," and he owed the public an unflinching account of what had happened.

Ker's notice, a copy of which lay buried in the haphazard records of the Jefferson County courthouse, seems to have anticipated an attack upon the character of the slaves, if not their potential for violence. Its chief interest lay in the debate over three key issues: fears and allegations that the Prospect Hill slaves were verging on insubordination; the supposition that Ross had written his will under the influence of "terrors of death and judgment, inspired by 'priests and fanatics'" and abolitionists; and the claim that Ross's slaves were by law rightfully the property of his family. Although he addressed each issue, Ker obviously considered property the only one worthy of lengthy debate. Like Turner Ross, he believed in the sanctity of the slaves as property, which meant that only Isaac Ross could, within obvious limits, determine their fate.

Ker began his account with this disclaimer: "Whilst I feel conscious that I am influenced by no intention of injuring any fellow man, either in character or fortune, a solemn sense of duty forbids that I should suppress or disguise the truth, whatever may be the consequence to myself.

"That said, during the last session of our Legislature measures were introduced into the House of Representatives, and passed by that body, which were evidently intended to annul the provisions of the last Will and Testaments of the late Captain Isaac Ross, and his daughter, Mrs. M. A. Reed, both of Jefferson County. Those measures were defeated in the Senate, but, I regret to say, not without difficulty, arising, as I believe, from misrepresentations by interested and prejudiced persons; and I have reason to believe that the purpose is not yet abandoned, but will be renewed." He portrayed the bill as "an attempt to legislate away one of the rights most dear to men and hitherto held sacred, the right to dispose of property, by will or otherwise, at pleasure. . . ."

Isaac Ross could not have had a more able or dedicated champion in the legislature, which convened at what is now the Old Capitol State Historical Museum, but was then a gleaming Greek Revival edifice built just two years before, in 1839. The building was actually the fourth devoted to the purpose, the first having been located in Washington, Mississippi, the territorial capital, and the second in nearby Natchez, which was the epicenter of political power throughout much of the nineteenth century. The third was a temporary assembly hall in the new city of Jackson, which had been selected for the capital in 1817 precisely because it was outside the controlling interests of the Natchez District. Relative isolation from the plantation stronghold may have reduced the influence of vested interests in the contest of Ross's and Reed's wills, but the subject of slavery was overarching. In one way or another, it mattered to everyone, in all parts of the state.

Jackson at the time was an inconsequential town, unimportant as either an agricultural or industrial center, but during each legislative session it became a political battleground, hosting a seasonal mélange of lawmakers from places as diverse as wealthy Natchez, the largely undeveloped Delta, the yeoman-farm country in the northeast hills, and the no-man's-land of the piney woods toward the coast, which included one region that would unofficially secede from the Confederacy during the war. It was a town where lawmakers could spend their free time playing chess or backgammon under the portico of a grand hotel, watching a horse race on the street running before the statehouse, or swilling ale in a basement saloon. One observer, Thomas Wharton, who visited the city in 1837, recalled a bar directly across from the capitol "crowded with a gay and festive party, making night hideous with their bacchanalian revels." Wharton wrote of his disappointment in finding that "Instead of the flourishing young city my imagination promised I should see, the population did not exceed, I would suppose, 900."

The capitol, and the nearby governor's mansion and city hall, represented significant departures from the typical buildings, which Wharton described as "wholly devoid of architectural taste and design." The House of Representatives met in an ornate and spacious chamber at the opposite end of the building from the more restrained Senate chamber, which was embellished with columns modeled after a monument in Athens, Greece. Immediately behind the building was the labyrinthine Pearl River swamp, while the front lawn served an array of public purposes, including occasional slave auctions. There was an odd mixture of pretense and recklessness about the place that provided fertile ground for the pitched battle over the slaves of Prospect Hill.

Ker's turf was the Senate chamber, and it was there that he led the defeat of the offending bill on the last day of the 1841 legislative session. The bill, which originated in the House, proposed to make it illegal to free slaves by will for any purpose, including emigration, without legislative authorization, and sparked heated debate over the "dangerous example the emancipation of the estimated 300 slaves of the Ross and Reed estates would set." In its original version the measure was retroactive, which meant that it would stifle the American colonization society's plan for the Prospect Hill slaves. After the Senate refused to concur, the bill returned to the House, where it was revised and returned. Sensing the danger of compromise, Ker successfully introduced a motion to table the bill until the following Monday, which would be after the close of the session. Tabling was equivalent to rejection.

"By joint resolution of the two Houses, the session was to close on Saturday evening, the 6th of February, at 7 o'clock," he wrote. "Long after 7 o'clock, perhaps 9 or 10, on the evening of the 6th, whilst I was for a moment absent from the Senate Chamber, an attempt was made to call up the bill." When Ker returned and realized the bill had been resurrected, he appealed to his peers in the Senate to abandon the effort, and prevailed on a parliamentary technicality. "Thus ended, for that session, this extraordinary attempt to legislate away the solemn decisions of the highest judicial tribunals of the State," he wrote.

Afterward, when he approached a member of the House with

whom he had been friendly and expressed his surprise that the representative had supported the retroactive measure, he recalled being told that "if the Wills should not be defeated by the Legislature, they would be by violence, and that every man in Jefferson County was opposed to the Wills, and that 200 men were ready to oppose their execution by force of arms, and that he wished to save that county from the odium or disgrace of such a procedure." Ker recalled telling the man that he could not fathom how a legislative act that superceded legal wills affirmed by the highest court "could exert any *moral* influence. Nothing that I can conceive of could be more *demoralizing* in its effects."

As for some lawmakers' claims that the wills were the product of a cartel of abolitionists and religious fanatics, Ker wrote that, on the contrary, the proponents were "emphatically men without reproach. One of them, it is true, is a clergyman; but this, I trust, can only be a subject of reproach, even among those who make no profession of religion, when the life and conduct is inconsistent with the profession." He posed the question: what was the accusation against Rev. Butler, who was one of the men Margaret Reed had named to receive the slaves on behalf of the American colonization society? The answer: "Attempting or desiring to remove, to Liberia, in Africa, *his own slaves*.

"Who will deny that Mrs. Reed had the right to make these gentlemen her heirs?" he asked. Who could question their motives, when they could not benefit from the bequest? Ker recalled being told that Stephen Duncan, another of the recipients, had "actually obtained his portion of the slaves by having them run away from the plantation, and secreted on the banks of the Mississippi until a steamboat was hailed to take them on to Louisiana, whence he sent them to Liberia."

Considering that so many controversial court cases today are tried, at least in part, in the media, it is interesting to note that opponents of the will undertook their own newspaper blitz. "Publication was made in the newspapers of the briefs of the lawyers, and other exparte views of the case, for no other obvious purpose than that of operating, through popular prejudice, upon the Courts," Ker wrote. "There was nothing in this case to justify or even to apologize for such attempts to create popular excitement."

For Ker, the issue extended beyond his support for colonization. "If we quietly fold our arms and passively acquiesce to such proceedings, what security, I ask, have any of us for the protection of law to our property, or lives, or our liberty? Has it indeed come to this, that the laws of the land are to be annulled by one man, or even 500 men, because certain testators did not happen to make their Wills in accordance with their views, or with public sentiment? Let us not deceive ourselves. Passive acquiescence in such doctrines or in such measures is criminal. 'The poisoned chalice may soon be returned to our own lips.' *We may be the next victim of the ruthless hand of lawless usurpation and violence."*

The defeat of the retroactive provision was a major coup for Ker and other defenders of the will, despite contemporary accounts cited in the New York colonization society's 1848 report "that 500 men 'are pledged and ready to prevent' the full administration of the laws of the land." The report added, "Truly, the spirit of anarchy is stalking with a bold front in our land, when 'people have been called upon to rise up and put the laws at defiance'; when calls have been made upon the Legislature to usurp power not granted to them by the people in the Constitution, to annul the solemn decrees of the Courts—to wrest from the hands of the citizens, property which has been devised to them under the laws of the State."

As for the sentiment that the potential for freedom would undermine the ability of slave owners to control their slaves, Ker was dismissive— perhaps overly so. "It was alleged," he wrote, "that insubordination existed among the slaves of these two estates, to such an extent as to produce great and general alarm in the neighborhood, and even lively apprehensions of an insurrection, &c. I cannot do justice to the eloquence which was called into exercise in the description of the dangers and the horrors which impended over this ill-fated neighborhood. But, like many other splendid passages of poets and orators, this eloquent description had much more of fiction than fact for its foundation. Subsequent investigation has enabled me to say, that on the estate of Capt. Ross there never had been the slightest insubordination; and on that of Mrs. Reed, none more formidable than frequently occurs from the change of overseer; and none that was not promptly quelled by the energy and resolution of a single citizen. But for the sake of argument, suppose it had been true, that the negroes were a vicious, insubordinate and dangerous set. What would have been the danger to the neighborhood, or to the State, of sending them off to Africa?"

The slaves, he added, were first and foremost the possessions of Isaac Ross, who "ardently desired to provide for their welfare and happiness after his death. It is not for others to determine whether the plan he adopted was wise or unwise."

As Ker predicted, the affair was far from over when the legislature failed to circumvent the first round of judicial rulings. Although the courts ultimately ruled that the law that was later passed, without the retroactive clause, did not apply to the Ross and Reed wills, there was still the matter of forcing Isaac Ross Wade to relinquish his claim and allow the transfer of those slaves who had not already been spirited away. The majority of the slaves were still marooned at Prospect Hill, despite the courts' rulings, and were growing increasingly restive, according to the traditional family account, which attributes the burning of Ross's house in 1845 to an uprising of those slaves who had lost patience with the delays.

The threat of slave rebellion was at the forefront of the debate over Ross's and Reed's wills, so it seems remarkable that there is no documentation of the alleged uprising or the burning of the Prospect Hill mansion in April 1845. Every reference I initially found could be traced only to Thomas Wade, who cited the recollection of his father, Isaac Ross Wade, who clearly had his own spin.

Wade's version, chronicled in his emphatic letter to the Port Gibson newspaper in 1902, is accepted as gospel by most of the heirs of the slaveholding family, although others I would find—particularly from the descendants of slaves—are not convinced of its veracity. There is no doubt that the house burned and that Martha Richardson died. The date is on her tombstone in the family cemetery a short distance away. It also seems plausible, despite the lack of documentation, that the lynchings took place. Beyond that, I found no record of the uprising.

For Thomas Wade, setting the record straight appears to have been a lifelong mission. In his letter to the Port Gibson *Reveille*, he referred to the doomed Prospect Hill house as "Judge Wade's residence," despite the fact that his father (who, indeed, later became a judge) did not have legal title to the property at the time the estate was being contested. According to his account, "this commodious and most substantial old plantation home with all the handsome furniture, valuable books, and beautiful pictures, the accumulation of a lifetime by wealthy, educated and refined people, was burned on April 15, 1845, at 1 A.M., by Captain Ross' slaves more than nine years after his death."

This was to be the nexus of every account that came after.

Among the occupants of the house at the time of the fire, Thomas Wade wrote, were his parents and the three small children they had at the time; his mother's niece, Mary Girault, of Grenada, Mississippi; his father's sister, Adelaide Wade Richardson and her three small children, including Martha, who was about six years old; and Dr. Wade and his business partner, a man named Bailey. Thomas Wade also offered the first written account of the cook spiking the coffee with a drug or herb, and carefully noted that Girault and Dr. Wade, Isaac Ross Wade's uncle, were the only adults who chose not to partake.

"The house was a large, two-story house, and Dr. Wade, Mr. Bailey, Mrs. Richardson and children and Miss Girault occupied the rooms in the second story," he wrote. "Dr. Wade was the first occupant to discover the fire, and immediately set to work to arouse the family." The doctor apparently had difficulty waking the others and "probably would not have succeeded, owing to the size of the house, had it not been for the assistance of one of my father's own slaves and body servant Major, who was faithful, and rendered every assistance in his power."

Richardson, the mother of the fated girl, "was dazed and stupefied," while Girault, who was staying in the same room with her, took charge of the youngest children, Cabell and Addie, and instructed her to take care of Martha. "She did not discover that Mrs. Richardson, in her dazed condition, had left the child in bed until they all met in the yard," Wade wrote. "When this was discovered, Mrs. Richardson, terror-stricken, frantically appealed for assistance and volunteers to go with her to the second floor to save her child. To this appeal, a brave and faithful slave, Thomas, responded, and started with her up the steps to the second story, but before ascending far the steps sank under them into the fire. They were both rescued from the flames, but badly burnt. Mrs. Richardson was pulled out by her hair. The next morning the child's heart was found and buried in the family graveyard, only a few paces from the spot where she met her tragic death."

Thomas Wade credited his father with throwing open the doors of the house to enable the others to escape, but said the front door at first appeared to have been jammed. Once he managed to swing it free, he waited before escaping himself, which Wade believed saved his life. When Girault ran through the door, he wrote, "to her horror there stood Esau, one of the estate's slaves, with a drawn axe, evidently for the purpose of killing my father, whom he expected to pass out the door, as it was nearest his room. Miss Girault bounded out unexpectedly, and seeing Esau with a drawn axe, quickly remarked, 'Uncle Esau, are you here to help us by cutting away the door?'" According to Thomas Wade, Esau replied, "'Yessum, Mistus,' and walked away. My father afterward learned that Esau had been standing at the front door for some time, and did not make any effort to arouse them or knock the door in, and that he had gone there for the purpose of killing my father should he escape from the flames," Wade wrote. "Esau, with six or seven other leaders, were burnt or hung. This was all done by the neighbors without my father's knowledge, as he was then with his mother, Mrs. Ross, at Oak Hill, two miles away."

It is hard to imagine how the scene could have been more horrible: the house quickly engulfed in flames, the frenzied occupants struggling to escape, the trapped girl screaming, the terrifying and disastrous rescue attempt. Thomas Wade noted that the house was completely destroyed in a very short time, and under the circumstances it seems remarkable that anything was saved, yet somehow, someone managed to rescue the portraits of Isaac Ross, his wife, and her sister. Also saved was the piano—unless, of course, Wade had made off with it prior to the fire. The fire was no doubt so intense that the crowd of distraught family members and slaves was forced to move farther and farther away as the flames lit the sky, accompanied by a fusillade of containers exploding inside. The aftermath, too, must have been particularly devastating for the survivors, who knew that Martha Richardson had died a terrible death, even as the family was saving themselves and their portraits. For days after, the lawn would have been littered with debris while the stench of the fire and perhaps even of the corpses of the lynched slaves hung in the air.

Thomas Wade wrote that the family members sought refuge at Oak Hill, and it seems safe to assume that they spent the following days sifting through the ashes, even after finding the remains of the girl. Such

a fire would have smoldered for a long time, and the ruins would have
been riddled with dangerous, hidden hot spots for days, although some
remnants would have survived—cast-iron hinges, clumps of melted
silver and gold, even fragile items like a glass saltshaker or a piece of
fine china, protected, perhaps, by a metal trunk or left unscathed when
the collapse of a wall sent unburned debris tumbling into the yard.
Even the story of finding the girl's heart does not seem too far-fetched
to anyone who has probed the ruins of a house fire.

But in the absence of evidence or documentation, many questions
come to mind. Why would Girault have chosen such a tumultuous
moment to question Esau about his reason for being at the door, and
frame it in such carefully scripted language? Would a man who was
part of a murderous, secret plot simply walk away from a house on fire,
with people shouting and screaming, inside and out? How could the
slaves have expected to get away with such a bold murder, in front of so
many witnesses? And again, how could the cook—whether it was
Grace or someone else—have betrayed the family she was no doubt
close to, including the children? At the same time, how could Richardson have forgotten her daughter in a burning house unless she was
drugged?

Thomas Wade's account does not provide answers to those questions, but he claimed that the family account was corroborated by
some of the slaves, two of whom "ran off when the leaders were executed, but were caught in the woods . . . and were hung on the spot
and left there." His father, he wrote, "found their bodies afterwards by
the buzzards hovering over them." Wade claimed that the slaves had
been encouraged by certain whites to kill his father. "Ross Wade never
knew positively, up to the time of his passing, that this statement was
correct, but his descendants have the satisfaction of knowing that
those slaves told the truth, as will be shown in the ex-parte statement,
through letters over their signatures, from members and sympathizers
of the American colonization society, in [the] Mississippi Historical
Society's *Publications IX*. These letters, as reported, confirm without a
question of doubt that the advice given these slaves was responsible
for the burning of the old Prospect Hill dwelling and the attempted
murder of Ross Wade and his entire family and friends then in the
house, and the actual burning to death of his niece Martha Richardson. Some time after the fact some of the more intelligent slaves

admitted this fact to my father, and told him that they had been told by some white people that if they could get rid of my father the provisions of the will would be carried out; that they would be sent to Liberia at an early date. My father was charitable enough to believe that, if any white person had told these things, they did not mean it in the literal sense, but to get rid of him by the process of law as acting executor."

Armed with Wade's pronouncement, I read the letters in the Mississippi Historical Society's *Vol. IX*, but found no reference to the fire or any attempted murder. Perhaps it is necessary to read between the lines, or to be fervently looking for validation.

The letters from the Prospect Hill slaves who later emigrated to Liberia further muddy the waters. The immigrants corresponded with their former masters for years afterward, repeatedly expressing their affection and in one case entreating the recipient to "give my love to Master Isaac [Wade]." Tinker Miller cites this as evidence that there were "good and bad people on both sides—some of the white Rosses were for the will, some were against it, some of the slaves may have been in favor of an uprising, and some of them against it."

For Thomas Wade, the immigrants' letters represented a clear exoneration of his father's efforts to defeat the will. He wrote that his father received letters from the Liberian immigrants "as late as 1861, on the eve of the great civil war, but we have never heard of them since. The last letters received discussed their pitiable condition; they applied for help, and begged to have him send them some farming and mechanical instruments and clothing, especially calico dresses. Their colonization in Liberia, judging from their letters, was an absolute failure." He sounds a bit smug when he adds, "In fact they reported they were destitute and great sufferers. From these letters it was most natural to conclude that their condition was much worse there than it was in slavery, as they had always had kind and considerate masters."

Regarding the uprising, Wade wrote that for his father, "This great tragedy in his life was a favorite theme, when we were gathered around the fireside, especially in the declining years of his life." No doubt the story and the subsequent trials of the immigrants seemed to validate both the contest of the will and the fear gripping the surrounding countryside that should the Prospect Hill slaves go free, insurrections on neighboring plantations would follow. All of which makes it even more curious that the event did not garner so much as a footnote in the official written record.

Robert Wade, who is a descendant of both Isaac Ross and Isaac Ross Wade, says he does not doubt the story of the uprising. The slaves, he contends, "were waiting for their freedom and things like that took time because you had to go all the way to the Supreme Court. There was a Presbyterian preacher here in Port Gibson named Zebulon Butler who was an avid abolitionist. He came from Wilkes-Barre, Pennsylvania. He incited the slaves, told them there was no way they would get their freedom as long as Isaac Ross Wade and his family were living.

"So the night the house was burned the cooks drugged the coffee—or whatever it was—at supper, they set the house on fire, and one little girl burned to death. One or two escaped, but they hung the rest. There was a big old white oak tree back of Prospect Hill that I remember as a boy, and I was told that was where they hung them. A vigilante committee hanged eleven slaves. So this pastor, Zebulon Butler, was responsible for twelve deaths, and he is revered in my church. And that is a bitter pill to swallow."

Robert Wade's version diverges from Thomas Wade's account on one important point. In his version Isaac Ross Wade was either at his family's Oak Hill home or visiting at Rosswood, home of his uncle, Dr. Walter Wade, on the night of the fire. "A storm came up that night and he did not get back home and that's the reason he was not killed," he says.

CHAPTER SEVEN

FROM CORRESPONDENCE BETWEEN Isaac Ross Wade and his chief attorney, Henry Ellett, it is apparent that the restraints issued by the lower courts were making it increasingly difficult for Wade to foot the bill for the ultimately futile litigation. In July 1847 Ellett wrote to say that "the whole case in which I was originally employed—to resist the right of the colonization society to the negroes—has been settled against us by the High Court and the remaining controversy must relate entirely to the adjustment of your private interests with the Estate and the Society. It is now a question of the settlement of your accounts in the Probate Court." The letter referred to another legal tack that Wade was considering as a means of recovering some of his financial losses, and that Ellett agreed to pursue, with the caveat, "you cannot expect me to embark in this new litigation without some prospect of reward." For that, he required a contingency fee of 5 percent of the final proceeds to be awarded to Wade by the court.

Ellett initially had expressed confidence that they would win the suit against the American Colonization Society, which he referred to as "the Africanists." Later his tone soured. In March 1847 he admonished Wade: "In the settlement of your accounts as executor it will be well not to forget that you owe me $100 for going to Fayette in Sept. 1845 to attend to the settlement of your case." In May 1847 he wrote, "I observe a condition that you are to pay me $250. It is proper I should say that the account has been due since Jan. 1, 1841 and I shall expect to be paid 8% interest on it from that time."

In 1848, Wade had run out of avenues of appeal and could no longer prevent the colonization society from executing the will. But by then, fees paid to Ellett and other attorneys, along with the $28,699.50 salary paid to Wade as executor, and losses resulting from the alleged mismanagement of the plantation, had greatly depleted the funds of the estate. Further diminishing its value was the erection of the monument in the cemetery at Prospect Hill in tribute to Ross, which had been commissioned by the Mississippi Colonization Society in 1838 for an astronomical cost—reputedly, $25,000.

Annie Mims Wright, Ross's great-granddaughter, speculated that Ker had insisted on the erection of the grand monument, adding, "I have often heard my father say his grandfather had told him repeatedly that he wanted a plain box tomb, like others he had erected in the graveyard. I can't imagine why his wishes were not carried out, as some of the slaves had to be sold to help pay for the splendid monument, that being one of the unexpected drains on the estate along with the lawyers' fees."

To undertake the final repatriation, the American Colonization Society would be forced to resort to private fund-raising. In its 1848 appeal for donations, the New York Colonization Society noted that the Prospect Hill immigrants represented one of the greatest challenges of the colonization effort. The ACS had sent only 480 emigrants to Liberia over the past four years, while the number of applications for emigration exceeded 1,000 for 1848 alone. Among the recent immigrants were 129 aboard the *Nehemiah Rich* who set sail on January 7, 1848, many of whom were Ross and Reed slaves. The New York report observed that the slaves "are represented to have no superiors among their caste in good morals, industry and intelligence. The estimated 200 slaves for whom additional funds were needed would be the last from Prospect Hill to go." The long wait, the report lamented, had "deferred the hopes of these poor slaves until their hearts are sad with waiting."

The ACS noted at the time that the next crop year was looming, "and unless they can leave before arrangements are made for it, they will certainly be delayed another year, in slavery, and risk a final disappointment in their hopes for freedom." Banking on the belief that there would be no delay, the ACS reported, "a vessel is authorized to sail from New Orleans on the 1st of January with about 300 immigrants, among whom are two hundred slaves on one plantation in Mississippi, emancipated by Capt. Ross, whose peculiar condition makes a most urgent appeal upon our sympathies."

Apparently the society got the desired financial response. Although there were no funds to found the institution of learning that Ross had envisioned in Liberia, enough money was raised to pay the way of the last group of slaves to emigrate, and with their departure, Ross's house was finally, completely, and literally divided.

After more than a decade of legal wrangling, the seemingly endless rounds of political chicanery, the fire, the lynchings, and the threat of vigilante violence—followed by a midnight march for some of the slaves to a steamboat waiting on the Mississippi River, and finally, weeks spent in squalid New Orleans refugee camps, during which scores died of cholera—setting sail for Africa must have seemed like a dream for the newly freed slaves of Prospect Hill. Slowly but surely, small groups had been released, and on January 22, 1849, almost twelve years after Isaac Ross died, the largest group—142—departed for Liberia aboard the barque *Laura*. On board were the cook, Grace, her husband, Jim, and three of their four children, but not their son Levy, who appears to have either died or been among those who chose to stay behind.

After they were gone, the indefatigable Wade continued making ineffective court claims against the ACS, right up to the eve of the Civil War, in 1861. By that time all that remained of the estate was the land, the piano, the portraits, an array of farm implements and livestock, and whatever else Wade and his family may have secreted away. The "bounty of Ross's estate," including the coveted house, almost all its furnishings, and the majority of the slaves, was gone. That was not to say that Wade was destitute. In fact, he managed quite well. The court battles had cost him dearly, yet he was able to buy back Prospect Hill when it was sold at public auction, along with many of the slaves who chose not to emigrate, and in 1854 built an imposing new house on the site of the old one. According to the New York Colonization Society's 1848 report, he had also by then "reputedly become the possessor and owner of a large plantation, well stocked with slaves, in Louisiana."

Remarkably, Isaac Ross Wade continued to busy himself with trying to find some new mechanism for recouping his losses, even as the rest of the country turned its attention to the looming civil war. His attorney, Henry Ellett, however, had no time for litigation now—on January 7, 1861, he was participating in the Mississippi Secession Convention in Jackson.

Soon after war broke out and Mississippi voted to secede from the Union, companies of Rebel soldiers began forming under the Confederate banner across Jefferson and Claiborne counties. Among the family members who joined the cause were Earl Van Dorn, the father of Arthur Ross's widow, who became a Confederate general, and Arthur Ross's son, Isaac Allison Ross, who served as a private in a Confederate cavalry unit based in Natchez. Although Wade would have been in his mid-forties at the time, he apparently stayed behind at Prospect Hill.

Most of the local soldiers were shipped up the Mississippi River to Memphis and from there by rail to the eastern theater of the war, which is where nearly all the fighting initially took place. In 1862, when the Union navy captured New Orleans, the war moved closer to home. Soon after, President Lincoln issued the Emancipation Proclamation, freeing slaves held in rebelling states as of January 1, 1863, and Union forces fanned out across the Mississippi Delta and attacked Vicksburg, Jackson, and Port Gibson. Natchez, where many residents had opposed both the American Revolution and secession from the United States, surrendered without a fight, but smaller river ports such as Rodney, in Jefferson County, and Grand Gulf, in adjacent Claiborne County, were repeatedly caught in the line of fire.

The main focus of the Union effort in Mississippi was Vicksburg, about forty miles north of Jefferson County, which was a heavily fortified city commanding a horseshoe bend in the river from a series of steep bluffs. Union General Ulysses S. Grant attacked the city from the swamps of the Delta—only to see his troops become hopelessly mired in the gumbo mud—and from the river, where gunboats and transports proved easy targets for the lofty Confederate guns. Frustrated, he pressed freed slaves into service to dig a canal across a Louisiana peninsula in hopes of diverting the Mississippi away from Vicksburg, to no avail. Finally, with few other options to explore, Grant marched his troops around the city on the Louisiana side, crossed the river at Bruinsburg, Mississippi, a few miles southwest of Port Gibson, and fought his way into the interior. It was a bold maneuver to sever an entire army from its lines of supply in enemy territory, and it marked the first time the citizens of inland Jefferson and Claiborne counties felt the war's heat. Because Grant found that he could feed and supply his soldiers from the pillage of plantations, local slaveholding families now had more to worry about than just the safety of their loved ones on distant battlefields, or the fate of their new nation—they had to contend with the prospects of widespread looting, the torching of houses and barns, food shortages, the confiscation of their cotton stores, and most importantly, the liberation of their slaves.

It soon became clear that no place was safe. First Port Gibson fell, next Raymond, and then Jackson. After subsequent Union victories at Champion Hill and the Big Black River, the Rebels beat a hasty retreat into Vicksburg, where frenzied residents watched in dismay as the troops entered the city at a full run, driving cattle and hogs before them. Surrounded on all sides, Vicksburg was besieged for forty-seven days, until Confederate General John Pemberton surrendered on July 4, 1863. With the surrender, the Mississippi River and most of central and southwest Mississippi fell into Union hands. The only remaining line of defense for area planters came from Confederate guerillas who roamed the countryside for the next two years, engaging Union cavalry in random skirmishes.

Many landowners chose to evacuate with their slaves and livestock, or to hide food, cotton, silver, and other valuables from the invaders. Today there are tales from seemingly every antebellum home in the area, including Rosswood, that involve the burial of silver by family members and their "faithful" slaves, which for inexplicable reasons was never found.

Confederate troops also hid what could not be hauled away. In a July 24, 1863, dispatch from Natchez, Union officer T. E. G. Ransom reported finding a stash of Rebel ammunition hidden in a nearby ravine along with 750 bales of Confederate cotton. Ransom noted that his scout "reports large quantities of private cotton everywhere in the country," adding that the Rebels had driven 2,000 cattle ahead of them as they retreated.

"The people of the country back of here have been running their negroes and horses into Alabama," Ransom wrote. "Very few good horses were found. . . . The people through the country are reported by Major Worsen to be discouraged and hopeless of the rebellion, and ready to do almost anything that will keep their negroes in the fields. There was a large public meeting at Hamburg on the 22d, to consider the question of abandoning the Confederacy. I have not heard the result of it."

There are surprisingly few references to the Civil War in the Ross and Wade family histories, but Robert Wade recalls hearing about a skirmish that took place in the nearby community of Red Lick, during which a Union soldier was badly wounded and taken for treatment to Prospect Hill. He does not know if Isaac Ross Wade was home at the time, nor who won the conflict.

"The occupants of the house at Prospect Hill were just young people, old people and slaves, and anyway they took him in," he says. "Of course there was no real medicine or doctors or anything, and they did what they could, but he died, and they buried him in the family cemetery. The family got his family's address from his personal effects and wrote them in Indiana and said they'd given him a Christian burial, and after the hostilities were over the family came down and removed the remains. His rifle is on display at the Grand Gulf museum. My mother and I gave it to the museum."

He says he heard the story often as a boy growing up in the second Prospect Hill house—much to his dismay, because it frightened him. "I slept in one of the old tester beds, and there was a jar with an old tarnished spoon in it on the mantle," he recalls. "It was always there on the mantle. And if I acted up, they'd say, 'You better watch out, because you're sleeping in the room where the Yankee soldier died.' They told me that jar and spoon were from his last dose of medicine before he died, and that the spoon was tarnished because he was a Yankee."

It is not clear if the fighting at Red Lick was related to a skirmish known variously as the Battle at Coleman's Plantation or the Battle of the Cotton Bales, which was fought in the vicinity on July 4, 1864, during which the family's Rosswood plantation home served as a field hospital. Both sides claimed victory in that one. According to a later account by another descendant, B. D. Wade, Rosswood was looted during the war and its owner, Walter Wade, was captured and briefly held by the Union army in nearby Rodney. After a brief confrontation between soldiers of the occupying force and Walter Wade's son, who B. D. Wade wrote was unable to serve in the Confederate army, the Yankee soldiers appropriated Rosswood's prized thoroughbreds.

No one with whom I spoke knew how many of the remaining Prospect Hill slaves left during the war, but there is no question that some departed when Union troops arrived, or simply fled on their own. According to Laverne McPhate, among those who remained behind were a few who lived out their lives in the same cabins they had previously occupied as slaves.

Keeping the slaves on the plantation was a major priority for all of the area's planters, even if, as things were headed, it appeared that they would have to pay rudimentary wages or allow farming on shares. A large workforce would be necessary to plant another crop, regardless of the outcome of the war. Some area planters tried to keep their newly freed slaves from leaving by playing upon their insecurity in a world with which they were wholly unfamiliar. In testimony before the U.S. Southern Claims Commission, which was deliberating whether to award remuneration to former slaveholder Kate Minor of Natchez, former slave Lee Scott described her mistress gathering the slaves around her and telling them that they were, in fact, free to leave. According to Scott's account, Minor then warned the slaves that the Yankees "were coming to take and work us to death and put us to work harder than they did, and take us to Liberia or some other country, and work us to death . . . I believed it . . . she said they were cruel and would take all of us colored understrappers and carry us off to Liberia, that they were tight, but we would find the Yankees a little tighter." Minor's overseer, Thomas Spain, also recalled her telling the slaves, "You can leave . . . but you will repent it & I will treat you well. They will make out they are going to treat you well for a little while & then they will turn you loose & you will be treated like dogs. . . ."

Despite Minor's admonitions, the majority of the slaves left, although some would indeed return after the war. During the post-war deliberations the Southern Claims commissioners asked Minor why, if she was so concerned about the welfare of her hundreds of slaves, she had not prepared and then freed them before the occupation. She explained that she was "an abolitionist at heart, but I am not a philanthropist. I did not know how to set them free without wretchedness to them and utter ruin to myself. . . . We were very much attached to each other, and they begged me to continue my watchfulness over them."

In hindsight, Minor's comments seem laughable—and may have seemed so at the time to the commissioners, but in his interview with the WPA, former slave Charlie Davenport recalled feeling an affinity with his owners, and remembered the war itself in unexpected terms. Although he was glad to be freed, Davenport said, he remembered the war less for the emancipation it brought than as a time of tumult and waste. When his owners made the painful decision to burn their stores of cotton to prevent them from falling into Union hands, the destruction was equally distressing to the slaves who had labored to plant, cultivate, harvest, and gin the crop, he said. He also lamented the death of his master's son in battle, saying that he had been a favorite of the slaves.

Some of the freed slaves who left their plantations made their way into the Union army and fought in the Vicksburg campaign, including James Lucas of Natchez, who conceded that freedom proved to be a mixed blessing. "Slaves didn' know what to 'spec from freedom, but a lot of 'em hoped dey would be fed an' kep' by de gov'ment," Lucas explained to a WPA interviewer. "Dey all had diff'nt ways o' thinkin' 'bout it. Mos'ly though dey was jus lak me, dey did't know jus' zackly what it meant. It was jus' somp'n dat de white folks an' slaves all de time talk 'bout. Dat's all. Folks dat ain' never been free don' rightly know de *feel* o' bein' free . . . When de sojers come dey turnt us loos lak animals wid nothin'."

Among the freed slaves who joined the invading armies were several in Mississippi named Ross, but it is unclear if any of them hailed from Prospect Hill or other Ross plantations. Two Ross veterans are listed in the records of the U.S. Colored Cavalry rolls for Vicksburg, with the space for birthplace left blank, and another, Jackson Ross, a member of the U.S. Colored Infantry, is buried in the nearby Grand Gulf cemetery (Jackson Ross's body was exhumed and reburied by the Sons of Confederate Veterans in February 2003, along with another black Union soldier, after erosion threatened their graves).

Historian Paul Escott noted that some former slaves recalled troubling encounters with Union soldiers to whom they had looked for salvation. "When the Yankees arrived they brought theft, destruction, and even mistreatment of slaves with them," he wrote. "Instead of acting as friends, the soldiers caused suffering and hardship for many bondsmen. In the context of the war between North and South, destruction of southern foodstuffs and property served to bring Union victory and emancipation nearer. But for the individual bondsmen, Yankee depredations only made a burdensome life more trying still. How was one to eat when the soldiers had gone?" In addition, he wrote, "There was considerable racism in the northern armies that found an outlet around the slaves."

Although there are numerous accounts of Union troops coming to the aid of freed slaves, giving them food and money, the uncertainty of how the freedmen would be treated is evident in the account of Hester Hunter, a freed slave in Marion, South Carolina, who was cited by historian Belinda Humence. "Remember the first time the Yankees come," Hunter recalled. "I was sitting down in the chimney corner and my mammy was giving me my breakfast. Remember I been sitting there with my milk and my bowl of hominy, and I hear my old grandmammy come a-running in from out the yard and say all the sky was blue as indigo with the Yankees coming right over the hill. Say she see more Yankees than could ever cover up all the premises about there.

"Then, I hear my missus scream and come a-running with a lapful of silver and tell my grandmammy to bury and sew that up in the feather bed, 'cause them Yankees was mighty apt to destroy all they valuables. Old Missus tell all the colored people to get away, get away and take care of themselves, and tell we children to get back to they corner, 'cause she couldn't protect us noways, no longer."

Hunter's account seems to indicate that her plantation mistress was concerned not only with her personal valuables, but with the well-being of her slaves, but in many cases such care vanished with the abolition of slavery. Another former slave quoted by Humence recalled his father saying, "the War wasn't going to last forever, but that forever was going to be spent living among the Southerners, after they got licked."

As it turned out, the cataclysm that was visited upon the South during and after the Civil War was not the exclusive burden of whites. The majority of the freed slaves could neither read nor write, and had comparatively little knowledge of finances and few means to support themselves, which is why so many returned to plowing the very fields in which they had been enslaved. The fact that some freedmen turned to looting made it more difficult for the law-abiding among them to coexist with whites who no longer had even a tangential vested interest in their well-being.

The war and Confederate defeat also brought hardship to Union loyalists such as Stephen Duncan, one of the Natchez area's largest slaveholders, who had been instrumental in helping the Ross and Reed slaves emigrate. Duncan, who had once been held in high esteem as president of the Bank of Mississippi, found himself ostracized in Natchez both during and after the war for his pro-Union stance. A Pennsylvania native who had arrived in the Natchez District the same year as Isaac Ross, Duncan reportedly grew disenchanted with the South and moved to New York, where he died in 1867. His mansion, Auburn, is now part of a Natchez city park.

Henry Ellett, meanwhile, suffered the indignity of being ejected from his home by black and white Union troops. The prominent lawyer, a New Jersey native who was also a state senator and a former U.S. senator (he had been appointed to fill the remainder of Jefferson Davis's term in 1847) was at home with his wife in Port Gibson when a skirmish broke out between Union and Confederate forces in September 1864. Following the Union victory, the troops arrived and put the family out in the street. After the war, Ellett managed to adapt to his new situation. In what must have been a gratifying turn of events for him, after having been rebuffed by the courts during the Wade litigation, Ellett was elected to the Mississippi High Court of Errors and Appeals, where he served from 1865 to 1868. Afterward he moved to Memphis, where he died in 1887 while delivering a welcome address for the visiting President Grover Cleveland.

Although the Wades and Rosses had landed on their feet following the long crucible of the litigation, after the war they experienced the same reversal of fortune that broke slaveholders across the South. At the outbreak of hostilities they had been among the more prominent planters in the Natchez District, but afterward, with slavery abolished, they saw their considerable fortunes evaporate, and found themselves struggling simply to maintain their properties.

They were able to put many of the former slaves back to work in the fields, utilizing a system that involved their cultivating and harvesting the crop in exchange for a share of the profits. It was a system ripe for abuse, because the sharecroppers depended upon the plantation commissary for their seeds and supplies, and typically, once the ledger was tallied at the end of the year, their debts exceeded the profits from the sale of the crop. No one with whom I spoke knew how Isaac Ross Wade treated his sharecroppers, and no doubt many planters were fair, but for decades those who were cheated had no choice but to stay put.

Isaac Ross Wade stayed put himself, in a diminished yet comparatively powerful role, until his death at Prospect Hill in 1891.

Laverne McPhate describes the Civil War as a time when "everybody got their heart broke," but it seems likely that "everybody" did
not include the remaining slaves of Prospect Hill. Despite the uncertainty of their future and continuing restraints, they were now free,
and some of them surely felt relieved that they had chosen to remain
behind when the majority had left for Africa.

CHAPTER EIGHT

"IT'S A HELL OF a lot of Rosses in this town that aren't related to us, that we know," Delores Ross says, over the phone. "They're a darker complexion, the ones I'm talkin' about."

She is referring to the descendants of the Prospect Hill slaves who did not take the one-way trip to Liberia, whether by choice or because they were not given the option. Delores, is descended from slaves from other plantations, but, surprisingly, also traces her ancestry to the slaveowning Rosses, which means she is no blood relation to the Rosses whose slave ancestors remained at Prospect Hill.

The Rosses have made and sometimes written history in both Mississippis, American and African, but the descendants of the slaves who stayed behind—presumably, the least mobile among them— have managed to slip through the historical record largely unnoticed. Part of the problem is that slaves were poorly documented, having been listed in census records by first name only, if at all. Surnames do not appear in the census records for African-Americans until 1870, and often the names were selected at whim. Sometimes freed slaves chose the name of their most recent master, while in other cases they chose a former owner, or a name they simply liked. As a result, the direct lineage of their descendants can be extremely difficult to determine.

From talking with Ann Brown, I have reached the bewildering conclusion that I will have to descend into the genealogical maw to find descendants of the Prospect Hill slaves who stayed behind. This is not something I really want to do. I have seen the family historians sitting bleary-eyed before the microfilm readers in the research room of the state archives, and I am not eager to join their ranks. It is as if the world can only be validated by reconciling certain significant names and numbers from the past, by proving that someone from whom you are descended lived and died in a way that is more important than someone else. My thoughts inevitably wander as the genealogists in the research room reel off these beatitudes with the zeal of rabid sports fans reciting players' stats. Perhaps the safely completed record of an ancestor's life can give context to one's own, but the process seems mind-numbing and looks a lot like math. Still, as Ann pointed out, it will be hard to make sense of things without knowing who is who. Genealogical records often contain pertinent information that can be found nowhere else, and could lead to other descendants.

Ann is all about connecting the dots. I have received stacks of records that she has collected from old censuses and from tombstones in abandoned African-American cemeteries, which I compare with listings in Jefferson County phone books. I have noticed that some of the genealogical records contain errors, and not just differences in the spellings of names, but actual dates of births and deaths, which means that I will have to subjectively judge their veracity just as I have the Ross family lore. It is daunting. Yet there are also some interesting genealogical side-trails to explore, such as the fact that Isaac Ross Wade and his branch of the family did not share the Ross family's predilection for slaves of mixed race, according to the slave census of 1860. Isaac Allison Ross owned 115 slaves, including nineteen mulattoes, while John Ross owned sixty-one slaves, only one of whom was of mixed race. The various branches of the Wade family owned approximately 170 slaves, all of whom were listed as black.

The probate court's inventory of slaves in Isaac Ross's estate and the immigrant ship registries are even more telling. Comparing the two, it appears that about twenty-five of the Prospect Hill slaves did not embark—four were freed outright, and the remainder chose to stay behind, were not given the option, and were sold. It appears that at least twenty-five also remained from the Reed estate.

Unfortunately, Ann has had no luck helping me find the missing Rosses. Delores, whom she had expected to be descended from the black Rosses, was her best bet. "There aren't many records for black people, and the ones I've checked don't show many Rosses at all, surprisingly," she says. It is possible that the slaves who remained did not take the Ross name, which would make it nearly impossible to track down their descendants now.

Tracing a black family tree beyond the limits of personal memories often involves scouting abandoned cemeteries and undertaking tedious searches of white genealogical and legal records for passing references and clues. The effort is complicated by the fact that slavery carries an enduring stigma, which is doubtless why so many Rosses I contact who are likely slave descendants decline to be interviewed. Slavery is a perennial source of political debate in Mississippi, and is sometimes a source of a sort of adverse power, but for a great many it remains a very personal and sensitive subject. And why wouldn't it be? Slavery was demeaning, and even freed slaves had to contend with second-class status among often embittered former slaveholders who steadfastly sought to maintain their own superiority. One freed slave recalled asking if slaves would still have to say "Master" after freedom, and being told by his fellows "Naw." But, the slave added, "They said it all the same. They said it for a long time."

Although there were certainly instances of bravery, courage, wit, and compassion among slaves, little of it was written down. According to historian Paul Escott, the WPA slave narratives prove "that if men have a body of culture on which to rely, they can endure conditions that are very unfavorable indeed," but in most cases, how they went about enduring those conditions has been lost. Old memories may not be the most reliable source of information, and it is certainly hard to find solace in the record of one's family's enslavement when the scant documentation that exists was compiled by people whose interests tended to be diametrically opposed. Typically, it was only the "faithful" slaves, or, at the opposite end of the scale, the violent or thieving ones whose actions were recorded. Beyond that, there is not much information to consider. There are no written accounts of the bittersweet day at Prospect Hill when the last of the emigrants departed. Those who remained behind would have had plenty of time to reflect on their decision to stay, particularly after they were sold at public auction, but the only reference I found in the historical record was a December 29, 1848, letter from David Ker to Isaac Ross Wade, informing him that his father would attend the Prospect Hill sale. The dearth of written records poses a significant obstacle to fully understanding the story of Prospect Hill, and to accounting for each of the key groups.

Some of the names of the slaves who remained behind are mentioned in the emigrants' letters, but always without an identifying surname. The same is true for slave births in the Prospect Hill plantation ledger for the years after the emigrants departed. There is a notation for a Daphney giving birth, for instance, but Daphney who? A female slave named Linder was listed as being sold after having given birth to a boy who lived only a week in 1853, with a notation by Catherine Wade that, "Richardson and Little Susan given to come in her place." Where did Linder go? Who were Richardson and Little Susan? Even as Catherine Ross recorded the births of Little Susan's three children, she noted, "I guess at their ages."

The task is further complicated by the mass dispersal of freed slaves after the war. According to the 1850 census there were fifty-four free people of color in Jefferson County, up from seventeen in 1830 and thirty-three in 1820. That number swelled into the thousands in 1865. The majority of the births recorded at Prospect Hill occurred after the transfer of the estate, from the 1840s to around 1870, and among them, thirty-two were born during the Civil War, and six more in the years after, which indicates that their families were among the most stalwart, or perhaps recalcitrant, of the slaves. Those slaves had foregone the opportunity to leave Prospect Hill twice, yet I found no record of who they were. Where are their descendants today? What, if anything, might they know?

It seems likely that many of those who stayed did not take the surname Ross. For one thing, the Rosses did not own them at the time they were freed, and hadn't for nearly thirty years. The list of freedmen's taxes for 1869, which is incomplete, includes only four Rosses in Jefferson County: David, Boswell, John, and Rankins. Others may have owned land, but their surnames were apparently different. Likewise the 1900 Jefferson County Enumeration of Children of black families lists only Henry Ross and his children Sam, Ann, Katie, Leota, and Mary. The U.S. Colored Cavalry rolls for Vicksburg in 1864 list two Rosses: Peter, age thirty-five, and John, twenty-two, both of whom also appear in the Freedmen's Bureau Register of Marriages in Mississippi. John Ross is again listed in the Freedman's Bank records in Vicksburg. It is a short list, but the names are common, spouses do not always share the same surname, and there is no way to definitively link them to Prospect Hill. Ultimately the records lead nowhere.

*   *   *

At no time is the dearth of information more evident than when I sit down, hopefully, with Susie Ross, who is among the few slave descendants I meet who is inclined to talk. Susie (to whom I was referred, again, by Ann Brown), greets me at the screen door of her Port Gibson home, hastily tying a scarf around her head, still in her housedress and slippers because she is recuperating from a recent illness. She is a quiet, unassuming woman, whose expression rarely changes. Though elderly, her face is remarkably unlined. Her home is small and nondescript, and stands on a knoll behind the county jail.

"The place don't look too good right now," she says, glancing doubtfully at her yard, which is devoid of landscaping and dominated by a rusty swing set. Her husband always kept the place neat, she says, but nine months ago he was run over and killed by a drunken driver at age eighty-four, and she hasn't mustered the energy to hire any help. Her dream is to have the place painted and burglar bars and an alarm system installed.

"My husband was a good man," she says, and motions for me to sit down in an overstuffed chair in her living room. "I had a good husband. He was raised to keep everything up. He kept things intact. He was a dutiful man. Now I don't have anybody much to depend on but the Lord and myself."

Before we are far into our conversation, it becomes apparent that the past is a vast network of gaping holes for her. Both her and her husband's family histories are discouragingly attenuated. She is a Ross by marriage, and her husband came from the vicinity of Prospect Hill. She knows little beyond that. She is related to another family, the Greens, some of whom emigrated to Liberia in the 1840s, but she was unaware of the connection until I showed her the records. She has little hard data to work with.

Her husband, Adel Crezet Ross, was from the community of Pattison. She hands me a framed photograph of him and points across to what she says was his favorite chair, which sits empty. "It's so much memory here," she says. His visage stares out from photographs on the coffee table and atop the TV alongside photos of other family members. His naval commendation hangs on the wall. "President Clinton mailed that to me after the death of him," she says.

The room is as crowded as a tiny Victorian-era parlor, with a mix of older furniture, electric fans, stuffed animals, books, a piggy bank, vases filled with plastic flowers and a large, framed print of Jesus. There is an antique buffet, which matches the dining room table, whose chairs, she tells me, are in a shed out back. "They need to be made over," she says of the chairs. She doesn't know the origin of the antiques other than that they belonged to her husband.

Adel Ross seldom talked about his family history, "but he had this picture," she says, and rises from her recliner to probe the dusty recesses behind the sofa. She first pulls out a .22 rifle, which her husband used to chase off stray dogs, then a very large, elaborately framed, late-nineteenth-century photograph of a dignified man with a neat goatee, dressed in a dark suit and vest and a starched white collar. She wipes off the cobwebs. The man in the picture is handsome, his expression is confident, and the portrait clearly did not come cheap. "My husband was a handsome man, too," she says. "I meant to clean this up before you came. I had it on the back porch for a long time, until one of the supervisors said it was important and I should take it inside." The gilding is flaking off and the plaster ornamentation is broken in places, but the photo is in good condition.

She leans the portrait against the sofa and returns to her recliner. "His father had that picture," she says. "That was his granddaddy on the Ross side. I don't even know his name. There's a lot I don't know."

She knows that her husband was born to George and Flora Patterson Ross and worked at a paper-tube plant alongside his father and brother until he was disabled. One of his uncles, Matt Ross, was a Claiborne County supervisor. The county administration building is named for him. "Most of his family is passed away," she says. Among her husband's family, she says she recently spoke with a brother-in-law, but he's not interested in talking to me, and he's the last one in the line. I tell her I have found a scattering of records relative to the black Rosses, and that perhaps the man in the gilded frame is Henry, because he alone was listed in the freedman's tax records, but her own family documentation doesn't go back that far, and it would be a stretch to say that it matters that much to her.

She shows polite interest when I tell her that the ship registry of emigrants from Mississippi to Liberia provides a link between her and the Greens of Liberia, that the slaveholding Greens were friends of

Isaac Ross's. Then she brings the story back to its more immediate focus: the family she has known. "My brother, Lesley Green, was a good man," she says. "My grandfather lived to be a hundred and seven. He was like a slave man." She says the Greens, together with her mother's relations, the Hills and the Fields, still hold reunions, most recently in 1999 at nearby Alcorn State University. "We all get together and they have barbeque and beer," she says. "I enjoy that." The distant past is not often a topic of conversation, she says. There is really no tradition for looking too far back. Yet this is a family that steadfastly holds together, which places great importance on reunions at a time when most American families are becoming increasingly fragmented. That is the irony of Susie Ross's family history—that its members so value their continuity yet know so little about their past.

As she thinks back on the reunions, she excuses herself to go into her bedroom and retrieve several T-shirts emblazoned with silk-screened photos and graphics commemorating the events. "These shirts mean a lot to me," she says, and holds up one with the image of an elderly woman's face. "This is my favorite one. That's the only aunt I have left. I try not to wear it too much, because I want it to last."

She says she wishes she knew more, but that she's hesitant to refer me to other family members who might be knowledgeable because they may not want to talk. She does give me one name, and wishes me luck. When I later call him and ask if he knows anything about his family's ties to Prospect Hill, he says, simply, "No," and then, "Good-bye."

When I ask Robert Wade what he knows about the slave descendants associated with Prospect Hill, he recalls a few whose family had remained. "They were old Negroes, as we called them, part of the family," he says. "They helped my daddy. He raised a big garden and let them come and get food out of it. They killed hogs together. You know, the old stories. I don't know if there's any of the families left out there now."

He confirms that the black families at Prospect Hill were not all named Ross. "The ones I knew of, in my time, their surnames were Bruce, Foster, Davis, Odom. These were families that were sharecropping on the place with my daddy. Then Daddy got tired of fighting Bermuda grass, and we moved to town. I can't say I really know what became of them all."

CHAPTER NINE

THE SIGN, SET AGAINST a backdrop of used car lots, convenience stores, and nondescript houses along U.S. 61, offers a curious introduction: WELCOME TO PORT GIBSON, TOO BEAUTIFUL TO BURN. Even without the incongruous setting, it seems a dubious boast.

The quote is attributed to General Grant, whose army passed through after defeating the Confederate forces in the area during the Civil War, and who, it is said, spared the town the torch for aesthetic reasons. At first it is easy to imagine that Grant, at war behind enemy lines and preoccupied with chasing the Rebels back into Vicksburg, literally had no time to burn, but after you cross the bridge over Bayou Pierre, the idea that a hostile general could be smitten by the place seems strangely plausible. Church Street, the main boulevard, presents a rich tableau, which is what tourists now come to see. The sunlight glints off the steeple of the old Presbyterian church, with its giant golden hand on top, one finger pointing skyward, and a wide boulevard opens up, lined with immaculate, painstakingly restored churches, gracefully arching live oak trees, and block after block of columned mansions that float serenely in clouds of pink and white azaleas in the spring.

Port Gibson bills itself as a quintessential antebellum town and in many ways it is, but the unlikely context of the welcome sign tells you that there is more to the place than meets the eye. This is clearly no set piece for the Old South, unless it was for a movie directed by Spike Lee. During the Spring Pilgrimage tour of antebellum homes, low-slung Delta 88s cruise Church Street, rattling the old window panes with music from far distant streets, while on the galleries of the mansions girls dressed in crinoline and lace smile and greet paying visitors at the door. There is the requisite statue of a Confederate soldier standing guard before the restored courthouse, but nearly all the elected officials who work inside are black, and the building was said to have been riddled with gunfire during the 1980s, when the county was beset by bitter intraracial political fighting. History is a palpable presence in a place like this, and it encompasses far more than tourist sites and events dutifully commemorated on historical markers.

No one knows that better than Delores Ross, whose family has lived in the area longer than she knows, and who has occupied the same house, a weathered, Queen Anne–style cottage just off the road leading from the courthouse to the Mississippi River, for nearly forty years. Delores knows all about the racial tumult that has characterized so much of the history of Port Gibson and surrounding areas in Claiborne and Jefferson counties—the oppression, resentment, condescension, the efforts at reconciliation, the unlikely alliances, the awkward shifts in power. She knows all about the struggle for dominance by both blacks and whites, but manages to straddle the lines of racial demarcation because she was born there, right on the line, the product of an interracial union. In a town where so much seems to come down to black and white, she is an anomaly.

At first glance, Delores's lineage is difficult to discern. Before now we have spoken only on the phone, after I was given her number by her niece, Laura "Butch" Ross. During my research into the story of Prospect Hill, I have often conducted first interviews on the phone rather than in person, and sometimes have found myself deliberating whether the person I am speaking with is descended from slave or slave owner, because many have similar accents and frames of reference. I wait for their perspective to reveal itself through some telltale sign—a verbal marker such as the use of "aks" in place of "ask" by blacks, or a reference to "faithful slaves" by whites. Sometimes the clue lies in what is left out of their account. The prevailing white version of the story of Prospect Hill always includes the slave uprising, but the prevailing black version never does. In many cases my assumptions have turned out to be entirely wrong, and I might be deep into a conversation before I know for sure.

In Delores's case, neither her speech nor her perspective gave her away on the phone. Finally she said, "I'll just be frank with you, it was kinda hard growing up in the South with a black mother and a white father."

After greeting me at the door and inviting me in, Delores launches into one of the more curious genealogies that I have come across.

"I tell you, *Roots*, the best movie ever made, don't have nothin' on the Ross family," she says. "We're all over the place. Go way back, all over the place. Here some of 'em started out in Africa, come to Mississippi, then end up back in Africa. And a whole lot of 'em—black, white, you name it, been right here all along—and I'm talkin' a long, long time."

Delores's hair is long, wavy, and black, carefully molded with pomade, her skin midway between black and white. Her house is a catchall sort of place, with furniture from the 1960s and 1970s, potted plants and vases of plastic flowers, and every available surface crowded with memorabilia and framed photos of people, both black and white. Many area residents have a tendency to reduce key figures in local history to archetypes and stereotypes—good guys and bad guys, everything black and white, but not Delores. She listens patiently to a summary of the history of Prospect Hill, then leans back on her sofa and takes a long drag off her cigarette. She is unpretentious and self-possessed, and has no qualms about entertaining my questions about her family history—in fact, she relishes the opportunity.

"One thing it ain't, is black and white," she says, and blows cigarette smoke toward the ceiling. She glances toward the front door as it swings open.

Her niece walks in, smiling broadly, and extends her hand to me. "I'm Butch," she says.

"Sit down, Butch," Delores says. "We just gettin' started."

"You're gonna hear a different version of the story now," Butch says, and smiles at Delores as she pulls up a chair.

"Here, pass me that picture there, Butch," Delores says, and Butch hands her a framed photograph from among the group clustered on the coffee table. "That's Thad Ross, my daddy," Delores says, and passes the photo to me. "He was a descendant of Isaac Ross." The photo looks to have been taken in the 1930s. A white man is seated on a sofa beside a dark-skinned girl with a black woman seated in a chair nearby. There is no mistaking that they are a family. "It was taken down in Jefferson County," she says. "That's my father there. The girl is Jimmie, my sister, Butch's mother. The lady's Queen Esther Polk, Jimmie's mother."

The photo would be right at home in many family albums across the South but for the mix of skin colors. There are many people of mixed race in this part of the country, but they are usually the result of clandestine encounters. Racial mixing is rarely documented for posterity, particularly by members of prominent white families like the Rosses.

Delores awaits my response, but all I think to say is that the average Mississippian would not know what to make of the picture.

"Mm-hmm," she says, agreeing with me.

"Probably think Queen's the maid," Butch says, and laughs.

Delores points to a group of framed photos on the mantel, and adds, "That's all my family up there." She goes down the line, naming names. Most of the faces are black, but some are white, and others are in between. She pulls out her albums and shows me snapshots of blacks and whites intermingling unself-consciously—fishing on a lake, visiting in someone's living room, gathering for a graduation. She points to a painting above the TV set of one of the local white community's beloved landmarks, the Presbyterian church with the gilded hand atop its steeple. "My uncle painted that," she proclaims.

Butch hands me another photo of her mother as an adult. She is beautiful, and Butch favors her. When I mention this Delores says, "She was pretty from a baby on up. All the way through."

It is tempting, studying the photo, to see the beauty of these women as the heart of this particular outcropping of the Prospect Hill story, yet there is no discounting the exceptional circumstances that gave rise to the love affair, particularly on the Ross side.

The family of Isaac Ross is best known for his controversial will. The saga of his descendants, and particularly that of Thad Ross, has not been so widely circulated. Thad Ross's family, it turns out, had a reputation for being mavericks, and in many cases for being randy and high-strung. More independent than most, and prone to grand gestures, the family exhibited a strong penchant for sometimes wildly contradictory behavior, the one constant being their apparent distaste for being told what to do. Thad Ross did his part to maintain the family's reputation, fathering children by three black mistresses, including Delores's mother, Consuelo Conti, as well as Queen Polk and Rosie Lee Jordan, the latter of whom lived in Natchez before moving to Illinois, where she died. By the time Thad Ross was born, the once wealthy family was landed but poor, with little to call their own other than acreage and a scattering of old houses and barns that had been handed down through the generations. He resorted to logging to make ends meet and became acquainted with Conti at a logging camp near Harriston, Mississippi. She had drifted up the river from New Orleans to Natchez and lived with him at the camp for a while. They never married.

"She was of mixed nationality," Delores says. "She knew all about my father's family, but she died in 1987."

"There was just something about those Ross men," Butch observes. "They liked black women. And nobody said anything about it. Back in the sixties people were ready to kill over a black and white living together, and here they were doing it back in the thirties, and they didn't hide it. Of course, all the Ross men carried guns."

"Sure did," Delores says, and nods.

"My grandfather was the great-great-grandson or whatever of Isaac Ross," Butch says. "He was a fool. She [Queen] was, too. That's probably why nobody bothered them—they were both crazy. My mother told me very little, but I heard a little bit—how Isaac Ross freed his slaves and offered them land and money. I just know what I grew up hearing through the years."

Delores sits up, a fire suddenly rekindled in her eyes. "Thad wasn't the only one," she says. "Uncle Frank, he had two black girls. They're well-educated. One lives up in Virginia. She's on TV."

"She's my namesake," Butch says, proudly.

"Robert Ross—he's on the white side of us, too," Delores says.

"He's got a black history, too, though," Butch points out.

"It's just all mixed up," Delores says.

I ask how they reconcile their family history in a place like this, where everything, on the surface at least, seems so divided.

"I guess it's just different for us," Butch says. "Us and the Harrises, we're the only ones I know that are on both sides. I guess we just all been around each other too long." She glances over at Delores and

they throw their heads back and laugh. I ask if the Harrises are descended from Drew Harris, who accompanied Isaac Ross to the Mississippi Territory from South Carolina, but neither of them knows.

My expression must betray my surprise at this new twist in the
story, because Butch and Delores are clearly amused. They are aware
that such intermingling does not sit well with everyone, and is rarely
mentioned in most portrayals of the Ross family. This is the Deep
South, after all, known worldwide for its troubled racial politics. On
the morning we talk, there is another round of vitriolic letters to the
editor in the Jackson *Clarion-Ledger* about the Mississippi state flag,
which incorporates the Confederate battle emblem, and in my interviews so far the subject of race has been a constant undercurrent. One
slave descendant asked me over the phone, not suspiciously, but pointedly, "Are you a white person?" At the Claiborne-Jefferson County
Genealogical Society, where I would later speak about my research, I
received a few blank stares when I mentioned that some of the area's
black Rosses were actually descended from the slaveholding family.
One woman asked, politely but with obvious skepticism, "Can they
prove it?"

At this point the question presents itself: aside from those cases
where it is obvious, what determines whether a person is black or
white? What if, as Frederick Law Olmsted proposed following his Mississippi plantation visit in 1852, the light-colored slave had been a
house servant, had been given finer clothes, and had moved to the
North—if she had "passed," would she in fact have been white? In
antebellum Mississippi a person's "blackness" was defined by law: anyone who had ⅛ black blood was black. It did not matter if the person
was ⅞ white. That is why a slave on an antebellum plantation could
have light skin and straight, blond hair and still be a slave. But what of
the people who came after—people who, like Delores, are of mixed
race?

In the census of 1870, which was the first to include surnames for
African-Americans, there were three choices in the guidelines given to
census-takers: black, white, and colored (in addition to four other
racial types). In 1880, "mulatto" was added, but with no clear criteria
for making a distinction. The guidelines for 1890 were more explicit,
delineating anyone with ¾ black blood as black; ¼ black blood as
quadroon; and ⅛ black blood as octoroon. In the final analysis, all were

black. By 1920 the definition had again changed, defining any "full-blooded Negro" as black and anyone with some white blood as mulatto. The 1930 census narrowed the focus considerably: "A person of mixed white and Negro blood should be returned as a Negro, no matter how small the percentage of Negro blood. Both black and mulatto persons should be returned as Negroes, without distinction. In cases where an assessment was difficult, the race was to correspond to the non-white parent." Not surprisingly, the term "mulatto" eventually lost its official meaning, and although the wording of the instructions slowly became less "white," for lack of a better term, for the next sixty years the census limited the options to a determination by the census-taker of "black" or "white."

The census of 1990 for the first time allowed those being counted to make their own racial determination, selecting from sixteen categories. For those at issue here, the choices were simply black and white. It was not until 2000 that the racial designation itself began to lose its importance. That year, respondents were allowed to check more than one racial category, meaning there need not be an official racial designation. If that sounds like welcome news in a country that has at times seemed overly concerned with race, not everyone thought so. Because black voting power is dependent upon racial divisions— i.e., in districts where blacks are in the majority, some black leaders were concerned that the new system would dilute their constituency. The NAACP, notably, urged "blacks, regardless of the racial percentages in their blood, to mark only one race on the census form," which would return the method of census recording to the concept of "some black is all black."

Why would it follow that any amount of black blood makes a person black, while the converse would not be true—that any amount of white blood makes a person white? I have found no clear answer.

For whatever reasons, most people of mixed race consider themselves black. Delores Ross considers herself something altogether different, a free agent, but she lives in a predominantly black neighborhood and socializes, for the most part, with blacks. Usually the answer is determined by the racial makeup of the majority of the family. If a person grows up in a black family, they tend to think of themselves as black, regardless of the shade of their skin. The same is true for whites of similar circumstances. As a result, the actual skin color may belie a person's race. Black is not always black, and white is not always white. A "white" person can be darker than a "black" person, and vice versa.

The dilemma, of course, is how to prevent social and governmental systems from using race as a criterion and still maintain racial integrity when it seems sensible or useful to do so. How is one to ignore race and yet account for it?

Race is only one factor influencing people's views, but it can be a bewilderingly potent one. During the 1980s, when Claiborne County was beset by bitter political fighting, federal election observers and state officials (most of whom were white) were reluctant to intervene. Both of the feuding factions were black, and although one side actively sought outside government help, cries of racism followed even minor overtures by such officials to enter the fray. The legislature eventually passed a law that divided the lucrative taxes from the county's Grand Gulf nuclear plant, reducing the largesse and with it some of the political incentive, and the situation quieted down. A residue of mistrust remained, however. It still seemed to be about race, because the law did not divide the revenue from power plants elsewhere in the state among the counties they served.

The county prosecutor at the time, Bob Connor, told me that the area's divisive racial history was clouding what would otherwise have been a routine case of political corruption. In Connor's opinion, a small group of unscrupulous, corrupt elected officials were subjecting black voters to "the same tactics that they were subjected to by whites a hundred years ago." It did not matter that the officials were black, he argued; the effect was the same.

Claiborne County School Board President Jimmy Smith gave an opposing view: "The problem here is that whites don't want to see blacks controlling any money, and money is totally the problem in Claiborne County. There are a few decent whites, but most of them are rednecks."

Of the approximately 11,500 people who live in Claiborne County, 9,500 are listed in the census as black and 2,000 as white; of the 9,750 people in neighboring Jefferson County, 8,650 are black and 1,100 white, the highest percentage of African-Americans of any county in the United States. Together the counties also have the highest percentage of black elected officials in the United States, and because blacks control most of the politics while whites control most of the money, the region has found itself at the forefront of a contemporary power struggle that is as complicated and unpredictable as any in Mississippi, where the stakes of racial politics are always notoriously high. As much as it is an Old South town, Port Gibson is today a proving ground for those politics.

For all these reasons, the descendants of the various Rosses of Prospect Hill share a history that is even more complicated and conflicted than it appears on the surface. For an outsider accustomed to typical American neighborhoods, which are segregated both economically and racially, it is surprising to find that blacks and whites of different economic backgrounds live in close proximity to one another here. They see each other every day, they share meals at local restaurants, visit on street corners, chat on the phone. They know a good bit about each other's family trees. In many ways theirs is a remarkably integrated society. Yet there is always a rarefied space between the races. Talk with enough people and you encounter racial polarization and outright prejudice—whites who blame blacks for the area's surprisingly high rural crime rate, blacks who see discrimination enduring in subtle yet pernicious forms.

The 1980s were a racially contentious time, but only the most recent in a series of tumultuous periods that have gripped the area for more than 200 years. None of the more famous stories much concern themselves with what blacks experienced during the Civil War era, but this much is known: once they were freed and given the right to vote, they quickly assumed the reins of political power. It took a decade for the whites to wrest that power back, after Reconstruction, and another century before the majority ruled again.

Of all the upheavals that have beset the region, the Civil Rights era of the 1960s and 1970s is the one most people personally remember. With whites struggling to maintain political power, blacks encountered intimidation and the threat of violence when they sought to exercise their right to vote and to enter cafés and stores that had traditionally been off-limits to them. They faced incredible odds because the local white power structure was bolstered by a state government that often worked hand in hand with paralegal organizations such as the Ku Klux

Klan, which targeted, threatened, investigated, and sometimes attacked people who posed a threat to the status quo. The period brought less outright violence to Claiborne and Jefferson counties than erupted in other parts of the state, but injustices fueled boycotts of white-owned businesses, public protests, and voter drives that ultimately succeeded in ending a century of officially sanctioned racial segregation.

Those and other past injustices linger over the region today, but not all the tumultuous stories cast whites as villains. Butch cites as an example the lynchings that followed the murders of several white men by black men in the nearby community of Harriston in the early 1900s.

"I remember people pointing out the hanging tree," she says. "From what I understand, it started during a gambling game at the [cotton] gin. Somebody found somebody cheating and the next thing the streets of Harriston was running red with blood. Every white person they saw, they killed." Butch's family ran the Ross Café in Harriston and she was raised near the site of the mayhem, she says. "I'm still right there on the Ross place," she adds. "I had a trailer there and then I re-did the trailer. Now I've got a brick home."

Delores has a flare for drama and takes over the story, at points assuming the voices of the different characters. "The Bell brothers were gambling and they took a black boy's money and wouldn't give it back," she says. "He said, 'Why won't you give me back my money? I worked hard for that money.' And they said, 'We ain't gonna give it back.' He thought they had cheated him. So he went home and got his brother, his horse, and his gun, and they killed every goddamn one of 'em. My daddy, Thad Ross, stuck his head out the door and they said, 'Get back in there or we'll get you, too.' Apparently they was close to Thad. Probably saved his life."

I nod, unsure how to respond.

I ask Delores how other people view her family's mixed lineage. She shrugs.

"People think what they wanna think," she says.

I ask if she is close to the Rosses who are descended from Prospect Hill slaves, and she quickly shakes her head.

"But I tell you who you should talk to," she says. "Pet." She turns to Butch. "Pet could probably tell him some shit."

Butch agrees. Pet Houston, she says, is part of an old black family.

"They know all about the Rosses. We'll drive out to her house. I'll go with you, that way she'll talk."

Delores gives us directions to the place, and soon Butch and I are driving out into the rolling Claiborne County countryside. The area is surprisingly sparsely populated, with only the occasional cluster of mobile homes and modest houses punctuating long stretches of quiet road. Here and there old crepe myrtle trees and solitary chimneys mark old house sites, hinting at the population that has left. When we get to Pet Houston's small, 1970s ranch house, she is in the kitchen serving an early supper to her elderly mother, who does not seem to notice us as she eats at the small table. Butch explains what I am there for. "He's all right," she says. "He's doing a story of the Rosses. He wants the black version. He's already heard the white version."

Pet considers this. "Well, when Mama get through chewin', she may know somethin'," she says.

We sit down in the living room, where a young woman is working on a quilt in front of a football game on TV, above which hangs the ubiquitous framed portrait of Jesus. Butch and Pet make small talk and presently the old woman, Ruth O'Neal, inches her way into the room with the help of a walker. She is nearly blind and deaf but her eyes are bright. Her hair is braided into tiny pigtails.

"Careful how you get in that chair," Pet says. "There's a man in the room."

Ruth slowly lowers herself into the chair. "Do I know the man?" she asks in a tremulous voice.

"No," Pet says. "But he won't bite."

Butch makes Ruth guess who she is, hugs her, then repeats her endorsement of my purpose. She prompts Ruth to talk about the Rosses.

Ruth's mind is a triumph over her failing senses. She is ninety-eight years old but her recall is total. She has lived in the area all her life. She trains her eyes on empty space, as if peering into the past.

"I know Thad Ross and his daddy, Bob Ross," she says, summoning the players from the wings. "His mama named Kate. There was Willie Ross. Frank. Little Kate. Little Bob got killed in World War I. There was a Ross they called Sonny. Ollie. It's a Ross had a store on Russum Road—Robert, Delores's first cousin. I ain't no kin to 'em, just raised close to 'em."

"Which ones had black children?" Butch asks.

"Louis had two black children," she says. "One of 'em left the country, went to California. Thad had two girls."

"That's right," Butch says.

Pet, who has been silently listening as the parade of Rosses goes by, interjects, "Katie Bell ain't no half-white. She ain't bright—she's darker than me. The children have a beautiful complexion."

"Mm-hmm," Ruth says, staring wide-eyed into space.

"Did the Ross sisters have any black children?" Butch asks, and shoots me a glance. On the way here, she had told me that one of her family members raised a child borne of such a union.

Ruth says only, "Mmm."

I ask her where she grew up.

"I was raised back in the country close to the Rosses. My people farmed near Stonington. After my husband passed I moved to Fayette, in the projects. I was an O'Quinn before I married." She says her husband originally lived on Holly Grove plantation, and for a moment I feel a commonality, since Holly Grove is now my home. But I do not mention this because I am mindful of widening the gap between us, and perhaps putting her on guard, by pointing out that I own one of the inaccessible big houses of her youth.

She continues. "Bob Ross, that's the furthest back I know about," she says. "And Thad Ross. They was good people. We used to have revival meetings at Shady Grove church and he'd come. Way back yonder, eighty years ago. He's the only white person that come. He'd come around to Mama's house and sit down at the table and eat. He was a farmer. All the colored folk liked him. Some of the white folks'd take up with colored people. That's the way them Rosses were."

She pauses. The football game blares from the TV. I try to think of a polite way to ask if she knows any Rosses whose family were slaves. I have noticed that when I bring up the subject of slavery with whites they talk about it easily, as if they are discussing a war fought long ago, full of victories and defeats, and familiar names. When I bring up the subject in conversations with blacks, particularly older people, I sense a distance, as if I have mentioned a dread disease. Knowing that so many are reluctant to talk about the subject, it seems rude to confront this elderly woman, who has been reminiscing about old times in the quiet refuge of her daughter's home, with the specter of her people's enslavement, but it is a crucial point.

When I do, she says nothing for a moment, then shakes her head.

"I sure don't know," she says. The subject falls flat.

"Well, I wish I could remember things as good as you," Butch says. "I can't remember near about as much as you." She and Ruth resume their small talk, and a few moments later say their good-byes.

As Butch and I drive back through the countryside toward Port Gibson, she seems satisfied that her account has been verified by an unassailable source. "Didn't I tell you?" she asks. "Miss Ruth knows all about it, the whole story. And it's a very complicated story, too—whole lot more complicated than most people think."

CHAPTER TEN

LAVERNE MCPHATE DID NOT think of it as trespassing, though it sounds a lot like it. The land was posted and the gate locked, so she slipped through the woods to approach the stranger's house with her video camera. She wasn't there to film the decaying manse, which is hidden far down a dirt road that is almost impassable when it rains. It was the cemetery she was after, because Isaac Ross is buried there. Although Laverne never lived at Prospect Hill, and she is aware that the current owner jealously guards his privacy, she felt she had every right to be there, as a descendant.

"It's quite an impressive thing," she says of Ross's monument, which she shot from every angle before hightailing it back to her car. The monument is an icon for descendants because it is all that is left to show for Ross's legacy, and any cemetery is sacrosanct in Laverne's mind. She was once appalled to find that someone had stolen tombstones from another of the Ross family burial grounds, most likely, she believes, to use for a sidewalk. She pauses to let the gravity of the affront sink in. "People's tombstones," she repeats. "For sidewalks."

Such remnants have become increasingly important to Laverne as her family has dispersed from the area. Most of the family members have not moved far—she and her husband, who operate a logging business in Jefferson County, live just across the river in Ferriday, Louisiana, and her brother Turner Ross lives in Vicksburg, but over the years all of the old home places have slipped from their grasp. What remains of their family's long occupation is now largely unattended. Their sense of ownership is derived from ghosts. They are holdouts, in absentia.

The family's regime is slow to fade because it lasted so long—nearly 170 years, from the arrival of Isaac Ross in the Mississippi Territory to the sale of Prospect Hill in 1973. When Isaac Ross Wade died in 1891, Prospect Hill passed to his brother, B. H. Wade, who lived out his life there. Family members also occupied several neighboring plantations, including Oak Hill, the original Rosswood, which was just down the road, and the second Rosswood, built nearby by Walter Wade for his second wife in 1857.

The Rosses' and Wades' continued occupation was more or less by default, because the properties were handed down through the generations. Until the 1940s brought the biggest wave of mobility, most of the old houses throughout the region were owned by their original families, but by then they were nearly all in disrepair, and there were few avenues available for making a decent living in the area, much less for maintaining houses built by wealthy men with large forces of free labor. Such families, according to Edna Regan, an elderly woman I spoke with at Vernalia plantation, just across the line in Claiborne County, were often "too poor to paint, too proud to whitewash." In the case of Vernalia, Edna and her husband had been reduced to setting up house in one of the dilapidated slave quarters, even as her mother-in-law continued to receive company in her threadbare brocade dresses, and forbade her son to take a job because she said it would ruin his hands.

This loss of financial stature did not exert a leveling influence on local society. Whites struggled to maintain a tenuous hold on the economic, political, and social status quo. When the WPA Writer's Project visited the area in the 1930s, its report noted that although many of the mansions were falling into ruin, "enough of them remain to stamp the scene with their character." Port Gibson, the largest town in the immediate area, was described in similar terms as "purely ante-bellum in tone."

Robert Wade, who is among the last surviving family members who actually lived at Prospect Hill, remembers when most everything was intact there—the main house, the separate kitchen, the slave quarters, a smokehouse, and several barns. All but the big house are gone now, rotted down. There are only a few reminders of Prospect Hill in Robert's Port Gibson home, including a scattering of photos and a parlor table. There are no oversized, gilt-framed portraits of his ancestors, no massive armoires, no shelves loaded with cracked leather books. When I ask why, he says, "It just all kind of got away through the years."

Robert is a tall, upright man in his sixties with a flat-top haircut, who looks more conservative than he is. He chooses his words carefully, and for someone who has lived his life in the quintessential Deep South town, has no noticeable drawl. He describes himself as "something like the fifth great-grandson of Isaac Ross," and is proud of his family legacy despite his belief that slavery was wrong. He and his family lived at Prospect Hill until 1956, when everyone except his mother moved to a more modern house in town. His mother stayed at the old place until her health began to fail, after which she moved into a trailer behind his house. That was in 1968, and afterward the family did not return to Prospect Hill, even for reunions. With the old house now weathered and empty, "People broke in and stole things out of it," he says. "They stole the stained glass windows, stuff like that. We cleaned it all out except an old upright piano, and they stole that, too."

The plantation acreage had over the years been divided among the heirs, leaving Robert's family with only the portion on which his father farmed. His father had inherited the place from his own father, and left it to Robert, who plans to leave the remaining 173 acres to his son. In the 1970s he made the difficult decision to sell the house and three acres to a Natchez man who planned to restore it but never did. "I realized it was a bad deal afterward but it was too late to get out of it," he says. The house was later sold to its current owner, John McCarter.

Most of the area's old houses were eventually abandoned or sold, Robert says, because they were isolated, expensive to maintain, and uncomfortable by twentieth-century standards. Prospect Hill, he recalls, was "cool in the summer and cold in the winter," and until the late 1940s was heated by fireplaces and lit by candles and kerosene lamps. As an only child, Robert spent a lot of time roaming the woods, playing Confederate soldier with an old rifle that he would sneak from behind an armoire in the hall—the same hiding place where the family kept the Union army gun left by the soldier who had died in Robert's boyhood room. Most of Robert's playmates were descendants of Prospect Hill slaves, although he sometimes stole away on his horse and rode for miles to play with white children whose families his parents did not approve of. He recalls being chastised by his family's housekeeper, who was herself a descendant of Prospect Hill slaves, for visiting families she called "poor white trash," and who threatened to tell his parents if he did not stop.

At this point Robert pulls a small album from a drawer beside his sofa and turns to a photo of a second housekeeper standing on the lawn before Prospect Hill, beside his mother. "Her family—those families, all of them had been on the place all along," he says. This housekeeper, whom he called Nonnie, moved with his mother to Port Gibson in 1968 and lived with her until she died.

Robert has visited the Prospect Hill house only a few times in the last thirty-five years, once when the Daughters of the American Revolution erected a marker near Ross's grave, and again when John McCarter had the family out to lunch and to install a second marker commissioned by the Isaac Ross chapter of the Colonial Dames. Robert retains the right of access to the cemetery, but he says it pains him to see the old house in its current condition. Likewise, "I haven't been through downtown Fayette since the courthouse burned. It made me sick when I drove through."

The sorry state of Fayette and Jefferson County in general is a common theme in conversations with Ross descendants, but Robert, who is more circumspect than most, is reluctant to criticize government officials who are responsible for an infrastructure that in many ways mirrors the old house at Prospect Hill. Still, he can't help but mention the poor quality of the county schools, the deterioration and later the burning of the courthouse, and certain black elected officials whose motivations he believes are as racist as some of their white predecessors. Because Robert had earlier suggested that Ross may have repatriated his slaves because he was concerned that emancipation would lead to problems, I ask how he thinks Ross would view the area today. He seems chastened by the question, and does not answer immediately.

"Well," he says, finally, "I wonder what my *grandfather* would think."

Considering the changes that have taken place since the antebellum era, he adds, "I'm glad I didn't live back in that time, myself. I do not believe in involuntary servitude in any way, shape, or form. I think it's wrong. Isaac Ross was antislavery and his belief was they would be more

trouble than they were worth in the long run. He created a lot of enemies among his neighbors because they thought he was an abolitionist."

Growing up at Prospect Hill, as a descendant of slave owners, he
says his racial views have at times been mixed. "Being raised like I was
down here, I can't help but admit that sometimes I was a little prejudiced. But I would never knowingly mistreat one at all. I have some
good friends that are black, that I would do anything in the world for,
and they would do anything for me. There are some white people
that . . . Anyway, in their case, I'd rather associate with the blacks."

Laverne McPhate's views on the state of Jefferson County are similarly mixed. She laments the hostility she says is increasingly common
today, but says she has had no racial problems herself. She realizes her
family history sets her apart in many ways, but not that far apart. Their
history, which she recorded her grandmother recounting on tape, is
more inclusive than one might expect. When I mention the racial mixing that Delores and Butch brought up, she says, simply, "As it came
down through the twenties and thirties, it was not uncommon for the
Ross men to have black mistresses. I just spoke with one yesterday, and
they're just as white as I am. We all knew that. They're proud of it and
I have nothing against it myself. They're well-educated people."

Her brother, Turner Ross, who runs a welding shop in Vicksburg,
actually seems to relish the idea of so many black Rosses and white
Rosses hailing from the same place, the same piece of ground. "Some
of 'em are actual kinfolk," he says, over the phone. "Some of the
Rosses had something to do with the blacks—I know that for a fact.
Years ago. And when they set 'em free, the federal government allowed
'em to take the name of their last master, and ninety-nine percent of
'em did. So it's all kind of Rosses, black and white."

Turner mentions an elderly man who picks up cans along the roads
around Vicksburg. "Black fella," he says, from Arkansas, which is where
his own grandfather, Thomas Alonzo Davenport, moved after the Civil
War. "And I'm here to tell you, that man that picks up tin cans on the
side of the road is named Thomas Alonzo Davenport—same damn
name as my grandfather. Whenever he comes around my shop, he
always says the same thing—he's glad to be around kinfolk again."

* * *

If such unconventional kinships are common in the history of Prospect Hill, the contest of Ross's will illustrates that kinship does not always imply affinity, much less harmony. While Isaac Ross and Prospect Hill occupy an odd middle ground, the region's history is beset by turbulent cross currents, and their pull is often influenced by race. Aside from comparative free agents such as Delores Smith, the line of demarcation is usually obvious, and despite concerted efforts to minimize the difference politically, economically, and socially, race still matters in a variety of ways. Not all whites are descended from slave owners, and not all blacks are descended from slaves, but how a person views Jefferson County today has everything to do with their own circumstances and the circumstances of their ancestors, and historically, those circumstances have been very different for blacks and whites.

The differences may manifest themselves in trivial ways, or may be extremely consequential, as during the Civil Rights era. But they present themselves again and again, sometimes as the context of a story that is otherwise generally agreed upon, as when Turner Ross mentions a long-ago mass murder in Harriston—the same story, it turns out, that Delores had mentioned.

While Delores couched the tale in terms of a misguided man who became enraged and sought vengeance over a perceived injustice, Turner calls it "the time the blacks went on a rampage." His version also begins at a poker game at the cotton gin, mentions the wounding of Thad Ross, and cites several victims, all white. Beyond that, it diverges.

As he remembers it, "There was seven or eight of 'em got killed. White men. Two of my uncles on the Ross side got wounded, one in the hand and one in the back of the leg." The sheriff, his deputies, and a group of other men eventually cornered the gunmen, who were hiding under the gin, and afterward, "They hung 'em, then shot 'em all night long." He summons the last, harrowing image with no apparent emotion—no satisfaction, dismay, or judgment in his voice.

The only documented account of the incident, which ran in the Fayette newspaper in 1913, tells still another version, under the headline CARNAGE AT HARRISTON; 8 DEAD AND 14 WOUNDED—SHERIFF HAMMETT KILLED AND CIRCUIT CLERK GILLIS WOUNDED; TWO NEGRO MURDERERS HANGED. Several black victims were also listed, which is something even Delores left out. The reporter took pains to discount the notion that the incident was "anything resembling a 'race war.'" According to his account, the main gunman was an eighteen-year-old mulatto man who began shooting "at a Negro house, where Willie Jones had some trouble with two other Negroes, whom he shot, at the same time shooting a woman. From there he proceeded to the village proper and shot everyone he saw, indiscriminately, with the exception of Shaw Millsaps, a Harriston merchant, whom he called to the door and asked for a drink of water, and whom he warned to stay inside."

Jones allegedly continued through town, shooting several men, including the sheriff, before being wounded himself. Eventually, he and his two alleged accomplices gave themselves up. By then a special train from Natchez had arrived with more men and arms and a supply of dynamite. The newspaper concluded: "Immediately following the orderly execution of the two murderers the crowd began to disperse, and before the noon hour the village of Harriston had resumed its normal appearance, except for the congregation of two small groups of citizens who discussed the affair."

In fact, people would be discussing it almost a century later.

Despite the newspaper's disclaimer, the incident clearly represented the white community's worst nightmare—a "black rampage"—and ended with the black community's worst nightmare—a lynching. It is not surprising that it is remembered in different ways today.

When I mention the melee to Robert Wade, he shakes his head but offers no comment. I ask how anyone can know what actually happened, when everyone, including the reporter who was responsible for the only documentation, seemed to have an agenda. He again shakes his head.

It seems a crucial point. But only when I offer as a similar example the different accounts of the alleged slave uprising at Prospect Hill does he sit up straight. "I have a copy of the original version of the burning of the house," he says. I ask if it is the account written by Thomas Wade. "Yes," he says. "That's the original account. I was shown the white oak tree where the perpetrators were hanged. That's basically true. Now, just exactly what the facts were, well, that's hard to come by."

As someone who was born in Jefferson County, yet who saw something of the world during World War II and later as a college student in Washington State and in the Naval Reserve, Robert is at once self-assured and cautious. He respects his ancestor's account but is aware that there is a lot he does not know. The same is true for many of his peers. Although Laverne McPhate might warmly embrace tales of happy slaves, she has no storehouse of information about what life was actually like in the quarters. It is one of the reasons so many black residents disregard local history: it was written by whites, whose agendas and personal knowledge were sometimes very different than their own.

Aside from a brief flurry of activity during Reconstruction, the first real opportunity blacks had to write local history came in the 1960s, and by and large they have been writing it ever since.

In the 1870s, during Reconstruction, parts of Mississippi were occupied by federal troops, which provided a measure of protection for newly franchised blacks. Soon blacks held elected office throughout the Natchez District and other parts of the state where they represented the majority of the population. After the troops left, though, whites found methods for regaining control. Literacy tests at the polls, harassment of potential voters and violence against black leaders soon vanquished black voting strength. Dissatisfaction with the return of white power brought about the first wave of emigration by black residents, and the trend continued, with a few intermissions, for the next hundred years.

During the Depression and after World War II, more whites joined in the exodus, mostly in search of jobs. The loss of population proved nearly fatal to many communities, particularly places such as Rodney, which was already grappling with survival after being abandoned by the wandering Mississippi River. Although Rodney once had its own newspaper and opera house, fewer than fifty people call the place home today, and the remaining historic buildings are slowly succumbing to fires, floods, and preservationists bent on relocating them to more viable locales. Rodney's most notable structure—the Presbyterian church, where Confederate guerillas captured Union officers attending services during the war, and which still has a cannonball lodged in its front wall—is an empty shell. Rodney resident Laura Piazza, who lived across from the empty church, once recalled a carload of intrepid tourists asking her if they'd found the "ghost town." She replied, indignantly, "Do I look like a ghost?"

The departure of whites from Jefferson and Claiborne counties escalated when black residents reasserted their political power. The Civil Rights era reached its stride in 1964 and 1965, and activists began to fan out across the state during what was known as Freedom Summer. The pivotal event in Jefferson County came when state police fired on demonstrators at Alcorn State University with rubber bullets, which energized the fledgling movement in the area. A year later black boycotts were imposed on white-owned businesses in Fayette and Natchez, which led the Ku Klux Klan, the Louisiana Citizens' Council, and a group called Americans for the Preservation of the White Race to stage "buy-ins" in support of the store owners. In 1966, a similar boycott was brought in Port Gibson to try to force store owners to address black customers with courtesy titles such as "Mr." and "Mrs." and to wait on them in turn, which led to a successful lawsuit by eighteen stores against the NAACP and other supporters—a ruling that was later overturned by the U.S. Supreme Court.

In 1968, Fayette Civil Rights activist Charles Evers defeated six white candidates in the Democratic primary for the district's congressional seat before losing in the general election. He garnered 43,000 votes, the majority of them cast by newly registered black voters. Later that year, Evers helped overthrow the state's whites-only delegation to the Democratic National Convention in Chicago, and in 1969 he was elected mayor of Fayette, the first black to hold such a post in a racially mixed Mississippi town since Reconstruction. Two years later, during his unsuccessful gubernatorial campaign, Evers stood on the old courthouse steps in Fayette and lambasted Theodore Bilbo, a former governor whom he had heard speak as a boy, recalling how he "spit that ol' racist fire." Evers then proclaimed, "But look out Bilbo, we comin' at you!"

By 1980, when about 200 white residents organized another "buy-in" in response to a boycott of a Fayette business that had fired its black employees, the majority of elected offices in both the town and the county were held by blacks, and in Fayette, at least, both white stores and white shoppers were clearly on their way out.

Hobbs Freeman, a descendant of Isaac Ross who was born in Fayette and lived there until the mid-1990s, says there were only about ten whites in town when he sold his store and moved to the community of Yokena, on the outskirts of Vicksburg.

"I had just wasted enough of my life thinking it would get better, and it never did," he says, explaining his painful decision to move. "It seems like nobody cares about anything. And the crime. My store was robbed—burgled, rather—twice in one week. They tore the door off, and it was right next door to the sheriff's office. But I really do miss the people. I know a lot of good people there."

Hobbs, whose earliest ancestors arrived in Jefferson County in 1780, still owns a parcel of land granted to the family by Spain. The original house on the property, which was known as Indigo plantation, was abandoned and decaying when a black family bought it and renovated it. "I was glad to see that," he says.

"The white people in Jefferson County for the last fifty years have encouraged their young people to get out—to get out and start a new life," he says. "And after the Civil Rights movement, a lot of blacks who had gone to Chicago and Detroit, they moved back, so there are more of them, and less and less whites."

Hobbs's mother is among those who have stayed, and he returns often to visit. He says most of the county's residents, black and white, try to get along. They have different ways of viewing local history, just like there are different versions of the story of Prospect Hill.

"It's kind of like a car wreck," he says. "Everybody sees something different, but you know that there was definitely a wreck."

Robert Wade says that he, too, is optimistic that area residents will eventually come to terms with their differences. In fact, he believes most of them already have. But he has experienced his share of racism, he says. In the 1980s he was among several whites who crossed swords with Claiborne County tax assessor Evan Doss, the first black elected to the position in Mississippi, after Doss allegedly refused to sell them license tags because they opposed him politically. Robert felt vindicated when Doss later went to prison on embezzlement charges.

The biggest stumbling block to the region's progress, Robert says, is the local economy, particularly in Jefferson County. "When they took the tax money from Grand Gulf away from Claiborne County, that was wrong," he says. "But why is there nothing in Jefferson County?" He mentions the Mississippi Band of Choctaw Indians, who have grown wealthy from casinos and industrial development in east Mississippi, and says, "When you look at what the Choctaws have been able to accomplish, and you consider how they've been treated, you wonder why something can't be done in Jefferson County."

The lack of jobs is just one reason so many young people leave the area, he says. Because the area has such a small tax base, anyone who owns anything of high value "is just taxed to death. In Jefferson County they have no other way to produce revenue. But the main reason for young people with children is the schools. It's so expensive to send them to private schools, and they can't go to public schools, they just can't. It's not possible."

Of Robert's five children, only one has stayed in Port Gibson. The others are scattered from Jackson to the Gulf Coast. Of his grandchildren and great-grandchildren, all who are of age have left. He says that when he sold the house at Prospect Hill it was already clear that none of the family members would ever return there to live. Because four of his children were born while the family was still at Prospect Hill, and they were the last generation of the family to live there, I ask if the story matters to them, if they ever go back to visit, to see the monument over Isaac Ross's grave.

"Not really," he says, sounding more empathetic than sad. "They all have their own lives now."

The same is true for Turner Ross's children. Although his sister Laverne would surely beg to differ, he says, "None of 'em was ever interested in all this but me and my mama."

CHAPTER ELEVEN

THE ROAD TO PROSPECT HILL is narrow and rutted now, threading its way through the depopulated Jefferson County countryside, past abandoned houses and barns, and old cotton fields long since grown up in trees. Great mats of purple wisteria bloom over entire groves, marking the sites of forgotten houses with a psychedelic display each spring. Here and there fallen trees funnel the road down to one lane, which poses no real problem, because we pass only two trucks and a handful of houses over the last ten miles or so.

Aside from a couple of posted signs, there is no evidence of Prospect Hill from the road, just an unremarkable metal gate, a seemingly random and obscure portal through the green. Today the gate is open, which is unusual because John McCarter, who owns the place, does not welcome uninvited guests. He has agreed to let me visit the family cemetery because he recognizes that its importance transcends his ownership of the surrounding area, but he has told me that the house itself, his personal domain, is off-limits.

I met John when I was dismantling Holly Grove, which originally stood in the vicinity, in 1990, and during a subsequent visit to Prospect Hill was amazed by the house's contradictions. The structure itself is near ruin, the ground visible through the rotten floor of the elevated porch, slivers of sky peeking through the rotten lath of the crumbling plaster ceiling. The late Tom Perrin, with whom John owned the house, let me go inside on that first visit. The interior was a showplace of antiques and nineteenth-century Southern decorative design—great tester beds draped in mosquito netting, Victorian-era sofas, side chairs and marble-topped parlor tables, and freshly painted walls.

Passing from one plane of existence to the other—from the external ruin to the exquisitely preserved time capsule within—was surreal.

The approach to the house ends in a quagmire a few hundred feet before the structure itself, and when my friend Scottie Harmon and I roll to a stop this day, we see John standing on the lawn amid his chickens and his English shepherd and two Great Pyrenees. Beyond him the house looks like a grand, weathered barn with six monumental chimneys. Attached to the fence is the Colonial Dames' brass plaque, which reads PROSPECT HILL PLANTATION HOME AND GRAVE SITE OF ISAAC ROSS PATRIOT-HUMANITARIAN-PHILANTHROPIST.

John greets us on the lawn. Beyond him, the setting of Prospect Hill is as tragically beautiful as I remembered it. The house is surrounded by ancient, storm-damaged cedar trees from which Spanish moss hangs to the ground. Architectural remnants are crammed beneath the gallery and flow into the yard. The fine facade of cypress siding, scored to resemble stone, stands exposed to the elements by a massive hole in the gallery roof. The roof has been leaking for years but the hole is large enough to have been made by a bomb blast. John says one of the old cedars fell on the house during a tornado a few years back. The gallery is elevated perhaps ten feet off the ground, and the ceiling rises to fourteen feet or more, and with its scattering of antique chairs and faded bunting over the door, it has the appearance of a ruined stage set floating in the air.

The once purple fabric draped over the elaborate doorway with a wreath of blackened magnolia leaves at the center are the remains of a funerary display for Perrin, who died in a car wreck several years back. John says he has had no real interest in working on the house since then. Everything about the place—the storm damage, the decay, the funeral bunting—brings to mind a gaping, long-untreated wound. Although the house has a haunting beauty that seems apropos for the Prospect Hill story, John notices the camera slung over my shoulder and asks that I take no photographs of the structure itself, because he does not want it to be remembered this way.

The grounds are a lush, overgrown garden of traditional Southern landscape plants—camellias, jasmine, irises, dogwoods, azaleas, blue phlox, and wisteria. The cemetery stands in a field of blue and white flowers. Two old cedars also fell onto the cemetery during the tornado, toppling several tombstones and narrowly missing Isaac Ross's monument, which is a towering, cupola-like marble structure ringed with columns. It is as impressive as everyone has said. The whole family is here: Ross, his wife, his sons and daughters, their husbands, children and wives, and little Martha Richardson, who died in the fire. Curiously, Isaac Ross Wade's tombstone faces away from the others. All of the tombstones except his are oriented toward Ross's monument, and, like most I've seen, are read from the side facing the grave. Wade's faces away from Ross's monument, and away from his own grave. It seems backward.

When I mention this, John says, "Yes, it's unusual. A lot of people have different ideas of what it means, but what's the point in speculating? There's no way to know about that sort of thing." Of the massive, toppled tombstones he says, "I don't like seeing them like that, and if I had a gang of slaves, I'd get them to stand them back up, but it's not a priority for me right now."

John appears dubious about the history that frames his life at Prospect Hill. He appreciates its physical evidence but seems weary of long-running disputes and efforts by certain "old families" to stake their claim to fame. The cemetery at Prospect Hill is one of many historical crosses that he has to bear. It is a demanding remnant of an overwhelmingly significant history, right in his own backyard, but none of the interested parties seem inclined to help him keep it up.

The majority of the graves belong to Wades, several of whom fought for the Confederacy, with the most recent dating from 1908. There are three Isaac Ross Wades. The first two died as boys, one in 1846 at age five, the other in 1847 at age one, and the third, the one who contested the will, in 1891 at seventy-six. Isaac Ross's monument is the centerpiece. John says he hopes to resume work on both the cemetery and the house eventually, but he has no firm plans right now.

Few people would take on a project like this, sinking incalculable time, energy, and funds into a huge, crumbling house in a remote corner of Jefferson County, Mississippi. Red Lick, the community nearest to Prospect Hill, is now largely the domain of a Muslim group that operates a small school known as Mohammed's University of the New Islam, which shares the neighborhood with a perfectly preserved antebellum estate and the Good Ole Boys hunting club. Nearby Church Hill was for a time the site of a Hare Krishna compound, based at an old plantation known as The Cedars, which had previously been owned by actor George Hamilton. The roads between are scenic tunnels through overhanging trees, but the pavement is pocked and the shoulders are uniformly littered. Here and there are empty mobile homes, overgrown with vines, the windows broken out. It is hard to imagine anything more forlorn-looking, or more telling, than an abandoned mobile home—something designed specifically to be mobile, which has been left behind. The nearest town of any size, Fayette, is dominated by federal housing projects and empty storefronts.

There are a few prominent holdouts of the Old South scattered around the region, and many people showcase their homes during the annual pilgrimage tour in Port Gibson. Most of them, with poetic names like Disharoon, Idlewild, and Collina, are repositories for a vanished way of life. On our way to Prospect Hill, Scottie and I stopped by a few of the tour homes in Port Gibson, which had all been spruced up for the pilgrimage, their lawns neatly mowed and tables set up on galleries to dispense tea cakes and punch. The first, Tremont, was filled with antiques, family memorabilia, and decorative arrangements of artifacts that serve as tiny Civil War shrines, mostly for local Confederate General Earl Van Dorn. A pretty young woman in a lavender and blue floral hoopskirt guided us through several rooms, reading from index cards. The furnishings were a hodgepodge from the 1830s to the 1960s, and unlike tour homes that faithfully mimic a specific historical period, this one had clearly been occupied by a single family for a very long time. The tour's treatment of antebellum history was equally venerable, which is to say that it was not politically correct. At one point a second, incongruous-looking guide with tattooed cleavage pointed to an old tea cart and said, cheerfully, "Back in the days of slavery, your little maid would roll this out to serve you!"

A few blocks away, amid a hundred acres of lush woodlands, was Collina. The home, built in 1834, is now owned by Dr. David Fagan, a native of Portland, Oregon, who bought it more than a decade ago and carefully restored it. The house is grandly appointed and could easily be the subject of an article in *Architectural Digest*. It is a tour de force of interior design, yet the doors at either end of the wide hall stood open on this day, filling the rooms with the scent of wisteria and wild azalea, and enabling the family dog to roam through at will.

"The house has great karma. This place is like a sanctuary," said a friend of David's, Donna Smith, who was helping to greet visitors. "Mississippi is just such a wild place."

Donna is originally from Cleveland, Ohio, and said that when she moved south she was surprised to find that in addition to the familiar sources of conflict, Rankin County, near Jackson, where she works in forensic psychology, is overrun with drugs. "It's the crystal meth capital of the country," she said.

The world, in fact, seemed noticeably uncontrolled and unkempt after we departed the landscaped grounds of Collina. Out in the countryside the roadsides were again littered and the landscape had a lush, abused look.

Most of what passes for an economy in the rural areas is a sort of picking over bones. As we depart Prospect Hill we pass a man with a metal detector probing for artifacts at an old house site, of which there are seemingly hundreds to choose from. The most famous of the area's old sites is Windsor, the state's grandest antebellum home before it burned during a party in 1891. The ruins of Windsor are evocative, dominated by twenty-three towering columns topped by massive, cast-iron capitals embellished with acanthus leaves, and here and there linked by surviving sections of elaborate iron railing. Built in 1860, the house was new when the Civil War came, and was used as a Union army field hospital while the family was sequestered in its upper stories. Its ruins were later used as a set for a romanticized movie about the Old South starring Elizabeth Taylor and Montgomery Clift called *Raintree County*. Today it is owned by the state, and is a popular spot for picnics. The surrounding fields have been planted in pines, and the family cemetery is caving into a ravine. It is possible that it is even more impressive now, as a monumental ruin, than it was during its heyday.

Just beyond Windsor, the road leading to the old Mississippi River ferry has also caved into a ravine, and the ferry no longer runs. The remaining roads are occasionally closed for long periods by bridge failures and landslides.

Nothing epitomizes the region's decline more than the house at Prospect Hill, and nothing embodies the hypersensitive desire to hold on more than Rosswood, the only other Ross family house still standing in the area. Thinking it might be interesting to see Rosswood, I had phoned ahead, explained my research, and asked if I might visit. Jean

Hylander, who owns the house with her husband Walt, replied, "Yes, you may, for seven dollars and fifty cents." The admission fee is more than twice what other tour homes in the area charge, perhaps because the massive house is so expensive to maintain, but it seems a small price to pay to see the only surviving Ross home that retains its antebellum splendor.

After driving roads lined with substandard houses, many of which have burglar bars on the windows, and where refrigerators and sofas have been dumped into every eroding ravine, the approach to Rosswood is certainly impressive. The massive, gleaming white Greek Revival edifice surmounts a hill in the distance, surrounded by old trees draped with moss. It beckons visitors down the long, oak-lined drive, although signs clustered at the gate send a different signal, informing you more than once and in no uncertain terms that anyone who proceeds further will be charged admission. There is also a sign for a security service displayed prominently on the front wall, and when Hylander opens the front door the first thing that comes into view is a cash register.

The Hylanders operate Rosswood as a business, and have spared no expense in re-creating the sort of ostentatious display they think would have greeted guests during the antebellum years. An eclectic array of period sofas, china cabinets, and bookshelves brim with cut glass, china, and silver, and crystal chandeliers hang from elegant plaster medallions. Hylander is obviously proud of the history of the house, but it is clear that her own furnishings are her real passion. There is something overproduced about the whole affair, which was probably true in the antebellum era as well.

The Hylanders had no connection to Rosswood, or to the area, before they bought the mansion in 1975, but for personal credentials she points out that she is a fifth-generation Mississippian. "Walt's grandparents," she adds, "couldn't even speak English." I assume this to mean that her family has its Mississippi bona fides, while her husband's ancestors are comparatively recent arrivals.

As she goes through the litany of tour-home highlights, she offers an unexpected aside, noting that the house "has a lot of black history." For evidence she points out that the plantation was originally owned by Isaac Ross, whom she claims was "the first person to free his slaves before the Civil War." Ross's slaves, she says, "worked this land. As for my own part, I had black crews do all the work on the house." The restoration work included installing a new roof and applying 220 gallons of white paint. She goes through the cast of housekeepers and handymen she has employed over the years, some of whom she says she occasionally still talks with on the phone. She mentions one housekeeper who was "the best help I've ever had. There's no way I could make up all those beds myself."

We talk about Ross family history and I explain why I am here.

"It's too bad you can't go out to Prospect Hill," she says.

When I tell her that we have just been to Prospect Hill, she is incredulous.

"You've been to Prospect Hill? No one gets in there! You're the first person I know who's ever been allowed in. He has the fence electrified so you'll get shocked if you try to climb over!"

I am torn between defending John, who was unfailingly polite, and going along with the notion of the electric fence to aid in his effort to keep the tourists at bay. I say I don't know about the fence, but am aware that John values his privacy.

Hylander thinks this over for a moment, then says she has a book about Prospect Hill. She points to a group of folding chairs that seem out of place amid the fancy sofas and armchairs, and says, "I invite you to sit down here while I go find it."

It turns out I have seen the book, so she reverts to tour mode, pointing out the Mallard case where her collection of cut glass, Dresden china, and jade is on display, along with a fragment of a cannonball she says was fired at the house during the Civil War skirmish in July 1864 that involved the Second Mississippi Infantry, part of the U.S. Colored Troops, some of whom had previously been slaves in the area. "We found it when we put the pool in," she says. "The Rebels won that one."

Hylander says that Walter Wade, the builder of the house, was living in an earlier house by the same name at the time of the controversy over Ross's will, but that he happened to be spending the night at Prospect Hill the night of the disastrous fire. "He's the one who didn't drink the coffee, which had been drugged," she says, offering her own version of the night's events. "He was the one who woke everybody up. When they came out the front door there was a man with a sword or an axe or something, and the mistress of the house said, 'Did you come to rescue us?'"

She shows us a copy of Wade's plantation diary, which chronicles life at Rosswood between 1855 and 1862. One entry reads: "Go to Conrad's shopping for Negroes." Another reads: "Sat by the fire all day—dull—Negroes no fun."

Hylander recalls that Rosswood was in disrepair when she and her husband bought it and she began fulfilling her lifelong dream of owning an antebellum mansion. Then she turns toward the door and says, "I invite you to come into our parlor, our most beautiful room."

The parlor and the dining room adjacent to it are undeniably rich, with elaborate, gilded mirrors, a rosewood square grand piano, heavy drapes, and a gloomy, oversized dining room set embellished with carved boars and dogs. The china cabinet is loaded with more silver, cut glass, and china. "While we were living in different places all over the world, I was always collecting," Hylander says. A mirror in the hall "was collected in Berlin. It always reminds me of my life in Berlin." The dining room set "is from the Jacobean period."

The doorbell rings and Hylander excuses herself, leaving us in the dining room. We stroll into the hall, and beneath the stairway see a door with a sign that reads TO BASEMENT GIFT SHOP AND SLAVE QUARTERS. I have been hauling my camera around during the tour, and when Scottie suggests I snap a photo, I do. Hylander, who is rushing through a tour of the preceding rooms with a man from Kentucky—trying to catch up with where we left off—hears the shutter and hurries into the hall. "No photographs are allowed in this house!" she says, with surprising rancor. "Did you not see the sign?" She points to the corner where the cash register sits. I still do not see the sign.

"No, I didn't," I say. "But I won't take any more."

"I can't get insurance if you take pictures," she says. "That's why I have that sign." She glares at me from behind her darkly tinted glasses, then adds, "I'm going to have to ask you not to have that film developed."

I nod. The Kentuckian looks at the floor, bewildered. I am hoping that that's the end of it, but it isn't.

"Did you take other pictures when I wasn't looking?" she asks.

"No, I did not," I answer.

"Do you have some kind of card with your name on it that says what you're doing here?" she asks.

I do not.

It is apparent that her anger is building. I glance over at Scottie and say, "Maybe we should just go."

He nods. We head for the door.

Hylander leaves the Kentuckian in the hallway and hurries after us, protesting that we have not seen the entire house.

"We've seen enough," I say, continuing out the door.

"Did you take pictures of my *furniture*?"

As we pull out onto the highway, and I notice there are signs along the road, flanking the Rosswood estate, delineating the boundaries of a neighborhood-watch crime prevention program. There are no other homes within those boundaries, which makes it clear that the estate is a neighborhood unto itself.

CHAPTER TWELVE

THE MINIVAN PULLS TO a stop before a nondescript building in Stone Mountain, Georgia, and a woman gets out, wearing a striking West African dress of vivid purple with golden sunbursts and red embroidery along the hem. She bears an armload of bulging plastic bags, and eyes me curiously.

"Is this where the . . ." I begin to ask.

"Yes!" she says, and offers a wry smile. "You must be the man who's working on the book on Ross."

I nod.

"Well, you come to the right place. Everybody knows the Rosses." She pronounces the name with a strong Liberian inflection, so it sounds like "th' RUH sez."

Soon other cars pull into the parking lot and people begin to gather in front of the building. Among them is Sandy Yancy, a Georgian who is chair of the Sinoe County Association of America, which was formed by expatriates from the Sinoe County region of Liberia that included Mississippi in Africa. There are association chapters in several states, owing to a mass exodus of Liberians during the nation's two decades of unrest and civil war, which began in 1980.

Yancy left Liberia in 1982 and hopes one day to take his children to see their native land, but only for a visit, and certainly not now, when the country is still in the throes of something very close to anarchy. When things get better he would like to hold an association meeting in Sinoe County. "You know, ease back in, clean up the neighborhoods, not just send supplies," he says. "I want to help the people who remained behind."

Over the last year, as I have been trying to piece together the threads of the story of Prospect Hill, I have come to the unavoidable—and daunting—conclusion that I will have to travel to Liberia to fill in the most important blank—the fate of the freed-slave immigrants and their descendants. I have come to Stone Mountain hoping that some of the association's members will be able to offer leads in my search for the Liberian descendants of Prospect Hill. I have also posted notices on countless Internet bulletin boards, explaining my project, saying that I am planning on traveling to Liberia to do research, and asking in general about the Rosses, but the responses have been discouraging. Although many cite famous Rosses in Liberian history, none have provided names of descendants who live in Liberia today.

Ironically, most of the people I meet in Stone Mountain are searching for relatives in the United States, a sort of *Roots* in reverse. None knows of a Mississippi connection in their family, although Janice Sherman, whose mother's maiden name was Duncan, suspects she has one. I suggest that her ancestors may have been freed by Stephen Duncan, Ross's friend in Natchez, but that is as far as it goes. The meeting is primarily a social event, a time for the expatriates to eat traditional West African foods, hear news from home, and lament the current state of their native country. It begins more than three hours late because, as Yancy explains, the party the night before lasted until four A.M.

At the start of the meeting the association members sing the Liberian national anthem, which sounds like a mournful hymn, with one person counting time:

"We will o'er all prevail.

"We'll shout the freedom of a race benighted.

"Long live Liberia, happy land,

"A home of glorious liberty by God's command. . . ."

Then everyone holds hands and prays.

Wilfred Harris, chair of the Minnesota chapter, recalls celebrations in Sinoe County to which men wore tuxedos and top hats, and reminisces about people he once knew. I pick out the names David Ross, Hampton Ross Mosely, and Simon Ross.

"Gone are the days," he says. "Those were the days when so many people looked at Sinoe with so much conviction . . . there was so much pride. But it has changed. Brothers and sisters, things have changed.

We are scattered around the world, looking for things we do not have. But our being here is not a mistake. Just like Joseph in the Bible was sold as a slave, to prepare for the hunger, we were brought here for a reason." The reason, he says, is to help the people back home. He expresses gratitude for the opportunity America has offered, and suggests, "If you're in America and cannot advance yourself, then you go to Liberia."

During a break in the meeting, Evans Yancy, Sandy's brother, says that when he was growing up in Liberia, people heard his name and told him his family was originally from Georgia. "So when I came to the States, I came to Georgia," he says. He visited the state archives and found several Yancys in old phone books near Augusta, Georgia. "I found Isaac Yancy," he says. "Isaac Yancy was a common name in my family. I didn't know if he was black or white, but I figured, either way." He drove to the town where Isaac Yancy was listed as a minister, but found that he had recently died. As he inquired around town, he was shocked when one man recognized his relation to the Yancys. "He said, 'I knew you were related to Reverend Yancy—you have his eyes.'" Eventually Yancy organized a reunion of the two families—the Sinoe-expatriate Yancys and the native Georgian Yancys. He says he met a man there who looked more like his brother Sandy than he did, after 165 years of family separation.

Yancy says most of the expatriates do not expect to go back to Liberia to live. Why would they, when everyone else is clamoring to get out? They are only too happy to dream of Africa. Several other members suggest names of people in Liberia who may be related to Prospect Hill: Rosses, Reeds, Woodsons, but no one knows how to reach any of them. There are few phones in Liberia, and because the country is in turmoil, people tend to move frequently. Janice Sherman offers what proves to be the best lead I could hope for in the United States, a man named Nathan Ross who was in the Liberian congress and fled the country following the 1980 coup. But for now, as I am preparing to embark for Liberia, I have little to go on aside from warnings. Everyone is unanimous: this not a good time to go to Liberia. I heard much the same thing following my Internet postings, which prompted an array of responses ranging from concern to hostility.

✳   ✳   ✳

The Liberian conflict erupted from a variety of causes, but a major factor was the long-running conflict between the descendants of the freed slaves and those of the indigenous tribes. Most of the Sinoe association members are the former, who were once referred to as Americo-Liberians. Before the coup the Americos represented about 5 percent of the population, yet they controlled most of the nation's money and all of the elected offices. Their legacy included the recreation of something like the society of the Old South, where the slave-master system was all the immigrants had ever known.

The coup followed an incident in 1979 in which police in Monrovia, the capital, fired upon demonstrators who were protesting the government's intention to raise the price of imported rice. Looting followed. The police and the army were divided in their loyalty for Americo President William Tolbert Jr. and the demonstrators. The following year Samuel Doe, a military legend who was of native ethnic descent, overthrew Tolbert and the long period of Americo rule ended. The later civil war, which broke out during the Christmas season of 1989 and lasted until 1997, included fighting among rival ethnic groups and the Americos, but by then the lines had blurred considerably. By many people's reckoning, the civil war has never really ended, and in fact, more intense fighting will break out in 2003.

Because most Liberians now in the United States fled their homes in Liberia following the coup or during the civil war of the 1990s, nearly all of the expatriates I meet at the Sinoe meeting are fearful of going back. One association member offers to act as my guide and protector in Liberia if I will pay his way, but this proves unnecessary after I hear from John Singler, the linguist at New York University who responded to one of my postings. John says that he can make arrangements for a guide who is already there.

John proves invaluable to my search, not only because he has lived and taught in Liberia, including Sinoe County, but because he is intimately familiar with both the country's history and its current situation. He manages to keep in touch with old friends through haphazard phone calls and letters, and offers much-needed advice on the logistics of getting to Liberia and what I can expect once I am there. He knows of no Ross descendants himself but is confident that his contacts will be able to help.

Everyone at the Sinoe meeting correctly predicts that the biggest hurdle will simply be getting there. Acquiring a visa from the Liberian embassy in Washington, D.C., proves a formidable task. The embassy is understaffed and I get nowhere on the phone. When I visit the embassy in person, it is closed. On my third try the door is open, and I present my papers and the visa is granted. I notice that the wall of the waiting area, where framed photos of Liberian dignitaries hang, has been stripped almost bare. Where once there were perhaps thirty photos, there are now only a handful interspersed with the shadows of those that have been removed.

As I plan my trip to Liberia, I keep in touch with several of the Sinoe Association members, who each time sadly report that the situation is not improving. Although my trip is delayed numerous times by outbreaks of fighting, eventually I decide that it is simply time to go. If I am going to find the descendants of the immigrants from Prospect Hill, I do not have the luxury of waiting for the right moment in Liberia, because who knows when—or if—that will come. Also, my visa has an expiration date.

The logistics of the trip are complicated. Because flights to Monrovia are often canceled without notice, John advises me to fly direct from Europe to Abidjan, in the Ivory Coast, which is the most stable country in the region. Just before my departure, however, an attempted coup in Abidjan forces me to change my plans. I will now fly to London and from there to Brussels, then to Conakry, Guinea, and finally to Monrovia. I will have two weeks on the ground. The date of my departure, by coincidence, comes 165 years to the day after Isaac Ross died.

Just before my departure, the ubiquitous Ann Brown phones to say that even if I find the people I am looking for in Liberia, she is not satisfied that I have found everyone I need in Mississippi to tell the story. She is still searching for descendants of the Prospect Hill slaves who chose to remain behind, and is determined to find someone among that group who knows the history.

The same goes for Delores Smith, who says, over the phone, "Give me a call when you get back, baby. We gonna find who you're lookin' for."

The next day I am on an early morning flight to begin my search, in earnest, for whatever might remain of Mississippi in Africa, and for the Prospect Hill emigrants, who long ago disappeared from the local radar screen, but whose story in Liberia was just beginning.

Part II

LIBERIA

CHAPTER THIRTEEN

A RIVER GLIMMERS DIMLY in the gathering dusk as the jet banks for its approach to the Monrovia airfield. Fires burn in clearings of the jungle nearby, sending smoke through the ruins of the Roberts Field Hotel and the roofless hangars and aircraft graveyard edging the runway of the bombed-out airport. Aside from a scattering of lights within the reclaimed terminal and tower, the airport is dark. Passengers clamor to get out when the plane rolls to a stop before the terminal: doe-eyed missionary volunteers from Minnesota; furtive businessmen from Libya, Germany, and France; ebullient young athletes on the Liberian Lone Star soccer team; women resplendent in traditional African dress toting large, ersatz Louis Vuitton bags filled with supplies from abroad.

Inside the terminal the atmosphere grows chaotic. The windows and doors are open to the tropical night as everyone jockeys for position in the queues for Immigration, for the baggage carousel, and finally, for the baggage search. Carts crash into one another at bottlenecks. Surly inspectors struggle to maintain order. Slowly the crowd pours through the turnstile into the night.

The shadows of soldiers with automatic weapons hover near the terminal. Across the darkened street a hundred or so people wait, cordoned off. Somewhere among them is Peter Roberts Toe, a friend of John Singler's who has come to meet me, to take me to Greenville, Liberia, the former center of Mississippi in Africa, where I hope to find the descendants of Prospect Hill.

I have been unnerved by Liberia before I even arrived. I have read harrowing news accounts of its wars and related atrocities, including stories of militia forces and rebels who tortured and mutilated women and children and drugged young boys and forced them to take up arms, and of the starvation and disease that have accompanied them over the last two decades. The U.S. State Department has issued repeated warnings against traveling to the West African nation, and while the warnings might fall upon deaf ears among seasoned foreign correspondents and rogue businessmen, I am a novice. My greatest fear was that there would be no one waiting for me at the airport, which lies an hour outside of Monrovia, a city that is itself hardly a safe refuge. And it is night. I have been told that it is too dangerous to travel in Liberia after sundown, although, like so much of what I have heard before coming here, this proves debatable.

My trepidation must be evident, even in the darkness, because a policeman standing alone in the wide street sees me and asks if there is someone to meet me. He seems relieved when I say yes. "Welcome," he says, and smiles.

I am elated to find Peter and his friends waiting for me, and they are relieved as well, because a rendezvous is a chancy thing in Liberia. It is not uncommon to make the expensive and time-consuming trip to the airport only to find that a flight has been canceled or, even if the plane does arrive, to discover that the person you are looking for is not aboard. There is no phone at the airport, and the few phones found elsewhere in the country are unreliable. Peter has driven ten hours on a notoriously bad road from Greenville, where he lives. After quick introductions he happily grabs one of my bags and leads us to the car he has hired, an old Nissan Sentra painted bright yellow, with a decal of an American flag stuck to the windshield.

Peter is a nurse who functions as a doctor in a place where there are almost no health care workers, and has brought with him Edward Railey, a young man originally from Louisiana, Liberia, who is to act as my guide in Monrovia, along with a student activist from Monrovia, who is to be my fixer, and a driver, whom he introduces simply as John.

We set out from the airport in high spirits and make it about a mile before the car breaks down. The engine sputters to a stop in front of a cluster of mud and thatch huts in which oil lamps glow dimly. John gets out and opens the hood, his face silhouetted by the headlights as he pries the gas line free and blows through it. He replaces the line and slams the hood. We lurch forward through the curious crowd that has emerged from the huts, but continue only a few hundred yards before the engine cuts out again.

This time everyone gets out. I have a flashlight in my bag. We try again, the engine fails again, and we coast to the shoulder of the road, scattering women with loads of firewood and fruit and other burdens on their heads. Again the young men emerge from the huts to check us out while the shiny Land Rovers bearing the soccer players, the businessmen, and the missionaries fly past.

I tell myself that had I known I would end up broken down on the side of the road, in the middle of the night, I would not have come. But I am here and everything is fine. After two more breakdowns, John manages to solve the problem, sucking and blowing on the gas line until whatever is blocking it comes free. We make our way toward the first checkpoint, where a gate blocks the road to Monrovia.

I have heard about the checkpoints, and have dreaded them. They are common all over Africa but have a particularly bad reputation in Liberia, where they are usually manned by former combatants in Liberia's civil war, many of whom had been pressed into military service as part of warlord (and now president) Charles Taylor's "Small Boys Unit," where they were given drugs and beer and AK-47s, then unleashed upon the terror-stricken countryside. There are many horror stories, of drunken soldiers at a checkpoint who slashed open the womb of a pregnant woman to settle a bet over the sex of the fetus, of travelers robbed, tortured, and shot. Most of the stories originated during the wars of the 1990s, and although the worst ended in 1997, there is still fighting along Liberia's borders, which increases the likelihood of encountering trouble, or at least facing its uncomfortable and sometimes dangerous aftermath.

There are fifteen or twenty men at the first checkpoint, mostly in their teens or early twenties, many of whom appear to be drunk or stoned and most of whom are armed with old automatic weapons. One of the soldiers, dressed in a T-shirt and dark khaki pants with his gun slung across his shoulder, approaches the driver's window and peers into the car. The interior light is on out of necessity, because cars with unknown occupants are sometimes fired upon. John, the driver, exchanges a few words with the soldier, delivered rapid-fire in a strange patois that sounds like southern American English with African inflections and is hard for the untrained ear to understand. Most Liberians speak English, the national language, but the influence of numerous ethnic languages complicates things. The word "flashlight," for example, becomes "flah-lah."

I gather that there is a demand for money or beer, and that John will have none of it. The exchange becomes more heated until finally the man with the gun gives up, the makeshift gate swings open, and we zoom away.

A few miles down the road we reach a second checkpoint. The scene is repeated. This time the demand by the man at the window for money or beer is echoed by men lurking beyond the light of the car. Again the exchange becomes heated. Finally the man with the gun says, very distinctly, "I'm speaking to the white man."

Until this point I have tried to stare straight ahead, at the gate illuminated by the dim headlights of the taxi, where a group of men are waiting for directions. Now I turn toward the rheumy eyes of the man with the gun.

He stares at me for a long moment before saying, simply, "Hello."

"Hello," I say, with all the enthusiasm I can muster.

We stare at one another. Finally he says, "Welcome."

It sounds like an ultimatum but the word is *welcome*.

"Thank you," I say.

He stares a moment longer, then signals toward the gate, which swings open. We speed through.

Soon we are passing the Land Rovers that earlier passed us, careening around blind curves, scattering dark figures on foot, barreling toward Monrovia.

"Could someone explain what just happened?" I ask. Everyone in the car bursts out laughing.

"They want money or beer," Peter says. "Next time, maybe you don't say anything."

CHAPTER FOURTEEN

THERE IS A LONG historical backdrop to the unrest that has gripped Liberia in recent decades. Beginning as early as the 1500s, the coastal region, which was crucial to trade with Europeans, had been contested, first by competing indigenous tribes and later by freed-slave immigrants, including those who arrived from Prospect Hill in the 1840s. Wars, revolts, and blockades have repeatedly swept the coastline, often spilling over into the interior. Although there have been periods of calm and prosperity, sometimes for decades at a time, the area's settlement history—even before colonization—has been hard fought.

The region that was to become Mississippi in Africa, on the southeast coast of Liberia, was first occupied by a complex amalgam of ethnic groups who were later lumped together by Europeans under the name Kru. They occupied autonomous villages and began trading with the Dutch and English in the sixteenth century, exchanging first rice, pepper, and slaves, and later coffee, cocoa, palm oil, ivory, and wood, for products such as cloth, iron, tobacco, and liquor. Beginning in the late eighteenth century, European vessels also began recruiting Kru members as shipboard workers.

As many as forty separate social, political, and dialect divisions were identified within Kru culture by the 1970s, when historian Mary Jo Sullivan conducted a definitive oral history project in Sinoe County, the site of Mississippi in Africa. The groups traditionally competed with one another for the most productive land, for other natural resources, and for trade, which often led to bloodshed and forced migrations, Sullivan wrote. Only after the arrival of the freed-slave

settlers, who provided the tribes with a common foe, was there anything resembling unity among them, and even then, some of the
groups broke away.

Although the Kru farmed and fished, trade was their most lucrative
enterprise. Those groups who were accustomed to plying the rough
coastal waters in canoes were able to control the landing, loading, and
unloading of European ships, which would give them an edge and be a
source of controversy for settlers and their descendants well into the
twentieth century.

Historically, Kru villages were formed when family groups from
the interior splintered and some of the members gravitated toward the
coast. Within their villages, political power was wielded by councils
comprised of the eldest members of each family in consultation with
religious oracles. The elders were responsible for appointing a governor, who presided over meetings, and a mayor, or chief, who was
responsible for ensuring order and maintaining trails and bridges.

Another important position was that of the *bodio*, who was charged
with keeping the community's idols, consulting the oracle, and making
sacrifices, to ensure successful trade, crops, and female fertility. Essentially, the *bodio* got the blame if things went wrong in a big way. His
house was considered a sacred place, but he was never allowed to leave
the village, and, according to Sullivan, "the office was not popular and
new *bodios* had to be conscripted against their will. . . ." Negotiations
between rival groups were usually left to women, including the *bodio*'s
wife, who could settle disputes.

Alliances between villages were rare, and always temporary. This
aspect of Kru culture would pose a significant impediment to good
relations with the freed-slave settlers, because the indigenous groups
did not consider their grants of land to the settlers permanent.
Another source of conflict would be the slave trade, in which the Kru
had been active for centuries.

When settlers began arriving in the 1820s, they attempted to interrupt the slave trade, and were aided in the effort by the U.S. Navy,
which was charged with seizing and freeing the human cargo of slave
ships. The subsequent addition of so-called "recaptured slaves"—people
who were neither indigenous to the area nor among the freed-slave
elite—only added to the colony's volatile cultural mix.

The settlers also competed with tribes for other types of trade—in such products as coffee, cocoa, palm oil, and ivory—that had become ever more integral to Kru society during the fifty years preceding the emigrants' arrival. In addition to selling goods to European traders and working on their ships, Krus acted as guides and interpreters and handled cargo. There was a highly developed trade hierarchy. It was not simply a matter of the settlers interfering or competing with those activities, although they did. It was also a matter of the Kru being in a comparatively strong position to defend their livelihood.

The settlers typically viewed the Kru culture condescendingly, as primitive and pagan, although they themselves had arrived, in many cases, with few possessions, no knowledge of the area, few trade contacts, and no land to call their own. As Sullivan noted, access to capital and contacts with Europeans gave the Kru a certain advantage. "This edge not only prevented the settlers from becoming established commercially, but also enabled the Kru to resist settler control for almost 100 years," she wrote.

Among the first emissaries of the American colonization society was Jehudi Ashmun, who arrived in what would become Liberia in 1822 to lead the colony, but who died of fever in 1828. Ashmun had envisioned an American empire in Africa, and from 1825 to 1826 arranged leases, annexations, and purchases of tribal lands on the coast and along the rivers leading inland. The first treaty with native leaders conveyed rights to land in exchange for tobacco, barrels of rum, powder, five umbrellas, iron posts, and ten pairs of shoes.

A few Mississippi immigrants arrived on their own in the 1820s, but it would be 1835 before the first sixty-nine sponsored by the Mississippi colonization society arrived in Monrovia. Of the latter group, two had been born free, eighteen had bought their freedom, and the others had been emancipated by Judge James Green and Mary Bullock from their plantations near Natchez. Three years later, thirty-seven more immigrants arrived in the new colony established by the society, Mississippi in Africa, which encompassed the land near the mouth of the Sinoe River. At the time, the Mississippi colony was distinct from the greater colony of Liberia, with its own administration and funding.

The Prospect Hill group was among thousands who made the crossing. Between 1821 and 1867 the American colonization society sent an estimated 13,000 immigrants to Liberia, but because the Mississippi colonization society reportedly did not feel that the American colonization society was placing enough emphasis on the Mississippi settlers—and, according to some accounts, due to their perception that the ACS was abolitionist in sentiment—the group eventually bought its own land down the coast from the other Liberian settlements. The immigrants were first sent to a settlement on the St. Paul River near Monrovia, but in 1837 the colony was shifted to the mouth of the Sinoe River and christened Mississippi in Africa. The Mississippi society members pledged $14,000 annually to establish and maintain the colony.

"The slaves of the Ross/Reed estate had been working in Mississippi since Mrs. Reed's death with the understanding that their labor would produce money which would be used to give them a start in Africa," John Ker wrote, in an account cited by New York University linguist John Singler.

"However," John Singler added, "when they arrived, they found out that this aid was not forthcoming."

Letters from the Prospect Hill immigrants include only passing references to the arduous journey to what was to be their promised land, but the accounts of others included recollections of strong gales that tossed their ships for days, resulting in broken windows, toppled masts, swamped holds, and widespread seasickness. Former Prince Ibrahima, who would die in Monrovia soon after his journey, recalled the "unforgettable motions and smells" and "creaking masts and thumping hull on the trip over," and described his first sight of land, Cape Mesurado, as "a majestic promontory covered with a rich mantle of green." Behind the beach was a solid wall of foliage rising up the cliffs, beyond which spread Monrovia, protected by cannons and companies of richly uniformed volunteers.

Many arriving immigrants described the scene as beautiful, although at least one lamented the sight of so many naked and "uncouth" people who came out in canoes to meet them. Immigrant Thomas Johnson recalled encountering native huts decorated with the skulls of enemies killed in battle, and hearing nightly communication by drums from village to village, indicating that "white men"—which is how the indigenous tribes referred to the African-American immigrants—had arrived.

✿   ✿   ✿

The immigrants faced an uphill battle from the start, particularly those who settled in Mississippi in Africa. In addition to epidemics of various African fevers, and conflicts with indigenous tribes, the Mississippi colony was underfunded and did not enjoy good relations with the Liberian government in Monrovia, partly due to disagreements between the Mississippi colonization society and the American colonization society. The Mississippi society was active only from 1831 to 1840, after which the colony was incorporated into Liberia, but by then its government was essentially bankrupt and its residents were isolated and reeling from depredations by tribes that had also been responsible for the murder of the governor, Josiah Finley, in 1838. The colony would have no official leader again until 1844.

"Difficulties plagued the settlement," Sullivan wrote. "Its small size, lack of communication with other settlements, little support from the American colonization society and the Mississippi Society, lack of knowledge of the human and physical environment, and sporadic hostility from African neighbors hampered progress."

The majority of the immigrants were unskilled laborers, and most were illiterate. "Those who were literate and educated went into international trade and commerce," according to Joseph Guannu, who teaches at the University of Liberia in Monrovia and is a former ambassador to the United States. "Those who became affluent because their slave masters put something in their pockets—gave them money—took to trading with the states from which they came," he says. "Those who were illiterate and came with little or nothing, most of them took to agriculture—field Negroes, as Malcolm X referred to them." Their primary crops included cocoa, coffee, rice, cotton, sweet potatoes, cassava, collard greens, cabbage, eggplant, and okra.

The passengers aboard the ships that brought the Prospect Hill immigrants were a mixed lot. Some were literate, some were not, and some were farmers while others were trained in more specialized tasks. Hilpah Ross, at sixty, was the oldest aboard the *Laura*, while the youngest was an infant born on the voyage over. Among those who died while waiting to board the *Laura* in New Orleans were Frederick and Sillah Ross, whose five children made the passage without them. Mechia Ross, sixty-five, was the oldest passenger aboard the barque *Nehemiah Rich* when it set sail from New Orleans in early spring 1848 on a voyage that took sixty-four days. Accompanying her was her husband, Hannibal, sixty-two, and daughter Lucy, twenty-five, who died the following summer in Liberia, according to an ACS representative, Dr. J. W. Lugenbeel, who attended to the medical needs of the Mississippi colony. Among those who never saw Liberia was Grace Ross, who died aboard the *Laura* en route from New Orleans at age thirty-eight. Her husband and children safely completed the passage.

A few years after the *Nehemiah Rich* and the *Laura* arrived, the *Renown* brought seventy-three more immigrants from Mississippi, sixty-seven of whom were slaves emancipated by the Ross and Reed estates. The *Renown* actually did not make it all the way to Liberia, but wrecked off the coast of the Cape Verde Islands. All of the passengers survived and completed the voyage on another ship, but they lost their possessions. The next year, sixty-nine more of the Ross and Reed groups followed on the *Lime Rock*.

The majority of the Mississippi immigrants hailed from the Natchez District, which had the state's largest concentration of slaves. Although blacks were the majority in southwest Mississippi in the 1820 census, only about 450 of 33,000 were free, and in 1830 the district had thirty-four percent of the state's white population but 65 percent of its slaves. In 1840, the average percentage of enslaved people among the total population of the six Mississippi counties that sent emigrants to what would become Sinoe County was 76 percent.

The freed slaves from Prospect Hill were the largest group to emigrate, and from the surviving letters they mailed home it is evident that they remained cohesive despite dispersing to various sites throughout Mississippi in Africa.

In a February 16, 1853, letter to Catherine Wade, the wife of Isaac Ross Wade, one of the Prospect Hill immigrants, Granville Woodson, recalled setting sail from New Orleans on January 7, 1848, and landing at Monrovia on March 19, 1848. During a long delay in New Orleans, the group had been held in open quarters with no sanitation facilities, and among those waiting to board the *Nehemiah Rich*, sixteen had died of cholera there and three had succumbed to the disease en route to Liberia. There was a particularly deadly outbreak of cholera, a type of dysentery, in New Orleans the following year, which took an estimated 3,000 lives, including about twenty-five would-be emigrants from Prospect Hill waiting to board the *Laura*.

In May 1848, Sarah Jane Woodson, Granville Woodson's sister, wrote Catherine Wade from Greenville "to inform you of our safe arrival to our destination in Africa and to let you know that we had a long and tedious passage to Africa of some sixty some odd days and I can assure you that we experience a very severe gale wind in the passage." Echoing a sentiment expressed in most of the letters, Woodson wrote that the colonists needed many basic necessities that were not available in the new land.

"To your children remember my love to them and to all the Prospect Hill people and to all the Oak Hill people," she wrote. "I expect something from them when our people comes and tell our people to bring all their things when they comes out. The children is all going to school every day. Bring some seed of all kind with you and everything you possible can. Bring with you of your things, bring them for you will stand in need of them in this country." In particular, she advised the next immigrants to bring feather beds and not to spend their money on the way. "I am very sorry that I left my Bed," she wrote, "and there is no way to get another in this country." In closing, she wrote, "Daphne sends her love to her mother and all of her children. Jefferson Bolton's children say that they are not able to bring him but hopes that the exectors will open their hearts and send him out." Then, in a postscript she added, "Bring out some castor oil."

Another Prospect Hill immigrant, York Walker, wrote Isaac Ross Wade in April 1852 to say, "This is indeed a fine country for the coloured man but we have to live by the sweat of the brow for everything is scarce and high, such as provisions, clothing, etc., and I stand in need of many things. . . . You would therefore Sir confer a great favor on your humble servant by sending a few articles. If you can make it convenient please to send me a Whip Saw and some clothes and a pair or two of shoes and any other things that you may think proper to send will be thankfully received by your Humble Servant."

Granville Woodson also wrote to request schoolbooks, and noted that his sister had written to "Mrs. C. Wade and have not received no answer yet. You must excuse my handwriting. I was in a hurry as the Liberia boat had just return from Cape Palmas on her way back to Monrovia and had about two miles to go down the river."

The letters offer ample evidence of the physical challenges that faced the settlers. By all accounts, as many as half of the settlers succumbed to fever and disease, often within the first year or two after they arrived.

In one letter, Sarah Woodson wrote, "The last people of our State who came out are a great many of them dead, they came here so worn down with hard usage, and disease, that almost the one half of them were carried off in the acclimating fever. Tell Rufus that Rachel send her love to him and says will please to tell him her father is dead, and all the family except three, that is Rachel, Linthy and Garth. Rachel says she is doing tolerable well, as well as she could expect, but is quite lowspirited."

Joseph Tellewoyan, who maintains a website on Liberian history, noted that there were extremely high mortality rates among all of the immigrants from the outset. Of eighty-six immigrants who arrived on one ship in 1820, only eight were still living in 1843; of thirty-three who arrived in 1822, only five; of 655 who arrived in 1832, only 229; and of 639 who arrived in 1833, only 171. "Visitors who arrived in Liberia during this period were astounded by the number of fresh graves they saw," Tellewoyan wrote.

Many of the immigrants remained in Monrovia only long enough to acclimatize, or to die. According to immigrant Augustus Washington, all of the settlers had to endure the raw ordeal of acclimatization while living in small huts crowded with people, many of whom had fever. In Liberia, he wrote, "Where one succeeds with nothing, twenty suffer and die, leaving no mark of their existence."

Problems with the management of the Mississippi colony only made matters worse. In an undated letter to the American colonization society, which Sullivan cited, an immigrant from South Carolina observed the travails suffered by recent arrivals, including his family and a group of Rosses, due to mismanagement and corruption among local officials: "I am writing to tell you of our bad accommodations," he began. "When we landed, we were put into a small house with a very sick man in it. Raining and it took a long time to get out the dirt. The roof leaked. I have 7 children and they only gave me one quarter of an acre of land and near a swamp . . . Judge Murray [a local representative of the ACS] only had 18 rooms for 180 people. It is a shame that the Ross people are made to suffer. Provisions are sold for cash and poor people suffer. And now Murray have sold out all our pork and butter we have not received any but twice since we been here and he also sell our flour to a Dutch Capt and a English Captain my wife was very sick and I sent to Murray wife to buy some butter and she sent me word that they don't sell but would give me a spoonful. He had butter but we could not get any at all."

The accounts of Liberian immigrants often stressed the crudity of native culture, which is typical of many colonial efforts, including America's, but in Liberia both the settlers and the indigenous groups were of the same race, which complicated matters. Despite the claims of its chief proponents, the colonization of Liberia was not about going "back" to Africa, because "home" for the slaves had been America. Some had been educated by their masters and brought with them a devout missionary zeal, and although the native tribes held many advantages, the settlers' trump card was their knowledge of American capitalism and the occasional backing of American military power.

Guannu says the history of the Mississippi colony and of Liberia as a whole is both a transplanted African-American story and an African experiment with Western culture. "Since they came from the Deep South they brought with them the dominant culture of that region," he says of the settlers. "And that culture very much influenced their relationships with the indigenous tribes. The settlers, who called themselves Americo-Liberians, sought to build a society that melded certain African traditions with aspects of the culture they had known as slaves."

Historian Mary Louise Clifford contended that neither side had a monopoly on hostility. "The Free Negroes who came from America did not regard the Africans as their brothers," she wrote. "They were not returning to their homeland, but rather had left their homeland across the Atlantic because it denied them opportunity . . . few of the American Negroes even knew from which part of Africa their ancestors had been taken. Most of their memories and associations drew upon the agrarian society of the young United States. In their eyes, everything attractive and desirable had belonged to the wealthy masters of the plantations on which they had labored.

"Now, suddenly, they were in the incredible position of having not only escaped their degradation—and it had taken enormous courage for them to leave all that was familiar behind in America—but of assuming for themselves the mantle of command and aristocracy in their new Republic."

The settlers, Clifford wrote, adopted the eighteenth-century puritanism of the American colonies and "cultivated an elaborate facade of formal clothing (frock coats and top hats), stilted language, and porticoed mansions—everything they associated with elegance and gentility—in order to emphasize the social difference between themselves and the African heathens."

The Kru, for their part, seem to have recognized the vulnerabilities of the Mississippi colony, and although some subgroups were friendly with the settlers, most sought to exploit those weaknesses. Kru dominance of trade also hindered the colony's commerce, Sullivan wrote, because the Krus preferred to interact directly with British traders, who often undercut the settlers. Liberian government efforts to blockade ports against British vessels were only partially successful, and some local ethnic groups responded with their own blockades between 1846 and 1850, aimed at thwarting trade between interior groups and the settlers, which led to three years of outright war. Only two years after the fighting ended, in 1855, other tribes began warring with the settlers of the Mississippi colony.

"Resentment over trade and the expansion of the settlers led to surprise attacks on the Sinoe River settlements," Sullivan wrote. "Settlers and Kru were killed, houses burned, and crops destroyed on both sides. With the aid of European ship captains, the Monrovia government intervened to defeat the attackers."

The destruction of the tribes' crops led to years of famine, which further embittered them. And, as Sullivan noted, "The attack reinforced a siege mentality of a small group of immigrants in a foreign environment. Their presence, expansion, and interference in trade had brought about a reaction which many would have expected and feared from their African neighbors. With the size of the settlements reduced to earlier numbers, the small band who remained became even more determined to survive and more committed to resist than to cooperate with their Kru neighbors."

Even with these setbacks, the struggling settlement continued to receive new immigrants, and over time some of its residents prospered. From 1838 to 1847, Sullivan wrote, "the Sinoe settlement grew in numbers, began agriculture for consumption and export, traded with African neighbors and European traders, and began to expand geographically."

By 1845, the population of Greenville, the capital of Mississippi in Africa, had grown from seventy-nine in 1843 to 240, and new settlements had sprung up in the surrounding countryside. The greatest growth would follow the establishment of Liberia as an independent republic—Africa's first—in 1847. During the next seven years, 1,402 settlers arrived in what was then known as Sinoe County, including the last of the Ross and Reed groups, although immigration would taper off after word reached the United States in 1854 about settlers being killed, houses burned, and crops destroyed during fighting with the tribes.

As the immigrants settled in, the tone of the letters to Prospect Hill became more upbeat. In April 1851, Granville Woodson wrote to say that although the immigrants had experienced "a little difficulty since the attack of the African fever I have enjoy good health so have father. Mother had several severe attack of defness complaints but now enjoying good health both of them send there love to you both hoping that your latter days may be more prosperous than your former has been." His mother, he noted, "says she hope that the children are good and smart active children as they were when she left them."

Sarah Woodson wrote Catherine Wade in April 1852 to express her concern that in her last letter she may have sounded disappointed in her new country. "But it is improving so fast, that I am becoming quite satisfied, and especially since I have got my health as well as I have, my health has improved very much lately, so much so, that if I only had a little more means to start with I should like Liberia very well." She marveled at the prolific growth of crops in Liberia, explaining there was no winter and that, "we have all got our own land and the most of us are living in our own houses." That in itself may have made the effort seem worthwhile. It seems likely, too, that the settlers wanted to put a positive spin on the colonial endeavor—to proclaim success.

On June 17, 1848, ACS correspondent R. E. Murray wrote from Greenville to give his report on the fledgling Mississippi colony and described the immigrants who had arrived aboard the *Nehemiah Rich* as "clearing off the land quite fast." He said he had received word from the Louisiana colonization society asking that immigrants from that state be settled on the opposite bank of the Sinoe River from the Mississippi settlement, which mimicked the geography of their home states in the United States, in reverse.

The land at that location, known as Blue Barre, had not yet been bought, however. This would have facilitated the removal of the area's unruly inhabitants, according to a subsequent report by Luganbeel, in which he lamented "the uncommon treachery, barbarity, and thievish propensity of the Blue Barre natives, who are pretty numerous, and who I know are generally a cruel, roguish set of unprincipalled desperadoes— much more so than the natives in the vicinity of any of the other set- tlements in Liberia." The Louisiana colony was eventually located a short distance upriver instead.

On July 18, 1848, Luganbeel reported from Greenville that most of the Mississippians had become "quite reconciled to the place; and some of them express themselves as not only perfectly satisfied with their new place of residence, but much pleased with the appearance of things in and about this little settlement. Since the date of my last let- ter to you, none of the immigrants by the *Nehemiah Rich* have died. Most of them have got pretty nearly through the acclimating process. Those of them who have pretty good constitutions have required very little medical attention, during the last two months. A few of them, whose systems had become considerably impaired, in one way or another, before they left the United States, are rather feeble; and I fear that I shall lose one or two more of the company, especially one of the men, who, as his relations inform me, had long been accustomed to the too free use of ardent spirits."

Among the Prospect Hill slaves who died, Lugenbeel wrote, one was "a poor skeleton of humanity; who had been a helpless idiot from infancy, the daughter of Hannibal Ross. Another was a delicate girl named Catherine Witherspoon, and another, a youth, named Riley Ross, both of whom, according to the statement of their parents, had always been sickly. The other four were small children, the oldest of whom was less than seven years. None of the adults have died, except the idiot woman."

The ever prudent Luganbeel stressed the immigrants' enthusiasm for the colony. "Indeed, I have sometimes been obliged to interpose my authority to prevent some of the men from exposing themselves so much by laboring in the rain, and some of them have suffered consid- erably in consequence of being exposed," he reported. Of one group of Mississippi settlers, he added, "Nearly all of these people have drawn land a little back from the Sinou river, about two miles from this place. The tract which the Ross people have, being separated from that of the Patterson and the Witherspoon people, by a small creek, the former tract being sufficiently commodious to accommodate all the remaining people. . . . The location of these people is decidedly preferable to Readsville; the land being perhaps equally arable, more elevated, and farther from the river, and not being liable to overflows."

By then some of the settlers had taken to planting cotton, and although the plant survived from year to year in the tropical climate without replanting, the crop never really caught on. The plantation system did, however, and once the settlers became established, many built massive houses reminiscent of plantations back home, staffed with servants from the native tribes.

Architecture was perhaps the most striking aspect of Liberian settler culture. The many grand houses lining Greenville's Mississippi Avenue were impressive monoliths in a land of mud and thatch huts, graced by stately colonnades, spacious rooms, and breezy verandas. As late as the 1980s, the mansions remained in the hands of the Americo aristocracy, and although most had by then been faced with zinc siding, their lineage was unmistakable. The fighting during the 1990s doomed most of these structures. The rebels, seeing in them the physical manifestation of more than a century of Americo rule, would set many afire, while others would be damaged beyond repair by rockets and mortars.

The replication of Greek Revival architecture was not the only aspect of Southern culture that the immigrants imposed on the colony. They also subjugated the underclass of native tribes whenever they had the opportunity, creating a dynamic reminiscent of their former master-slave roles. Traditionally, the descendants of Isaac Ross have claimed that many of the Prospect Hill immigrants enslaved the native tribes of Liberia, and put them to work on their plantations and in their homes. Although slavery had been practiced in Liberia even before the settlers arrived, and continued to crop up as late as the 1930s (some say it continues in isolated pockets today), Guannu argues that there is no evidence that "classical" slavery was ever commonly practiced in the colony. Instead, most settlers relied for labor upon apprentices or wards who were financially dependent upon them, he says.

According to Sullivan, many settlers had difficulty making ends meet after paying wages to indigenous workers. "African labor was available," she wrote, "but few could afford even the low wages necessary." Still, in 1846, one immigrant, Washington McDonough, reported that his father had "twenty-four or five bound boys" working on his farm, some of whom had been taken from a slave trader.

Letters compiled by historian Wilson Jeremiah Moses paint a complicated picture of the relationship that resulted between the settlers and indigenous tribes. In one, dated 1855, John H. Harris wrote, "I have seen barbarous cruelties inflicted upon the aborigines by the Americans; whether the crime justifies the act, I am not able to say; but there is the same relation existing with many, as there is in the South among master and slave. . . ." Harris recounted occasional humanitarian acts by the settlers, but conceded that a kind of forced servitude "that strongly resembles slavery was also practiced by native traders. . . . An interior head man, or petty king, will come to them for a trade; he may have some three or four boys with him, that he has either stolen on the path (for there are no roads), or else captured in war; these he leaves as security with them for the return of produce for the goods; the probability is he will never come back; therefore, they become theirs, to work, feed and clothe, as they see proper. This the law does not recognize as valid, yet it is tolerated, and hard is sometimes their lot; and with many of the colonists here, they think they are naturally and morally superior; as superior to the native as the master thinks he is to his slave in the States."

By law the Americos were required to apply to the courts before binding their apprentices, who were free to go upon reaching adulthood, but in practice the system often skirted the law and was ripe for abuse.

There was little agreement about the extent of Liberian slavery, or its nature, among opponents and supporters of colonization. In his treatise *Four Months in Liberia: Or, American Colonization Exposed*, published in 1855, William Nesbit asserted that slave ownership was almost universal among the colonists. Nesbit, who immigrated to Liberia from Pennsylvania only to return, disenchanted, wrote that among the colonists, "There is not one who does not own more or less slaves." He added, "The great majority of the present colonists are from the South, and have adopted southern habits, the state of society being more southern than anything else. For instance, all love to have a servant to wait upon them, both gentlemen and ladies. If it is but to carry a lantern, or to carry a fish, it must be done by a servant."

Nesbit went so far as to argue that conditions for slaves in Liberia were worse than in the United States, partly because everyone in the country suffered from deprivations, and the shortage of beasts of burden meant that slaves had to do all of the work on the plantations, including the plowing of fields and the hauling of crops. According to Nesbit, the slaves were always members of indigenous tribes who had been sold by their families, and as in the American South, occupied "small buildings near to their masters' residence, known as the 'negro quarters'."

Nesbit took great pains to paint a bleak picture of every aspect of life in Liberia, and was accused by his detractors of exaggerating and in some cases outright lying. There is evidence to support some of the accusations, as when Nesbit wrote that the entire colony was inundated by floods almost daily. He also struck a nerve when he contended that the colonists were doing the tribes a disservice by seeking to interrupt the foreign slave trade, writing that, "I would a thousand times rather be a slave in the United States than in Liberia."

Among letters from other visitors to Liberia that Nesbit cites to support his contentions, one correspondent noted that all work on the plantations was indeed done by natives, but differed with Nesbit by pointing out that the laborers earned twenty-five cents per day. This was corroborated by other observers cited by Harris, one of whom noted that settlers who performed the same labor were paid seventy-five cents per day. Nesbit also included in his book a rebuttal written by Samuel Williams, who lived (and remained) in Liberia. Regarding the prevalence of slavery, Williams wrote that "Nesbit lied in making this assertion. Upon the contrary, our laws make it a criminal act for any Liberian to receive a native in any way that he might be held as a slave. The Liberians cannot receive them as apprentices unless they take them before the proper court and have them bound as such, and every one, as soon as he or she is of man's or woman's age, can leave at will and go where they please."

There seems no question that the labor on the plantations was rigorous, and that growing enough food to eat was often more critical than raising crops for export. Although cotton was grown in the colony, Harris cites sources who indicate that the primary crops on the plantations were more likely to be food for personal consumption (especially rice) and coffee or sugarcane for sale. Fields were typically twenty acres or less, rotated annually because impenetrable bush vegetation rapidly reclaimed the land. In most cases, male workers cleared the brush and trees with homemade knives, machetes, and axes, then burned the debris before turning over the prepared land to women for planting and cultivation.

The letters from the Mississippi immigrants make no mention of slavery. Aside from occasional observations about life in Liberia, they are more often chatty, and are invariably familiar and friendly in tone, which seems to belie the reported enmity between the Prospect Hill slaves and Isaac Ross Wade, who had fought to block their emigration. Was it possible that the immigrants had maintained a sort of friendship with Wade under the circumstances? If Woodson could hope for "more prosperous days ahead" for Wade, it appears that not all of the Prospect Hill immigrants begrudged the heirs for attempting to thwart their freedom. Under the circumstances, it may have simply made good sense to maintain amiable relations with their former masters, who occasionally sent them supplies, and who alone could keep the lines of communication open between them and the slaves who remained behind.

For all his acrimony, it also appears that Wade felt some sense of responsibility toward the former slaves. He and his wife continued to correspond with them until the outbreak of the American Civil War, when mail service was interrupted by a Union blockade of Southern ports. Perhaps Wade did not hold them personally accountable for the alleged uprising, but the correspondence seems to support Tinker Miller's contention that there were mixed motivations on both sides of the story of Prospect Hill.

As letters between the two Mississippis began tapering off, immigrant Peter Ross resorted to writing to an ACS representative, Reverend R. R. Gurley, to ask what had become of the bequests that the slaves had been promised in Ross's will, and the money they had supposedly earned while they were technically free yet still being held at Prospect Hill.

After Gurley apparently replied that the money had been spent on court costs, Ross sounded disheartened, and betrayed.

"Consider one thing, My Dear Bro," he wrote. ". . . old Captain Ross Leaves one hundred thousand Dollers for his People Be Said Land, stocks, &tc., &tc. and then we can not Get Twenty five Dollars. We ear Glad for all the advize you Can Giv us but while we speak to you we feild that Africa, yea Liberia, is our home and we will not Give up. . . . Please Do not Denigh me. Please send me one of those Dubble Boil Gun. Please be so kind. . . ."

Following Peter Ross's death as a result of sunstroke, his son, George Jones, wrote Gurley on January 7, 1860, offering to send him coffee or limes, and to point out, notably, that his father had not actually been the son of Isaac Ross.

"I would hav say or said Sum thing to you befor now," he wrote, "but the old man he thought it was best not. The old man or my father Claim the name of Mr. Ross So that you may know that he was one of his people. Old Captain Ross was my father master and were not his father. . . . My father's father name was Mr. Jones. We are all Ross people but have our father title."

In one of her last letters, Sarah Woodson asked Catherine Wade to give her love "to all who enquire after me, and to all the children," and passed along greetings from Paschall, her husband, to "Master Isaac" and others, along with his request that Wade "will please send him a cane or something to help him along. . . . Give my love also to old Mistress, and her daughter Jane, and say to Jude and Sissy, that I thought they would have sent me something as I do have come to a new hard country."

Woodson expressed gratitude for the supplies Catherine Ross had sent her and regretted that she had been unable to return the favor with a shipment of oranges, because she had found none growing in the woods and was unable to come up with the money to buy any.

"I suppose I shall never see you all again in this life, but I hope to meet you all in the pleasant house of deliverance," she wrote. "Do please answer my letter."

The correspondence between the Prospect Hill immigrants and the Wades apparently did not resume after the Civil War, perhaps because the Wades were by then occupied with their own travails.

Liberian settlement also began to trail off during the Civil War in America, but immediately after, "worry among African Americans as to their physical safety in the south induced a new wave of immigration that extended from 1866 to 1872," according to John Singler's paper. During the period, 281 more immigrants arrived in Sinoe. The last large group, including thirty-eight people, arrived in 1888—coincidentally, the year Brazil outlawed slavery and began its own repatriation program in nearby Benin.

Maps of Liberia during the period offer ample evidence of the original settlers' places of origin. In addition to Mississippi and Louisiana, there were communities called Georgia, Virginia, Kentucky, and Maryland, some of which still exist today. All of the settlements were clustered along the coast, with the interior still the uncontested domain of the various ethnic groups.

The freed-slave immigrants who rose to power to rule over the culturally divided nation were generally lighter-skinned or mulattoes, and that continued to be the case well into the twentieth century. Guannu cautions not to put too fine a point on this fact where the descendants are concerned, however. The settlers were often at odds, or at war, with the native ethnic groups, but that did not stop them from intermarrying, he says.

"There was seldom marriage between a settler woman and an indigenous man. More of the reverse. But in that case all traces of the woman's former culture were obliterated. She was baptized and given rudimentary education. She lost all of her tribal identification and was completely assimilated into the Americo-Liberian value system."

Guannu says the settlers, who have been reviled and even tormented at various times in Liberia's more recent history, "were really, really courageous, which is why the conflict with the indigenous people went on for so long. They shared nothing in common but color. Here were people who came to live among people who had sold them, essentially. That was a big source of conflict." Until the coup of 1980, many Liberians took pride in being Americos, he says. "They identified with this because it was the elite class. Were you a Ross, a Roberts, you had ready access to education and very few restrictions. There was envy because of this, but only after 1980 did it become very pronounced. What it comes down to is access to power."

CHAPTER FIFTEEN

AN AMERICAN IN THE bar of Monrovia's Mamba Point Hotel is giving Monica Morris a hard time. The selection of take-out pizzas doesn't suit him, his order takes too long, the beer is not cold. He glares at Monica, who listens politely as she leans against the bar, but appears unperturbed. Then he adds, "You've got something on your lip."

"It's my lipstick," she says, in a dulcet voice.

I glance over and see that her lipstick is flecked with silver sparkles. She is not looking at him. She gazes out the window at the long boats sliding past, on their way to the harbor from distant fishing grounds, loaded to the water line with people and fish, flags flying.

The American grabs his pizza box and swaggers out the door. I am amazed by a lot that I see here, but this exchange is particularly surprising—this example of pettiness and arrogance in a world that is so profoundly distressed. There is a lot of pettiness and arrogance and distress going around, everywhere, really, but in a place like this it stands out in bold relief.

"Jerk," I say, after the man is gone.

Monica smiles serenely, and says, "So tell me why you come to Liberia."

It is not a question I expect people to ask at the Mamba Point Hotel, although it seems natural to want to know. Sitting in the lobby bar, watching the curious mix of people talking intently at individual tables or on sofas clustered in the corners, I find myself wanting to go from group to group asking the same question, partly because everyone seems intent on concealing their purpose for being here. The place

is exactly as Associated Press reporter Alex Zavis, who covers West
Africa from the Ivory Coast, had described it: something like Rick's
Bar in *Casablanca*, peopled by an odd mix of curious allies and potential enemies—European and North African businessmen, some of
whom are doubtless trading illicit diamonds or guns; a few foreign correspondents; the odd missionary; and a handful of well-heeled locals. I
do a quick survey of the room. Table 1: two young Frenchmen talking
to an African man. Table 2: two Arabs. Table 3: a dark, bearded man
with two women, one of whom is wearing a fanny pack and looks like
she is from the American Midwest. Table 4: two French businessmen.
Table 5: a woman in high-style African dress.

A lot of the men smoke cigars. A parrot on a perch on the balcony
squawks. Pink geckos sun themselves on the rail. An Indian family
passes through, then an Asian guy with a shaved head. I hear singing
from the ruined mansion next door—haunting songs that sound part
tribal, part gospel.

The decor is unintentional kitsch, with bad paintings, cheap African
crafts, an obnoxious Big Mouth Billy Bass, a sign pointing toward Ireland, 3,000 miles away and the homeland of the owner's wife. Zavis
said the Mamba Point serves as a rendezvous point for much of what
matters in Liberia today, yet it is almost surreal in its disengagement
from the rest of the country. There is no African food on the menu
because the hotel caters mostly to people who want to forget that they
are in Liberia. There are guards at the gate and the rooms are unimaginably expensive by Liberian standards, about $120 U.S. per night.
Still, it is an interesting retreat from the raucous, battle-weary streets
of Monrovia, and proves to be a good opportunity for networking. I
spend many evenings in the bar trying to figure out what is going on.

I tell Monica that I am searching for descendants of people who
came to Greenville, in Sinoe County, Liberia, from Mississippi, in the
United States.

"I'm from there," she says. "That's where my family comes from."

I realize that her last name is on my list of Mississippi families who
preceded the Prospect Hill immigrants to the colony. She smiles when
I mention it. "My mother knows all about it. My brother, too," she says,
but before I can ask more she sashays off to wait on a Frenchman who
has snapped his fingers for another beer.

Earlier, in the lobby, I had met a young artist selling watercolors of village scenes, whose name was Michael Mitchell. His surname was also on my list. When I asked about his family he said, "I'm from Sinoe." He knew little about their history other than that they came from a place called Mississippi.

Charlie Kollie, the bartender, laughs when I tell him that everyone who works at the hotel seems to be from Sinoe. "Not me," he says. "But I know the place well. Most of them, they were driven here by the war."

Charlie is of native descent. He grew up at Harbel, where Firestone operated the largest rubber plantation in the world from the 1920s until the war reached the area in the 1990s. The plantation became the scene of intense fighting and numerous detainments, executions, and atrocities, and was later used as a refugee camp. Charlie says he occasionally works at a hunting lodge run by California-based West African Safaris, which hosted big-game hunts near Sinoe's Sapo National Park until recently, when the tours were suspended. The safari company's owner, Tom Banks, told me over the phone before I traveled to Liberia that he was canceling the hunts due to the threat of economic sanctions by the United Nations. He then offered to make my reservations at the Mamba Point.

The debate over the sanctions, which were proposed as a way of forcing Liberian president Charles Taylor to end his involvement in neighboring Sierra Leone's civil war, contributes to my own feeling of uncertainty in Monrovia. In recent weeks the government has sponsored two protests against the sanctions proposal, and the U.S. State Department has warned of the potential for anti-American backlash should the measures be imposed. Charlie scoffs when I mention this.

"I don't know why Tom wants to scare Americans," he says, and laughs. He says he expects no trouble.

Charlie says the wildlife at Sapo actually flourished during the war because it drove people, including poachers, from the region. He has seen his share of wildlife, he says, including forest elephants, pygmy hippos, leopards, monkeys, tigers, duiker, parrots, and crocodiles— icons of Africa that I, for one, will not be seeing on this trip. It was in Sinoe, he recalls, that he learned one of the laws of the jungle: "If you see a tiger, you don't trouble him, he won't trouble you. But if you shoot at him and fail to kill him, he eat you up."

Charlie is interested in my story because he loves history, which he says is the subject he would have studied had he been able to go to college. He asks me the name of the family I am looking for and brightens when I answer.

"There is a Ross staying here in the hotel," he says. "An American. Nathan Ross." He picks up the phone and dials Ross's room, speaks to him for a moment, then hands me the phone. By a strange coincidence, it turns out that I have spoken with Nathan Ross before, by phone, in the United States, although at the time he did not seem inclined to talk. Now he agrees to meet me on the hotel terrace in the morning.

When I hang up, Charlie beams and says, "So, you're off to a good start." Charlie is the kind of person who makes you feel good about the world—any world, really, even this one.

I stroll onto the terrace to watch the sun set over the Atlantic. Boys are playing soccer on the beach with a ball fashioned from a tightly stuffed canvas bag. Children climb atop two statues of lions surmounting the grand staircase of the ruined mansion next door, where perhaps a score of families are encamped.

The mansion is one more indication that there is no such thing as an abandoned building in Monrovia. All over town, families squat in roofless buildings with blown-out windows and doors, the most dramatic being the marble ruins of the Masonic temple, situated on the heights overlooking the city, not far from Mamba Point. Gunfire, mortars, and scavengers have stripped away most of the temple's architectural adornments, which makes the massive, Greek Revival building even more darkly imposing. Children balancing five-gallon jugs of water on their heads scurry in and out while mothers prepare meals of rice and whatever else they can find on coal stoves, crouching under the shelter of tarps stretched between nails in the walls.

Meanwhile, in the bar at Mamba Point, CNN reports on Laura Bush's decision not to wear a hat to her husband's inauguration.

I hear someone ask, "Having any luck with your story?" and turn to see an Englishman whom I had met on the flight to Monrovia, who invites me to have dinner with him. He says he has come to Monrovia to set up "physical security" at a new bank, something he does in trouble spots all over the world—Lagos, Nigeria, most recently, and before that in Pakistan, Colombia, Tanzania, and Yemen. I ask how Liberia compares.

"It's dangerous if you go to the wrong place," he observes, "but then again, the same could be said of Plymouth." The problem, he says, is that in Liberia it is often hard to know if you're in the wrong place. There may be no clear answer to the question, "Is this dangerous?"

Before coming to Liberia I talked with everyone I could think of who might give me useful advice on dealing with the unstable regime, and pretty much everything I had heard was bad. In the newspaper, in magazines, and on the Internet were accounts of torture, cannibalism, and random violence committed by juveniles dressed in outrageous costumes—Batman masks, life preservers, or women's wigs—and armed with automatic weapons, often drunk, high, or drugged. Some observers reported that during the war packs of dogs fed on human corpses on the streets of Monrovia and were in turn killed and eaten by hungry refugees. I read that it is possible to buy, on the streets of Monrovia, a home video showing warlord Prince Johnson drinking Budweiser and singing gospel songs as he cut off the ears of President Doe, who was slowly executed. The accounts were too numerous to be discounted as inflammatory journalism.

Bewildered by what I had read, I had tracked down Alex Zavis, who told me that despite all the guns, she found the place surprisingly hospitable. "The people are incredibly warm, and as a woman traveling in Africa I actually feel less threat there than anywhere else," she said. Another journalist, Sebastian Junger, who has faced his share of danger in places like Afghanistan, Bosnia, and Sierra Leone, told me that the government in Liberia should be my main concern, because it is corrupt, violent, and ridden with factionalism.

Otherwise, much of what I had been told about Liberia before coming here has proved irrelevant, overstated, or simply off the mark. Liberia is not a country where you can easily assess the dangers and act accordingly. There is no going forth from and returning to a secure point. When you ride down streets teeming with former combatants, it doesn't matter if your fellow passengers in the cab are happily singing along to Celine Dion on the radio. Something virulent is in the air. You are in potential danger, and so are they, and everyone knows it. The potential for trouble can appear out of nowhere and dissipate just as mysteriously, like the gently rolling sea rising up, at the last instant, in a huge wave that thunders down upon the beach. Only in a place like Monrovia, where trucks loaded with soldiers are constantly speeding past, the streets are defiled by sewage, and the air is filled with the sounds of children singing, transistors blaring, horns honking, and men chanting angrily from within the prison walls, could the unexpected booming of a wave send a chill down your spine.

The government of Liberia, the very foundation of the society, is notoriously unpredictable, and although in general the people are remarkably genial, they live in the ruins of a nation where anything can happen, any time. Liberians have lived with social conflict and contradictions off and on for 160 years—and with the ever-present threat of danger and deprivation for the last two decades—but they are not used to it. They face threats from ethnic factions, the government, disease, starvation, former combatants, thieves, and overloaded, speeding log trucks. Yet, the Englishman points out, it is in many ways a safer place for visitors than hot spots elsewhere. Pointing to the white skin of his arm he says, "Sometimes this comes in handy."

I have to concede that this seems to be the case. Whatever unwelcome attention might be focused upon me, it will not likely be because I am white. Back in Mississippi, either despite or because of the high level of racial integration, resentment and hostility between the races are common, but I never sense it here. On the contrary, no matter how much I protest, I am repeatedly ushered to the front of lines. Children greet me politely on the street. The taxi driver calls me "sir." Edward Railey, my local guide, says this is partly because people interpret the appearance of a white person on the street as a positive sign. When things start looking bad, the white people vanish, so when they start trickling back in the assumption is that things are looking up.

Using that barometer, I reckon that the situation remains precarious. I will walk the streets for a week without passing another white person, although I find many inside walled compounds protected by razor wire, with guards stationed every hundred feet or so, and inside a few surprisingly well-stocked neighborhood grocery stores where few locals can afford to shop. These stores, almost all of which are owned and operated by Lebanese, are the exception to all the rules in Liberia, which include rigid physical boundaries between the wealthy and the impoverished. The Lebanese have been in Liberia for a long time, and constitute the closest thing the nation has to a middle class. They first came during their own diaspora in the late nineteenth century, which also took them up the Mississippi River in the United States, where they founded grocery stores in cities like Vicksburg and Natchez. The grocery stores of Monrovia are spotless, in stark contrast to the streets outside, and stocked with American food. In one, the cashier was a friendly young man wearing a Texas A&M T-shirt. Strolling the aisles of the store, it is almost possible to forget that you are in Liberia. There is an armed guard, but mostly he just holds the door for customers. No doubt the stores are vulnerable at night to thieves who are actually hungry, but I hear no reports of burglaries during the time I am here.

I occasionally see a few white faces staring balefully from behind the windows of air-conditioned Land Rovers. When I ask whites whom I meet why they don't venture into the streets, most say it is because their skin color readily identifies them as someone carrying a lot of cash. Credit cards are accepted nowhere, and simply by traveling to Liberia a visitor has clearly demonstrated his comparative wealth. Unemployment in Liberia hovers around 85 percent, and money changers on the street, many of whom are college graduates, will trade a grocery-size bag full of Liberian dollars for $100 U.S.

Sad stories, I find, are the real hard currency of Liberia. While there is less outright begging and hustling than a visitor encounters in most Third World countries, friendliness has its cost. Everyone seems intent on meeting you, and sooner or later, you will have an opportunity to help. They say hello, how are you doing, what's your name, where are you from, and slowly weave the details of their troubles into the conversation: the brother who is dangerously ill with malaria, with no money for medication and no public hospital to go to since the only one in the country closed a few weeks ago; the dead mother whose bereaved have no money to pay for her burial, who lies waiting, embalmed, in a funeral home where the air-conditioning is as erratic as the power supply; the boy helping his blind, half-crippled mother hobble down the street, who can't afford his next meal, much less a cane to prop her up on; the children selling candy or peanuts on the street to try to pay their way through elementary school. The list goes on and on. The presumption is that after you have heard the sad tale you will feel compelled to offer cash, and you often do. Each time I find myself mentally affixing a price tag to the story—$1, $5, $20. I have an over-whelming urge to save the world one Liberian at a time, because so lit-tle money can have such a profound effect, but by the time I realize that even selected needs are too great for one person, it is too late to turn back. Everyone, it seems, now knows my name and where I stay.

At one point a man shows up at my door at the Mamba Point saying he has traveled seventy-five miles through the bush "to meet the white man who loves to sponsor students to study in the States." I am mind-ful of my diminishing cash. I tell him that he has unfortunately received some bad information, give him $5, and send him on his way. I wonder how he managed to get past the guards.

The common apology offered by visitors for the poverty is that the people have never really known better, but Liberians actually have. As recently as the 1970s the economy was robust, partly because the country was relatively stable and partly due to a massive influx of U.S. aid.

The current lack of money has made it impossible for most Liberi-ans to rebuild their lives after two decades of devastating war and eco-nomic hardship, and there seems little hope for change on the horizon. What passes for an economy is really a type of large-scale, international looting. Malaysia's Oriental Timber Company is rapidly clear-cutting some of West Africa's last remaining virgin rain forests in Sinoe County; illicit brokers are moving tons of diamonds mined with slave labor in neighboring Sierra Leone to trade for East European arms; and someone—I could never determine who—is exporting shiploads of rubber from the former Firestone plantation, while Liberians travel in ramshackle taxis on dangerously bald tires. Schools have no books, pharmacies have no medicine, and the National Museum, which was looted three times during the fighting, has only a dozen or so items left from a collection that once numbered nearly 6,000. The commemora-tive park on Providence Island, where the first settlers arrived in the 1820s and where the Prospect Hill immigrants landed, lies in ruins.

Even businessmen who manage to get by reasonably well from legitimate income are aware that the situation in Liberia can deterio-rate further. At the American embassy, where I stop by to register, I wait to talk with the consul, Abbie Wheeler, as she is emphatically rejecting yet another request for a visa by a Liberian woman. An African-American businessman named James Roberts, who is staying in Monrovia, walks in, nervous. "Things are getting a little hairy now," he tells me. "The sanctions, and other things as well. I need to get on a list in case things change." When she finishes with the hapless visa applicant, Abbie Wheeler tells him that the embassy has "wardens" in each part of the city whose job it is to notify U.S. citizens if there is trouble. The last time the embassy had to evacuate American citizens, by helicopter, was in 1996. Satisfied, the businessman asks me what I am doing in Liberia. When I tell him, he offers a few contacts. "I live in Virginia, in the States," he says. "My ancestors came to Virginia, Liberia."

The embassy is a tantalizing piece of America dangling right before Liberia's eyes. It is not just a building, it is an entire, enclosed section of Monrovia, and the scenery there is by far the most striking in the city. The grounds, high above the ocean, are meticulously landscaped and make a dizzying, dreamlike descent through palms toward the crashing surf, compromised only by a white-painted wall topped with razor wire, which means that you can't get to the beach, and more importantly, that anyone on the beach can't get to you.

Most everyone I meet at the embassy lives and works there. Their children go to school there. Aside from intelligence about the political situation, few have much firsthand knowledge about Liberia. No one, not even an American citizen, is allowed to loiter on the street outside the compound, where guards are stationed every hundred feet or so, all of them comparatively lucky Liberians. If there is trouble in Monrovia, anyone who has half a chance of gaining entry will rush to the embassy compound, and the guards won't likely be among those left outside. The American embassy's reputation is such that several British citizens tell me they go there when they feel threatened rather than to their own embassy.

On designated days there is always a line of people waiting at the consulate gate to apply for visas. For them the embassy represents a kind of earthly pearly gates, and playing the role of St. Peter is the officious, highly skeptical consul, Abbie Wheeler. During each of my visits to the consulate, I observe her emphatically denying visas to a steady stream of unhappy Liberians at the window. It seems the whole country wants to go to the United States, and judging from the handful of exchanges I overhear, some will do anything to reach their goal. I listen to the consul chastise a woman for apparently falsifying documents, because there are notable discrepancies between some of her forms.

In such an environment a man like Nathan Ross, who managed to emigrate in the 1980s to the United States and develop a successful business there, is considered very lucky. Nathan's father, a member of the Liberian Congress when Samuel Doe ascended to power in 1980, escaped the resulting mass executions of Americo leaders by seeking political asylum in the United States, and he now lives in a suburb of Washington, D.C.

I am watching the long boats of the Krus depart from the harbor for another long day of fishing when Nathan appears at my table on the terrace at the Mamba Point. He is dressed in a tailored suit, open collared shirt, and black fedora. He looks splendid. He is in Liberia doing telecommunications work, he says, but before I can ask what the work entails, his satellite phone, the first I have seen in Liberia, rings. He talks for a few minutes, then stands up, clicks off the phone, and returns it to his pocket. "I'm on my way to Abidjan," he says. "Have you talked with my brother Benjamin Ross?"

I tell him that I have talked with no Rosses yet, and in fact have no names of Ross family members in Liberia.

"Perhaps you can talk with Benjamin," he says. "He works at Central Bank, here in Monrovia. A lot of the people you're looking for are here in Monrovia."

He says he is expecting a vote on the UN sanctions any day now, and apologizes for not having longer to chat. With that, he picks up his briefcase, says, "Have a safe trip, and good luck," and hurries on his way.

CHAPTER SIXTEEN

OUT OF A POPULATION of just over 3 million, only about 5 percent trace their ancestry to the United States, yet from all appearances in Monrovia, this is a nation of America-philes. On the streets I see "USA" T-shirts, American flag decals on cars, even a "Proud to Be an American" bumper sticker on the back of a pickup truck. On the radio I hear an ad for Showbiz Ladies Boutique announcing a new shipment of "American fashions." Despite its uneven record in supporting Liberia during its moments of crisis, America represents the promise of a better life. Everyone knows someone who has emigrated or otherwise benefited from knowing someone there.

Sometimes the associations border on the bizarre. The Liberian government, while making claims that America is conspiring against President Charles Taylor, markets coins on U.S. TV, minted in Liberia, commemorating U.S. president John F. Kennedy and Confederate General Robert E. Lee. Kennedy is popular for his support of civil rights, while Lee is revered because he freed most of his slaves before the Civil War and paid the expenses of those who wanted to emigrate. (There is a catch to the coins, however: the $10 Lee coins are sold for $10 U.S. but are valued at $10 Liberian, which equals about twenty-five cents U.S.)

Whatever affinity the average Liberian may feel with the United States, it is not generally shared on the other side of the Atlantic. News of Liberia's seemingly endless travails rarely garners more than brief mention in the American media. Americans may have founded Liberia, but according to John Singler, the colonial effort was essentially "an American solution to an American problem," and subsequent

American policy toward the nation has never been cohesive or pre-
dictable. Instead, that policy has been characterized by long periods of
disinterest and then sudden and significant intervention.

After the colonial era, and prior to 1980, the most vulnerable
period in Liberia's history was between the 1870s and the 1920s, when
renewed hostilities between the settlers and the tribes coincided with
disputes with Great Britain, which had claimed Liberian territory to
the west for Sierra Leone, and France, which had claimed Liberian
territory to the east for the Ivory Coast. At the time, Liberia was in
many ways teetering as a nation. There was even talk in Britain of making it a British protectorate, to ensure reliable trade. The Kru revolts
were ultimately defeated in 1920 with the help of the U.S. military and
U.S. economic aid, and the boundary disputes were eventually settled,
but by then Liberia's national debt had become unmanageable and its
economy had stagnated. In response, the Firestone Rubber Company
moved in to take over the nation's rubber production in 1926, and two
years later, the Firestone Plantations Company negotiated a ninety-
nine-year lease on up to one million acres of Liberian land at six cents
per acre.

The 1920s ushered in a period of reassessment of Liberia's cultural
and political identity, bringing the first tentative efforts to assimilate
the indigenous tribes into the political system. The Liberian government also found itself for the first time coming down on the opposite
side of the debate over repatriation of African-Americans. According
to Joseph Guannu, the historian at the University of Liberia, the government chose to distance itself from what was known as the "Back to
Africa" movement, sponsored by the Harlem-based Universal Negro
Improvement Association. The movement, led by Jamaican immigrant
Marcus Garvey and lauded by certain conservative whites in the American South, posed a potential embarrassment to the U.S. government,
according to the Liberian government's reasoning at the time, and the
country could ill afford to alienate its largest potential benefactor.
More importantly, Guannu says, "The feeling was, it was time to forget
the plantation, to recognize that you are an African. Then came the
crisis of Fernando Po, when it came to light that the government was
using indigenous tribes for forced labor, and the whole world began to
criticize Liberia, saying, essentially, 'Coming from slavery, and you

enslaved your own.' So people began to identify more with the indigenous people."

The crisis stemmed from a 1930 League of Nations report that
alleged that the Liberian government was involved in the sale of gangs
of tribesmen to work on coffee plantations on the small, Spanish-held
island of Fernando Po. The *Report of the International Commission of
Enquiry into the Existence of Slavery and Forced Labour in the
Republic of Liberia* claimed that high government officials who were
primarily Americo profited from the trade and allowed the pawning of
tribal family members as security for personal debts. It concluded that
"although classical slavery carrying the idea of slave-markets and slave-
dealers no longer exists as such in the Republic of Liberia, there are
cases of inter- and intratribal domestic slavery and cases of the pawn
system. . . . In one region unhappy wretches are forced to swim from
the harbour to a vessel anchored in the open sea, carrying hundred-
weights of goods of heavy luggage on their backs." Estimates of the
number of people in forced servitude in Liberia at the time went as
high as 400,000. Forced servitude was used primarily to provide con-
tract labor for road-building, the cultivation of private plantations, and
work in Fernando Po.

Among the key figures in the labor controversy was Samuel Ross of
Greenville, who is said to have been a native of Georgia, in the United
States, and not, apparently, among the Rosses who immigrated from
Prospect Hill. "Forcible recruiting and shipment of native labour to
Fernando Po from the County of Sinoe, with the aid of Frontier Force
soldiers, armed messengers and certain Liberian government officials
proceeded under Samuel Ross of Greenville as late as 1928, when he
was appointed Postmaster General of Liberia," the League of Nations
report noted, adding that even after Ross was transferred to Monrovia
he continued to recruit forced labor in Montserrado County. The
report alleged that between August 1 and September 21, 1927, soldiers aided in the capture of "a large number of natives to deliver to
Ross in Greenville," who were carried across the Sinoe River to a special compound in Louisiana and shipped off to Fernando Po aboard
the SS *San Carlos*. "The impression current was that Ross had powerful influences behind him in Monrovia, and any influence would be politically unwise. David Ross, adopted son of Sam Ross, testified that he

and another young man carried gin, tobacco, and rice to Firestone Plantation Number 7 'to attract boys for Mr. Ross. . . . For the 4 shillings given, one native policeman sent his brother to Mr. Ross.'"

A town chief testified, "We must give twenty labourers. If you do not agree, they fine you. My two children, I pawned them."

Although there were discussions of indictments, including of Samuel Ross, none were handed down. The League of Nations' follow-up 1931 report described Liberia as "a Republic of 12,000 citizens with 1,000,000 subjects" and included a letter to a Liberian financial advisor from American Lester Walton, who had been appointed to what was then known as the "Negro post" at the American embassy, in which he wrote, "Forced labor, vicious exploitation of the natives by the Frontier Force, unjust and excessive fines are some of the contributory factors to occasion resentment and dissatisfaction, impelling many natives to reluctantly settle in Sierra Leone."

Following the release of the second report, Liberia's president and vice president resigned.

Slavery has existed throughout Africa's recorded history, and still has not entirely passed from the scene. The nation of Mauritania only outlawed slavery in 1980, and some say the law only moved slave sales from public markets to private homes. In an August 2000 article in *Vanity Fair*, Sebastian Junger noted allegations of widespread forced labor in the diamond mines of neighboring Sierra Leone, and a March 1999 lawsuit filed by the governments of four Liberian counties sought damages against the Catholic Justice and Peace Commission and another human rights group, called Focus, for alleging that slavery still exists in southeastern Liberia, including what was once Mississippi in Africa. The suits, filed by the governments of Sinoe, Maryland, Grand Kru, and Bong counties, charged that the allegations "gave a wrong impression to the international community and made it difficult for the counties to obtain international aid."

Many Liberian households today have "foster nieces" and "foster nephews," sometimes known as "wards," who are basically indentured servants working for room and board. Although critics say the system is an extension of slavery, its defenders claim it is motivated by charity and enables people who are comparatively well-off to improve the quality of life of people who have, essentially, nothing. At one home I visit outside of Monrovia, I notice a teenaged boy and girl who had been left out of the family's introductions, and when I later ask who they are, the family members exchange a curious glance.

"Are they part of the family?" I ask.

"Yes," one of them replies, then adds, "We got them far into the bush. They're like a part of the family."

Such wards are free to go once they reach adulthood, but their willingness to depart is sometimes governed by their financial status, and the oft-repeated refrain—"they're better off this way"—sounds dangerously close to some white Southerners' apology for slavery. One need look no further than the sharecropping system of the Jim Crow American South after the Civil War to see that poverty can suffice where a method of coercion does not exist. And there is no guarantee that the wards will be educated in every household, as are the two in this particular family.

Still, the boy, who washes clothes in tubs while my host family and I have lunch, and later eats the scraps from our plates, seems as healthy, well-adjusted, and independent as any sixteen-year-old when he runs off to play soccer with his friends. The girl behaves more like a best friend to the daughter of the family, and cheerfully presents both cheeks for a kiss as we say our good-byes.

Before traveling to Liberia, I had met a woman who once worked in the Peace Corps in Africa, who said she had chosen to say nothing when she visited a friend's home and found children "who were a lot like slaves working there. It's the way things are done there, and who was I to say it was wrong?" she asked.

Such conundrums and disquieting scenes appear at every turn in Liberia, and it is often hard to know how to interpret or react to them. Watching the wards playing in the yard, it occurs to me that some of the myths I attribute to the traditional apologies for slavery may have been based upon truths that were misinterpreted for the slaveholders' gain. One of the more pervasive of those myths is the happy slave singing in the field, which is easy enough to dismiss as a racist idea. Yet, seeing so many hopeful—even joyful—people on the streets of Monrovia, where most lack basic necessities, I find myself wondering if it is simply human nature to maintain hope under unimaginably adverse conditions. I have never heard so much singing, whether in church, at school, in the cab, or on the street, anywhere else that I have traveled.

Liberia's ethnic and cultural mix was forever altered by the arrival of the U.S. military during World War II, which began what was arguably the most intense period of American involvement in the nation's affairs since the days of colonization.

Liberia initially remained neutral during World War II, but after German U-boats began sinking British ships in the nearby coastal waters, the government granted the United States a seaplane base and space for an airport near Monrovia, which later became Roberts Field. U.S. Secretary of State Cordell Hull wrote in a memo to President Roosevelt on September 14, 1943: "Our relations with Liberia from a strategic point of view have never been of more importance . . . as a result of the war, Liberian economy has been oriented almost entirely to the United States." Thousands of indigenous people flocked from the interior bush to the Americo-dominated coast to seek work with the military's massive construction projects. These included the airport, which was also used to support the Allies' North Africa campaign, as well as a network of roads and bridges and a new harbor in Monrovia, the latter of which was the base for a new trading concern known as the Mississippi Shipping Company. Most of those who left the bush never went back, which set the stage for lasting demographic change. No longer was Liberia as clearly divided, geographically, into different domains.

"Beginning in the 1950s, there was a struggle for African independence, and new interest in African identity," Guannu says. "There was a feeling in Liberia that it was time to reduce the cultural association with America. But in Liberia, even now, those who have settler blood in their veins still take pride in being described as settlers, while in America, only ten percent will accept that their ancestors were slaves. To some extent it's still a privileged class here, but not in America."

After World War II and throughout the Cold War, the United States continued to provide economic aid while using Liberia as a base for its covert intelligence operations in Africa. Among the recipients of the largesse was brutal, anti-Americo president Samuel Doe.

The U.S. government's stance toward Doe exemplifies its schizophrenic policy in Liberia. The old True Whig party government had been founded by a mulatto Americo elite and had ruled the nation since 1870 on behalf of the freed slaves and their descendants, who represented a small minority, at the expense of the descendants of indigenous tribes. Doe's overthrow of President Tolbert and the old-guard True Whig government in 1980 signaled the end of Americo power. Tolbert, who had served as vice president for nineteen years alongside President William Tubman before being elected president himself, had proved unable to find a middle ground between the Americo oligarchy and the increasingly dissatisfied indigenous tribes, who had seen colonial powers elsewhere in Africa overthrown in recent decades. Tolbert's effort to maintain Americo support and placate various ethnic groups led him to seek educational and economic assistance from nations such as Cuba and the Soviet Union, which did not sit well with the U.S. government. Although Doe was the enemy of the descendants of freed American slaves, the Reagan administration rewarded the new government with $400 million in economic aid, including $50 million for the military, which in many cases was used against the Americos. The U.S. government initially supported Doe due to concerns that communism would otherwise gain a foothold in Liberia, as was threatening to happen in other African nations such as Namibia and Angola.

The coup came as a surprise to many in the West, because Liberia had long been seen as a source of stability in West Africa, but in hindsight, the nation was a powder keg waiting to go off. Simmering unrest over the second-class status of indigenous ethnic groups for 150 years finally boiled over when the government proposed raising the price of rice during a particularly trying time for the poor.

"When the explosion came, it was violent, and it revealed the almost uncontrollable rage felt by the country's majority," journalist Sanford Ungar wrote in *The Atlantic* magazine. "The angry band of soldiers broke into the executive mansion, rushed upstairs, and surprised Tolbert in his luxurious quarters. They shot and killed the President, disemboweled him, stuck a bayonet through his head, and tossed his body into a mass grave.

"Ten days later, in a ceremony recorded by television and still cameras, the army took thirteen of the wealthy Americo-Liberian officials who had been arrested . . . marched them nearly naked through the streets of Monrovia, to ensure that they lost their dignity, tied them to seaside posts at the Barclay Training Centre, and executed them at point-blank range. A crowd of thousands cheered, and by all accounts there was jubilation throughout the country."

Other accounts described a frenzy of rapes, floggings, imprisonments without trial, castrations, dismemberments, executions, and mutilations of corpses following Doe's takeover. The victims were at first primarily Americos, but grew to encompass others who were simply weak or who posed potential opposition. During the ensuing crucible, *The New York Times* reported that Doe's militia arrived in the picturesque fishing village of Marshall, Liberia, and "quickly rounded up all of the Ghanian refugees they could find, marching them off together with Liberian friends and sympathizers for execution. In the massacre that ensued, perhaps 1,000 people were shot to death. Survivors say that children were swung by their feet by laughing soldiers as their heads were smashed against palm trees. Many say they can still hear the screams of the countless others who drowned as they attempted to swim across a river for the safety of a nearby island."

Alton Johnson, who later immigrated to America's Mississippi, where he teaches at Alcorn State University, was a college sophomore in Monrovia when Tolbert was executed, and remembers the night well. He was on the campus of the University of Liberia when shots rang out in the nearby executive mansion and a wounded man came running onto the campus.

"He was a Caucasian fellow," Alton recalled during a phone conversation back in America's Mississippi. "I personally helped him into a vehicle to go to the hospital. He was shot in the stomach." There would be much debate after that night about what had happened at the executive mansion, but the consensus, Alton said, is that the American embassy was directing the coup. "When you look at the executive mansion, there was something mysterious about it," he said. "To go into that building to kill the president—no Liberian could have done that on his own. The U.S.A. is not clean on that one."

Why would the United States assist in the overthrow of the Americo regime? Alton takes a cynical view, arguing that, "The United States has never supported highly educated people in Africa because they feel these educated people will not be puppets for them." He believes the United States was operating on its own agenda in allowing

Tolbert's overthrow, and later the overthrow of his successor, Doe, by Charles Taylor. In his view, the relationships of the various leaders toward the descendants of the freed slaves who colonized Liberia proved incidental to U.S. policy, and the U.S. government's current anti-Liberia stance is rooted in the same self-interest. "America founded Liberia, but they have been very much hypocritical toward the sons and daughters of the freed slaves who went over there," he said.

Until the September 11 attacks exposed the terrifyingly high stakes of foreign policy, diplomatic dallying by the U.S. government rarely registered on the radar of most Americans, but it has had profound effects in Liberia. As Alton sees it, when Tolbert sought to overcome a legacy of poverty by improving Liberians' access to foreign education, he found himself largely shut out of American colleges and universities. In response, he turned to nations with whom the United States was unfriendly at the time.

"Tolbert was looking for schools to send Liberians to get an education—in veterinary medicine, in medicine, in engineering—and he found that the United States does not take people from just any country," he said. "So what Tolbert did was to find Eastern European countries like the Soviet Union, Romania, Bulgaria, to send a lot of Liberians on scholarship. That did not go over well with the U.S. government. It was not that he was a Communist or a Marxist, but Liberia needed help. Those countries had something to offer. China opened their hands to us for development. The U.S. didn't like that at all."

Today, long after Tolbert's fall, there is still evidence of international aid for Liberia. The parking lot of the war-ravaged University of Liberia is filled with vehicles donated by the United Nations, Japan, and the People's Republic of China, but none from the United States. A Libyan firm, meanwhile, has announced a $20 million renovation of the empty Hotel Ducor Intercontinental in Monrovia.

It is hard to know how much credence to place in allegations of U.S. involvement in the 1980 coup, particularly because there is a lot of wild speculation about the time and about the civil wars of the 1990s. Many Liberians, after all, believed that the warlord known as General Butt Naked could fire bullets from his anus. Still, it is impossible to entirely discount the role of the U.S. government, because it is well-known that the CIA was very active in Africa at the time. For

Alton, seeing the wounded American fleeing the mansion that night told him all he needed to know. Five years later some of his family members were executed by the Doe regime and, he claimed, "all were betrayed by the U.S. government."

Alton believes that the United States concluded that Doe was unmanageable and so shifted its support to Taylor. When Taylor turned out to be intractable—he has since been accused of fomenting wars with and within neighboring nations and of his own human rights abuses within Liberia—he, too, fell from grace.

Taylor is unique among Liberia's leaders in that he is a descendant of both slave immigrants and indigenous groups, and that, from all appearances, he has been both attracted to and repulsed by the United States. Born in Arthington, Liberia, near Monrovia, to an Americo father and a mother of the Gola tribe, he enjoyed a comparatively privileged upbringing due to the family's Americo ties. He was sent to private preparatory schools (although he was ultimately expelled), and in 1972, at age twenty-four, received a student visa to the United States. He moved to Rhode Island and Massachusetts, ostensibly because he was interested in the region that had been the point of departure for so many of Liberia's immigrants, and enrolled at Chamberlayne Junior College. He eventually transferred to Bentley College, where he received a degree in economics in 1977. Whether he felt antipathy toward the ruling regime in Liberia before moving to the United States is unclear, but after graduating from college he remained in Boston and became an outspoken opponent of Liberia's President Tolbert. He was elected chair of an opposition group called the Union of Liberian Associations, which staged a protest outside the Liberian mission in New York City when Tolbert visited in 1979. Tolbert responded by challenging Taylor to a debate, after which Taylor declared himself the winner and announced that he was taking over the mission. Although he was arrested, Tolbert refused to press charges. Instead, Tolbert invited Taylor and a group of his compatriots to Liberia, with all expenses paid, in the spring of 1980, hoping to win them over. As it turned out, the timing of the trip was fateful. In April 1980, soon after Taylor's group arrived, Tolbert was overthrown and murdered by the forces of Samuel Doe. Sensing an opportunity, Taylor worked his way into Doe's confidence and was appointed head of the nation's purchasing agency, serving in that capacity for three years, until he was accused of approving the transfer of $900,000 to an apparently bogus company based in New Jersey.

After investigators in Liberia found that the money had actually been deposited in Taylor's own U.S. bank account, he was removed from his post and he fled back to Boston. The Liberian government then issued a warrant for his arrest on embezzlement charges, and in May 1984 federal agents arrested Taylor. He spent sixteen months in a Massachusetts prison before escaping with four other inmates, all of whom, except him, were eventually recaptured. Rumors later flew that the U.S. government had been less than zealous in its effort to track Taylor down, and he vanished. By most accounts he fled to Libya, where he was given sanctuary by Muammar Qaddafi, and where he set about planning his own Liberian coup. On Christmas Eve 1989, he resurfaced in Liberia with a force of several hundred men who called themselves the National Patriotic Front of Liberia. He had cultivated a rogue's gallery of allies, and joined forces with warlord Prince Johnson to attack Doe's army. The fighting, which swept the country before closing in on Monrovia, resulted in a bloodbath. In one of the most horrific acts, in July 1990, Doe forces shot and killed 600 and wounded 150 refugees being fed in a Lutheran church in Monrovia. Later that year Prince Johnson executed Doe, and in 1992, Taylor launched his own offensive to take Monrovia, which pitted him against his former ally. Johnson surrendered his command to peacekeepers a few months later and was exiled to Nigeria as the United Nations sought to reimpose order on Liberia. The shaky disarmament process that followed broke down after other factional militias began to proliferate.

The U.S. State Department responded to the increasingly unstable circumstances by advising Americans to depart Liberia immediately, and in the early morning hours of October 29, 1992, forces of the National Patriotic Front of Liberia fired three artillery or mortar rounds that struck or passed close to the U.S. embassy compound on Mamba Point, according to a U.S. State Department dispatch. The following June, 600 civilians were massacred at the former Firestone plantation in one of many such atrocities committed by rival warlords. Later that year, hundreds of civilians were allegedly beheaded. By then, hundreds of thousands of Liberians had been killed or had fled the country.

By 1994, *The New York Times* reported, Liberia had "come to bear little resemblance to a modern state, becoming instead a tribal caldron governed less by commonly understood rules than at any time since it became Africa's first republic in 1847 under freed American slaves." The newspaper quoted Amos Sawyer, Liberia's interim president from 1990 to 1994, saying, "'If we don't arrest the situation quickly, we will soon be back to where we were at the end of the nineteenth century, when this country was a stage for roving tribal gangs that fought back and forth for territory.' Others say the country has already deteriorated to that point."

In April 1996, Liberian forces again fired upon the American embassy, and a flotilla of five U.S. ships manned by 1,800 marines soon arrived off the coast of Monrovia. Navy Seals and Green Berets were sent to the embassy to evacuate hundreds of Americans and more fortunate Liberians and other foreign nationals by helicopter to Sierra Leone. The evacuees dodged bullets to reach the helicopters while the stench of rotting bodies filled the air. Some Americans remained trapped outside the embassy compound. One Liberian who was left behind recounted watching Taylor's security forces murder his brother, cut out his heart, fry it in a pan in palm oil, and eat it. Most of the refugees watched helplessly as the U.S. helicopters flew off overhead.

After the civil war subsided, in 1997, Taylor was elected president by a landslide, some say due to fears that if he were defeated he would make the country ungovernable. Such was the fear of a return to fighting that the common refrain prior to Taylor's election was, "You killed my Ma, you killed my Pa. I will vote for you."

By all accounts, Taylor has since grown extremely wealthy through the exploitation of Liberia's gold, diamonds, oil, iron ore, timber, and rubber resources, even as the quality of life of the average citizen has spiraled downward. Because his overthrow of Doe coincided with the collapse of the Soviet Union, Liberia no longer held much strategic importance for the United States. When American aid was subsequently cut off, Taylor's looting of Liberia's natural resources in exchange for East European arms began—an effort that is now part of the focus of the UN sanctions debate.

Not surprisingly, Taylor has been unable to generate diplomatic support in Washington, and instead has cultivated some very dangerous allies elsewhere, including, by numerous accounts, the terrorist network al Qaeda. He also has allegedly sought to destabilize his neighbors, arming rebels in neighboring Sierra Leone, engaging in border clashes with Guinea, and supporting a failed coup in the Ivory Coast which later erupted into civil war. By March 2003 the war in the Ivory Coast had resulted in the deaths of more than 3,000 and displaced more than one million people, and it was happening simultaneously with a new outbreak of fighting by rebels in adjacent regions of Liberia.

Journalist Tom Kamara, writing in the Liberian expat journal *The Perspective*, published in Smyrna, Georgia, attributed Liberia's current turmoil to its "culture of crime," and what he saw as a related trend, that the "centuries old tradition of accepting authority and wisdom of an elder's verdict, has been replaced with the 'wisdom' and authority of armed and drugged rebels. . . ."

"The worst disaster for Sierra Leone came when the neighboring state of Liberia was transformed from a symbolic one-party state into an essentially criminal polity," Kamara wrote. The diamond trade brought "a world of shadowy South African, Israeli, and Ukrainian businessmen" and "eastern European weapons bought with the proceeds from the sale of illicit gems." Taylor's associates, Kamara alleged, ferried out suitcases full of rough Sierra Leonean gems on presidential trips overseas, aboard jets loaned by Libya's Muammar Qaddafi. "Middlemen deliver the stones to the traditional diamond capital of Antwerp in Belgium, and increasingly to Tel Aviv where they are cut, polished and sold," he claimed. Kamara also accused Taylor of "brutal tactics of using drugged children as soldiers, terrorizing civilians, financing the war by exploiting diamonds and kidnaping peacekeepers."

There is evidence to support some of Kamara's allegations. In 1999, Liberia exported $300 million worth of diamonds, although the country is said to have a maximum mining capacity of about $10 million per year. The bulk of the diamonds were believed to be coming from Sierra Leone, whose "blood diamond" exports had been banned by international merchants due to charges that the gems were mined with slave labor, and the revenues used to fund military groups responsible for the upheaval in the region.

Since December 1999, the Association of Liberian Journalists in the Americas has sought a UN war crimes tribunal for Liberia, citing similar tribunals following revelations of war crimes in Nazi Germany, in the former Yugoslavia, and in Rwanda. Lamenting what it characterized as international complacency, the association has sought to bring international scrutiny to such crimes as the execution of leading opposition leader Samuel Dokie along with his family and bodyguard unit; the attack upon the Monrovia church in which hundreds of people, including women and children, were killed; the disappearances of dissidents and the murders of ordinary citizens, some for affronts as simple as overtaking or passing official vehicles; and the continuing harassment of both foreign and domestic journalists by the Taylor regime.

The media has been a particular target of Taylor's in recent years. In March 2000, the U.S. government officially protested the Liberian government's closure of two independent news radio stations, Star and Veritas, supposedly because they posed a security threat. Star was run by a Switzerland-based, nongovernmental organization that establishes radio stations in post-conflict countries, and although its shortwave radio frequency had been withdrawn in 1998, and the Veritas headquarters had been burned during clashes in Monrovia in 1996, both stations had continued to transmit until the government shutdown.

By summer 2000, when I began making plans to travel to Liberia, the situation seemed to have stabilized, and although a travel advisory remained in effect for U.S. citizens, the American embassy was again at full staff. Then, in August, a British film crew was arrested and charged with spying. The crew had been working on a documentary about Liberia for Britain's Channel Four network, and had briefed Liberian government officials on the nature of the documentary before being given permission to conduct filmed interviews. Their timing turned out to be particularly bad, as Liberia was under increasing international pressure for its involvement in the diamonds-for-arms trade. The members of the film crew, Britons Davie Barrie and Zimbabwean-born Timothy Lambon, South African Guglakhe Radebe and Sierra Leonean Samoura Sorious, were held in solitary confinement in Monrovia, where they faced the prospects of prolonged imprisonment and possible execution. The elder South African statesman Nelson Mandela and America's Jesse Jackson successfully lobbied Taylor for the journalists' release, but not before the crew was repeatedly threatened with mutilation and death. *The Perspective* reported that Taylor had publicly stated that the film crew had planned to poison him with a camera that he said would have caused him to develop cancer within weeks of the crew's departure. He also claimed Americans were involved in plots to assassinate him.

The next month, former U.S. president Jimmy Carter shut down his Carter Center in Monrovia, saying that "prevailing conditions and the actions of the government have made it increasingly difficult for the Center . . . to be effective in supporting democracy, human rights and the rule of law." In a letter to President Taylor, Carter cited human rights abuses and intimidation of journalists as part of the reason for the closure.

During all of this, refugees continued to stream out of Liberia, and many have ended up, ironically enough, in the United States. An estimated 150,000 Liberians died during the civil war of the 1990s, and an estimated one million fled to refugee camps in neighboring countries. Few of the refugees return to Liberia for more than brief, uncomfortable visits, often to care for less fortunate relatives, which poses a conundrum for U.S. Immigration officials. When about 10,000 Liberian refugees in the United States faced the loss of their protected immigration status in the fall of 2000, which would have required that they be sent home, Attorney General Janet Reno vowed not to extend the protection. President Clinton overruled Reno, citing Liberia's shortages of food, electricity, hospitals, and schools, the crackdown on the Liberian media by the government, the disappearance of political dissidents, and the fact that the U.S. State Department still considered Liberia too dangerous for Americans to visit.

Soon after, the U.S. State Department again advised U.S. citizens in Liberia to maintain contact with the embassy and to "carefully consider whether to remain in the country." In November 2000 the State Department issued a new travel warning, and prohibited family members from accompanying U.S. government employees to Liberia, noting that, "the ability of the embassy to provide direct assistance to U.S. citizens outside of Monrovia is severely limited. Many ill-trained and armed government security personnel continue to constitute a potential danger."

That same November, more than a hundred disgruntled former combatants severely beat two Taylor critics, former interim president

Sawyer and Commeny Wasseh, director of the Centre for Democratic Empowerment. Both men were hospitalized. Some alleged that the attack was made with Taylor's backing to divert attention from the diamonds-for-arms trade and the related UN sanctions debate.

"Under the current political climate in Liberia, no one is capable of organizing over 100 hoodlums without the President's blessings," *The Perspective* editorialized. "It is not possible."

As it turned out, the sanctions debate would loom over my entire stay, with the threat of flight cancellations, political unrest, and retaliation by the government against the United States for its efforts to push the punitive measures through. Although there is widespread dread of the potential sanctions, which were expected to worsen the plight of the average Liberian, most of the people I meet in Monrovia express growing resentment over Taylor's policies and hope that he can somehow be reined in. While the old economy favored the Americos, few people, whatever their family background, have ever felt as financially hopeless as so many feel now.

As one young man in Monrovia whose family was dispersed by the fighting tells me, the current situation is debilitating and unnerving for the average Liberian. His family, he says, is both fearful of a return to war and concerned about where their next meal will come from.

"My mother isn't working, my uncle who I live with isn't working, I'm not working," he says. "We are just making it because of God."

CHAPTER SEVENTEEN

THE CAB BARRELS TOWARD a bomb crater so large that there is only room for one car to pass. A Mercedes approaches from the opposite direction, lights flashing, which prompts our driver to step on the gas. Suddenly we pass into a different zone—from manageable disorder to chaos, just like that.

We careen toward a young, one-legged man who hobbles on crutches near the curb, blocking our only escape route should we lose the contest with the Mercedes. The passengers in the backseat begin shouting at the driver as we head toward the crippled man, who watches us bear down upon him but makes no move to get out of the way. At the last moment the Mercedes shoots past, and we skid to a stop beside the crippled man. The passengers go wild, berating the driver, growing so angry that I expect someone to reach over the seat and begin hitting him. I watch the crippled man's stoic face drift slowly past my window.

The driver shouts back, and the cab lurches onto the sidewalk, causing a young girl to spill an impossibly massive load of clothes that had been balanced on her head. She falls to the ground and disappears beneath the mound of clothes. I cannot understand much of what anyone is saying but hear the word "dead." As the angry passengers pile out of the cab, the driver shouts, "Why you say I be dead? Why you say such a negative thing? You be dead!"

The passengers continue shouting as they walk away in search of another cab. The driver drives on. Edward Railey and I say nothing.

It is the first sign of overt hostility I encounter in Liberia, though the evidence of turmoil is painfully obvious—in the buildings, in the

faces of people, in the large number of cripples on the street. Everywhere we go, we see injured people, mostly young men in wheelchairs,
on crutches, some missing one or both legs. They mark the line
between the planes of existence we crossed just moments before. Few
of them ask for money, although one man, hobbling on crutches with a
broken leg, approached me earlier in the day on crowded Broad Street
and introduced himself. I had noticed him before because his leg is
excruciatingly swollen and badly bent. It is painful to look at, yet
impossible to ignore. I imagine he is among the patients who were literally put out on the street when the John F. Kennedy hospital closed a
few weeks before, due to lack of funds and because frequent power
outages made it impossible to properly operate the morgue. The man
said his name is Sheriff, and offered the local handshake, a combination of seemingly every handshake in the world, with a twist—the traditional grasp, then something like a soul-shake with a finger snap off
of the other man's index finger at the end (I'm not sure where the
handshake originated, but it became popular in some parts of the
United States in the 1990s, usually without quite the same finesse as I
observe here). I reached into my pocket and gave Sheriff a few dollars.
He smiled, said, "Thank God," then turned to Edward and his brothers, Kaiser and Augustus, and said, "Thank you for your friend." Again
we shook hands, and when I failed to get it right the first time he made
me practice until I did.

It is hard to reconcile such friendliness, which you encounter
everywhere in Monrovia, with the pervasive scent of violence in the
air, and with the accounts of depravity that characterize the recent
war. There is no question that Liberia and neighboring Sierra Leone
have both dissolved into terrifying anarchy on numerous occasions,
with armed young men fighting, in some cases, because they have little
else to do. Many of the young rebels are orphans who have known little besides war. Some claim the youths are excited by the smell of
blood, which seems possible when you consider that they were weaned
on it. But walking the streets of Monrovia, I wonder how it can come
to this, particularly in a place where everyone's emotional default setting seems to be friendliness and warmth. How can a society based
upon such lofty ideals, where people say "good morning" to everyone
in every cab they enter, descend into such absolute chaos?

Although I rarely see its evidence in the interaction of people on the streets of Monrovia, I had heard a good bit about the historic enmity between the descendants of freed slaves and indigenous tribes in my Internet research. Typical of the articles was one in *The Perspective*, in which editorialist Tarty Teh cited a comment by Jesse Jackson that the Taylor government has failed to deliver Liberia from its nightmare. That nightmare, Teh wrote, "began for us when the free American slaves hit the shores of West Africa. We only got a respite in 1980 when the first African, who packed a gun, ended the 130-year rule over native Africans by the self-proclaimed Americos who had fled slavery in America and founded Liberia in the name of democracy."

I was amazed to find that so much of the vitriol harked back to the arrival of those intrepid freed slaves, among them the Rosses of Prospect Hill. Even the American Civil War, which in the South has turned out to have the half-life of plutonium, no longer holds the power to induce mass violence.

"What more do the African-Americans and Americo-Liberians want from us?" Tey demanded to know. "We surrendered a century and a half of our lives to absorb the anger of the returnees on behalf of any African who had anything to do with selling our brothers and sisters abroad. . . . If these returnees still don't like us after 150 years, then they have returned to the wrong part of Africa."

Such bitterness pervades Liberian chat rooms and message boards on the Internet. In Ciata's Chat Room, a website where Liberians post messages, exchange information, and argue about the history and current state of the country, the discourse frequently becomes vengeful, despite repeated warnings from the webmaster and entreaties from other visitors. When I posted a query about the descendants of the Rosses of Prospect Hill, I received many helpful replies. Then came the following:

"Seek yee first IN-BRED, BREAD FRUIT EADING, BOLLD SUCKING EX-SLAVE BASTARDS, FREE LIBERIA AND EVERY-THING WILL BE ADDED UNTO IT. I hope you know that blacks in America are a minority so total payback for what white DID to them is impossible. You ELITIST BASTARDS ARE in the minority. Just wait we will 'SKIN' your ELITIST ASSES AND USE THE SKIN FOR SHOES. If there is any thing to get over I suggest you get over your 'NO MORE WAR' crap . . . Take Heed asshole you better start filling more INS forms to bring over your sole-foot great grand and

grand mother from up river or else when the shit hit the fan they will
become part of a sad history."

Subsequent postings tapped a deep reservoir of remembered
atrocities and resulting hatred. One person recalled a group of rebels
cornering a woman named Esther Paygar and forcing a sharpened bayonet into her jittering hands to kill her own children. " 'Noo! I can't do
that' the despairing woman cried. 'I can't kill my own children. You can
kill me if you want.' They didn't kill her, but one by one, while the
defenseless children cried 'Mama, Mama' to their wailing mother for
help, Charles Taylor's wicked 'freedom fighters' got to work [and] the
helpless children were beheaded right in front of their mother. Then
with laughter, the rebels attempted to give the bloody heads to the
children's mother, but Esther Paygar fainted before they could reach
that stage."

New York University linguist John Singler had told me that the
Liberian conflict is not solely about the long-running division between
descendants of freed slaves and indigenous ethnic groups. "The war
was about greed, not about ethnicity, not about ideology," he said. "It
was the armed against the unarmed."

The Internet discussions, however, inevitably find their way to the
subjects of slavery, oppression, and prejudice, and the lasting horror of
slavery is glaringly apparent in the unremitting, personal, contemporary hatred that spews forth from every chat room and message board.

One person wrote: "Natives vs. Congo, slave vs. master, light
skinned black vs. dark skinned black . . . white vs. black, Hutus vs.
Tutsi, apartheid, slavery, segregation, nazism, facism and neo-nazis,
and the list goes on. If you really think about it, all they are trying to do
is survive at the expense of the next man. . . . Think about it. How can
a person who was a slave in one land be a master in another?"

In response, another wrote: "The war in Liberia is a result of ongoing hostility and conflict between repatriated slaves and the indigenous people of Liberia. Today's war torn Liberia is not the result of the
modern day politics and internal strife, but result of over 133 years of
animosity between the 'haves' and the 'have nots.' "

"What I can't understand," came the next reply, "is why a people
that were practically driven out of a nation that hated and brutalized
them continue to cling to such a nation. And why would an African sell
another African? . . . The truth of the matter is that we should be a

shame of ourselves. We are a disgrace to all people of color. The first independent republic in Africa. Independent for over 153 years. What do we have to show for that? Not a damn thing. A bunch of American educated fools, a group of displaced people who practiced apartheid against their own, a group of citizens who murder their own people because they are Congo, a group of arrogant bastards who feel good by putting others down, leaders who murder, maim and raped for the sake of power."

The Internet discussions were bewildering, and yet I had devoured every detail. Because the fighting had ceased by the time I began planning my trip to Liberia, neither they nor the other warnings I received were enough of a deterrent. From conversations with foreign correspondents, I was aware that aside from the British film crew, journalists were continuing to travel to and from Liberia without incident, and overall, the situation seemed more stable than it had been in years. Sebastian Junger correctly pointed out that the government would pose the greatest threat, but he and other journalists offered practical advice that bolstered my confidence to go. Most importantly, Sebastian said, I was not to discuss the diamond trade with anyone.

Once I arrived, I had resolved to approach the Liberian government directly. It seemed crucial for me to establish my credentials because I had more than one mission during my stay. In addition to finding the descendants of the Mississippi immigrants, I needed to build a case for my own defense should the government focus unwelcome attention on me. So before proceeding any further in my quest for Mississippi descendants, Edward Railey and I stop by the Liberian Ministry of Information office, so that I can register as a journalist. We meet with J. Paye Legay, a gregarious, reassuringly friendly guy who is deputy director of research and planning.

As we sit in his office, he seems interested in the story I have come to research and offers suggestions for people to interview. He hopes the book will prove beneficial to Liberia by sparking American interest in the country's plight.

"It's a mystery why America doesn't care about Liberia, considering this is the only country America ever colonized," he says. "When there was trouble in Haiti, they got involved. You see the names of places here, just like in America, and if I name my son for you, I expect something in return." He runs through the list of American investments in the country—the airport, the Firestone plantation, then points out that, "Half of the population of Liberia is in America now."

"Liberia should be resting in the bosom of America," he says. "They created this country. But it's like they put a bowl of rice before a hungry man, then tie his hands. That's what America do to the free slaves."

I am encouraged by his straightforward approach but refrain from offering any meaningful response, particularly after he begins talking about diamonds and the election of President George W. Bush. He tells a story about an American or Dutch firm—I can't remember which, because by this point I have purposefully stopped taking notes—that extracted diamonds from its iron ore mines without the knowledge of the Liberian government. Finally I say, "It's an interesting story, but I made a rule for myself not to discuss politics or diamonds with anyone in Liberia. I hope you can understand."

He laughs. "Well, maybe you can help us develop tourism in Liberia," he says. "That is what I would like for you to do." He takes my $50 fee for journalists' accreditation, along with copies of my photograph, my itinerary, and the outline of my book, then stands and offers his hand. "Come back this afternoon and you can pick up your papers to do your interviews," he says. He laughs again when I am unable to manage the handshake and makes me try again and again until I get it right. This is becoming the routine of every adieu in Liberia.

After a pleasant lunch of jollof rice—a sort of jambalaya dish of rice, peppers, and chicken—at a nearby restaurant, with Donna Summer singing the disco hit "Don't Leave Me This Way" on a raspy speaker, Edward and I return to the Ministry of Information. This time I am referred to a different man, whose demeanor is a marked departure from J. Paye Legay's. He is overtly hostile. He does not introduce himself. "If you go to Sinoe," he says, pausing to give me a belligerent stare, "sometimes journalists pass this way and see things that embarrass us." I am unsure if this is a lament or a reproach. "If you photograph the executive mansion," he adds, "you will be arrested."

"I have no interest in the executive mansion," I say.

He glares at me for a moment, then passes me my papers and asks for the $50 fee. He is visibly angry when I say I have already paid.

I am a bit chastened by the exchange, but feel better now that I have my papers and return to the café to find that Peter Roberts Toe has arrived with a car. Next stop: Mississippi in Africa. There is only the matter of the summons to the U.S. embassy.

When I had earlier stopped by the embassy to register as an American citizen, the consul, Abbie Wheeler, had taken a noticeably greater interest when she found that I was a journalist. After hearing of my plans, she had stressed that it would be important for me to maintain contact with the embassy while I was in Sinoe County, which I already knew would be impossible, and said she was concerned that the situation in Liberia could suddenly change as a result of the UN sanctions debate stemming from the country's involvement in the diamonds-for-arms trade. Then, this morning, I had received a message from her at the hotel, calling me back to the embassy to meet with the ambassador.

Edward is both impressed and bewildered when I tell him that I am to meet with the ambassador. He stares at the broken pavement as we walk, mulling things over, occasionally wondering aloud what this new development may mean. He waits out the meeting across the street from the embassy gate.

As it turns out, when I arrive at the consulate Abbie Wheeler greets me and tells me that I will not meet with the ambassador, but with the directors of security and politics for the embassy. She also mentions that she is processing papers to ship home the body of an American missionary who was killed on the road to Greenville the previous week. The missionary's car was overrun by a log truck operated by the Oriental Timber Company, and although the Liberian government officially blamed the accident on the woman's driver, the embassy has questions about that, she says. She adds that the embassy has some information particular to my own travel, then ushers me in to meet with Lon Fairchild, the director of security.

Lon Fairchild looks completely out of place in Monrovia. He is all-American, with gym-muscles bulging beneath a bright red polo shirt. His air-conditioned office is an oasis of comfort and control in a country where both are in short supply. I outline my travel plans for him. He is friendly but direct.

"I advise you not to go," he says. "If you worked for the government I wouldn't let you go. The Liberian government may turn you back. There's no security outside Monrovia. Our radios won't reach there. Supposedly there are dissidents in that area, dropping off caches of weapons—fighting, basically. We cannot help you there."

I have prepared myself for this lecture. By anyone's standards, traveling to Greenville is risky, but I have been told that once I get there I will find the place peaceful. It is the ten-hour drive through the bush, through countless unsupervised checkpoints, that worries me, although I have the utmost trust in Peter Toe, and on the flight down I had met a group of elderly Minnesotans who were traveling to Greenville to build a playground at a Methodist school. I told myself that if a group of elderly Minnesotans could go to Sinoe, so could I.

I thank Lon for his advice, then throw the Minnesotans on the table.

His response is, "The rules are different for you. Missionaries are accepted. They're here to spread the word of God. Journalists are perceived in a completely different light. Even though your interest is innocuous, you're here to gather information. That changes everything. The last ones to attempt what you're talking about doing was the British film crew, and you know what happened to them."

He then broaches the subject of the UN sanctions debate. "They are poised to impose the sanctions, and there's a very strong likelihood that they believe you're part of that effort," he says, and pauses, meaningfully. "I'm concerned for your safety. The biggest threat we face are the people who are supposed to protect us. They fly choppers sixty feet high over the embassy—that's what we deal with every day. It's aggression. Charles Taylor is paranoid, and in his mind the UN equals the United States. You're gonna be out there with a bunch of crack addicts with AK-forty-sevens who blame America for their troubles, and when the sanctions come down Taylor's gonna flip out. Anything can happen when he's in a cocaine-based rage, and you—you'll be out there someplace where our radios won't reach, where we can't help."

I have known all along that the sanctions debate could pose a problem. The UN discussions tapped into my two main fears about traveling to Liberia: the country's recent history of horrific violence, and its notoriously unpredictable, paranoid, and sometimes violent government. I have told myself that as long as the sanctions debate continued Taylor would have no incentive to implicate a foreign journalist in an alleged international conspiracy, as he had the British film crew, but that if they were imposed while I was in Liberia, he would have nothing to lose. It might not matter that I am a bit player in the grand scheme of things, because the government could confer upon me a starring role if it served its purposes.

Lon then raises the possibility that the government of Liberia does not believe that I have come here to research the Rosses of Prospect Hill—that, instead, they believe I am here for a more sinister purpose. It is an absurd notion, but, "What we deal with here is not reality," he says. "It doesn't matter if you're not here to gather information for the UN sanctions debate. What matters is what Liberia perceives as reality, which is skewed."

I concede that I was a bit unnerved by the guy at the Ministry of Information warning me that I might see things that would embarrass the government.

"That's not really a warning," he says. "It's a veiled threat."

This is clearly a battle of wits for him, and the ball is now back in my court. I tell him I understand that it is his job to keep people like me from causing trouble for themselves and for others. "I appreciate what you're saying, but I'm still going to go," I say. "I have to."

He doesn't miss a beat. "If you go, do whatever they tell you to do," he says. "Give them whatever they want. Comply with every order. Be very nice. Have two or three hundred dollars Liberian for each checkpoint because these guys haven't been paid in months. And if you do decide to go, call me." Then he adds, "If you stay in Monrovia, where they can keep an eye on you, you probably won't have any problem."

I thank him and move on to my next meeting, with Anthony Newton, who heads the embassy's political division. Newton is a spare, unassuming man who looks like he might just as easily be a high school principal, and his office offers no clue to the turmoil that has boiled over only a few hundred yards away. He speaks with quiet authority as he goes over the UN sanctions, the diamonds-for-arms trade, the possibility of a worldwide travel ban for Liberian government officials. I tell him I am aware of these things. "It's not just about diamonds," he says. "What also matters, in your case, is timber. The Oriental Timber Company is clearing old forests on the way to Greenville. It's very controversial, and you will see that. The government is frantic over the possibility of an embargo because it would cut them off from their source of income. The government says the sanctions debate is part of

an international conspiracy, and there's a chance they are going to por-
tray you as part of an effort to besmirch Liberia's image. That's the
context in which you've arrived."

This information seems more specific, and I am beginning to wonder if he and Lon Fairchild may actually work for the CIA, so I ask if
he has reason to believe that my presence has been discussed at the
executive mansion—if Charles Taylor actually knows that I am here.

"Yes," he says.

It is the one piece of information that I cannot disregard.

"Here's how it looks to them," he says. "They're looking for some
nefarious American plot, and it could not possibly be a coincidence
that you would arrive at this time, trying to go to Greenville. Maybe
you could go to Greenville and nothing will happen. Maybe some
moderates in the government will prevail and actually help you if the
situation gets bad. But I would suggest you go back to the Ministry of
Information and reiterate what you're here to do, say you recognize the
dispute, you're sensitive to the government's concerns. Then see how
that's received."

My second meeting with J. Paye Legay is markedly different from the
first. He now seems detached, impervious. He tells me a parable
involving African animals of equal intelligence, one of whom is clever
and manages to deceive the other. It is a long, cryptic story. I am
unsure if he is warning me, testing me, or . . . what? I explain that I am
now wary of going to Sinoe and wary of the government, which
prompts him to launch into another parable.

"If you go into a certain area and a snake bites you," he says, "the
next time you see a small tail, you think it is a snake. But we also have a
saying in Liberia: 'If you climb a tree and you fall, it shortens your
journey to the ground.'"

So much for getting a straight answer from him.

Leaving the meeting, I am bewildered. I think of something Sebastian Junger told me: "It's very easy to get accused of being a spy even
when they know you're not. It gives these types of governments a little
bit of bargaining power without getting branded a criminal state."

The question is whether to stay or go. I do not want to turn back,
having come so far, but neither do I want to embark upon a dangerous

folly that could result in my having my notes confiscated, or worse. In a place like this, it is hard to know if your fears are proportional. Unsure of what to do, I backtrack to the U.S. Information Service, a branch of the embassy, and talk with the media liaison, Sarah Morrison.

"If you stay in Monrovia, they probably will not bother you," she says. "Don't be alarmed if you're followed, because you will be, most likely, but the chances are you won't be bothered. It's possible there would be no trouble going to Sinoe. Anything is possible in Liberia—that's the problem, really." She says she visited Greenville a year ago. "It was beautiful. The people were delightful, the food was great. But then, I flew in and out in a helicopter."

My greatest concern is my notes, since the British film crew was relieved of all their footage, yet I am dubious about the embassy's advice, because the staff is paid to minimize dangers for people like me and no doubt errs on the side of caution. Still unable to make up my mind, I decide to put the question to Peter Toe, who is to take me to Greenville and host me while I am there.

Peter Toe is someone I would trust my life with. He is a caregiver, a provider, a brave and intelligent man, and is willing to lead. He has been hunted by rebels and twice has led groups of refugees through the dangerous bush, beginning when he set off on foot for the Ivory Coast with his wife and six children, aged three to twenty, on Christmas Eve, 1989.

During lunch at a Monrovia café, he recounts the ordeal. "I had to leave," he says. "I was being hunted. The fighting come, all the people rush into town. If you have money they want to kill you."

He and his family arrived safely in the Ivory Coast after an exhausting, frenzied journey through Liberia's coastal jungles and swamps, and remained there until 1992, after which the family returned briefly to Liberia, then fled again.

"We heard the gunfire in church," he says. "We left again. We walked to the Ivory Coast. It took us one month. The children were sick. I had fifteen in our house, and another group joined us, then another, and by the time we got to Ivory Coast we were more than a hundred and fifty. The rebels see us, they are beating us, but they left me because I am a doctor."

As Peter talks, I notice through the open window of the café one of the ubiquitous groups of destitute women sweeping the street with worn-out brooms. One of them glances through the window at us, her eyes alighting on Peter's. He reaches into his pocket and gives her a small Liberian bill. Next a group of soldiers stops by. Two enter the café while another guards the jeep, gun ready. Peter pays no attention to them, but Edward whispers, "These are the president's personal security. They are looking for someone."

The soldier standing guard glances at me through the window. I give him a nod. He nods back, and looks away.

Peter says that when the fighting ended in 1998, he returned from the Ivory Coast with no money and no way to start his life over again. John Singler, he says, gave him the money he needed. "Now I operate a drug store and a clinic," he says. "There is no doctor in the whole county. People give me chicken, rice, in payment. I have a lot of chicken." As a result, he is one of the few Liberians I talk with who has no interest in moving again.

I tell him what Lon Fairchild and Anthony Newton said about my traveling to Greenville, and his response is unequivocal. "I wouldn't go," he says. Peter is not one to overestimate danger. Although I have only known him for a few days, he inspires confidence, and I trust him. I would go anywhere that he was willing to go. But even if I were intent on taking the risk myself, it seems unfair to put him in jeopardy as well. If he does not think I should go, I cannot ask him to take me.

There is little else to consider. "Well, at least tell me what I'm going to miss," I say.

"You'll be missing my wife's cooking!" he says, the smile returning to his face. "She going to be very disappointed. She preparing for you. But really, two-thirds of the people in Greenville have left. Most of the old people who could have told you things—the ones it mattered about Georgia, Mississippi—they starve during the war. All of them are dead. The hunger kill all of them. There are only young people there now. Many people from Sinoe come here, to Monrovia, during the fighting. You can talk to them. I know you want to see Mississippi Street in Greenville, but most of it has washed into the sea. Most of the big houses, the houses with the pillars, were burned, destroyed in the fighting. All of the Southern houses are gone—the ones that did not burn, the rust eat off the roof."

I accept this, grudgingly. It is the people I am looking for, after all, more than the buildings. But if I stay in Monrovia, I will not be able to remain at the Mamba Point. All transactions in Liberia are cash, and I don't have enough on hand to be comfortable spending fourteen days there at $120 per night. The last thing I want to do in Liberia is run out of money.

Security, or at least the feeling of security, is a major consideration, and it is something that other, more affordable hotels in Monrovia cannot always provide. I ask Peter's advice, and he says that he needs to pick up some supplies to carry with him to Greenville and will try to come up with an idea while he is gone. In the meantime, Edward Railey and I will head back to Mamba Point.

I am disappointed that I won't make it to Greenville, that I may not get what I came for, that I may be chickening out. But walking back to the Mamba Point, Edward and I discuss the possibilities. He is an optimist, and is convinced that the change of plans will be a blessing in disguise. Plus, he seems upbeat about the fact that I won't be leaving him tomorrow.

We pass the imposing ruins of the old Masonic temple, its statues and balustrades damaged by mortars, toppled here and there, and I stop to take what I hope is an officially sanctioned photograph. I make a point of leaving out the antiquated artillery cannons on a bluff overlooking the building, aimed at the city below, which are rusting and partly overgrown with vines. The city lies in ruins, hazy with pollution, yet pulsates with life. A toddler is standing before the building when I take my photo. A woman who is washing clothes in buckets, out of sight behind a monument, hears my shutter click and hurries forth, talking excitedly. She is barefoot, pretty, wearing a bright red dress and bandana. I can't understand her accent but assume she is upset because her child was in the picture. Edward talks to her and she begins to smile. He gives her a few Liberian dollars.

Afterward he says she was concerned that I would get in trouble. She said guards sometimes patrol the building and that if they saw me taking pictures they might arrest me. She was relieved when Edward told her that I had my accreditation papers. Still, it makes him a little nervous, my taking photographs there. "Just take the picture," he snaps as I peer through a window opening at the ruined lobby, with its grand staircase partially stripped of its elaborate cast-iron rail. Clothes hang to dry in all the openings because the temple is full of squatters.

Edward says his parents taught him to be suspicious of the place
because a secret society, the Masons, once met there.

"It's funny," I say, as we walk away. "That the woman was concerned
for me."

"The Liberian people are mostly good people," Edward says. "They
are warm. It is only when the heat is on that things can get very bad."

"I don't understand why the people put up with the government," I
say. "They're doing nothing to fix the country, yet Taylor and his friends
are riding around in brand-new Mercedes and Lexuses and building
mansions outside of town. They're looting the country, and the average
Liberian has nothing, not even the basic essentials of life. It seems like
it would be in Taylor's best interest to keep people pacified."

He nods. "The Liberian . . . don't do nothing," he says of his countrymen's acquiescence. "And the reason is because no one wants the
war to come back."

I ask him about the underlying conflict of Liberia's civil war.
Although I have read much about the dispute between the descendants of the freed slaves and the indigenous tribes, in the short time
that I have been here, I have sensed more unifying despair than ethnic
animosity. Taylor traces his lineage to both sides, and with everyone so
uniformly polite, how could the country erupt into such unimaginable
violence?

"Everybody want to be the boss," Edward says. "I know what you
are saying—people so warm, so friendly. I've thought about it a lot.
Liberians killing one another. It all comes down to one thing: everybody want to be the boss."

CHAPTER EIGHTEEN

REVEREND CHARLESTON BAILEY LIVES in a small, cinder-block house behind St. Teresa's convent, where Peter Toe has arranged for me to take a room. The house is almost devoid of furniture, but is otherwise comparatively comfortable. It stands in an area that feels more like a neighborhood than a war zone, though no place in Monrovia, aside from walled compounds, feels in any way protected.

Edward has known Reverend Bailey, who is originally from Sinoe County, for years, and had hoped that he might be able to supply me with contacts in Greenville. Now that I won't be going to Greenville, he hopes for the same here in Monrovia.

At the front of the house is a swept dirt yard and a breezy porch. A large, horned lizard stalks insects atop the painted cinder-block wall as Edward and I wait for the reverend to amble out from the recesses of the darkened house. When he does, he shakes our hands and eases down into a chair on the porch. A younger man sits on the rail listening to world news on a boom box.

I explain myself. The reverend runs his tongue across his lips, thinking back. He is eighty-six years old, his eyes appear bewilderingly large behind Coke-bottle lenses, and most of his teeth are gone. He has a few teeth on the top on one side, and a few on the bottom on the other, which seems the worst possible combination. His memory, though, is sharp. He says he has ten living children, including two daughters in the United States. He says he remembers the soldiers torching the columned mansions of Mississippi during the civil war, remembers eating crawfish in Louisiana, and collard greens and okra. He remembers crossing the languorous river that flows between

Mississippi and Louisiana in a canoe. There is a strobe effect to these
images from old Liberia, juxtaposed with images from eponymous
places in the United States. Listening to him talk induces a sort of
mental vertigo. He switches back and forth often enough that sometimes I have to listen closely to know if he is talking about Liberia or
America.

The Baileys, he says, were originally from Georgia, in the United
States, and after being freed by their owner in the early nineteenth
century, immigrated to Monrovia and then sailed to Sinoe County
aboard a ship named the *Mayflower*. There they settled alongside earlier immigrants from Mississippi and Louisiana, who had built the Mississippi colony's first ocean-going vessel, which they christened the
Natchez. Soon after, the groups began to splinter.

"They had different ideas. Some of the settlers—the Baileys, the
Raileys, the Walkers, the Murrays—went to Louisiana," he says. "The
Reeds went to Readsville, the Rosses to Rossville. The Witherspoons
and Burches went to Lexington. They wanted to establish their own
place."

Establishing their own place was everyone's raison d'être, but some
of those places had already been taken by the tribes.

"My grandfather was killed in a war with the tribes," he says. "He
was shot in the stomach. The tribes wanted the settlers to go back to
America, but after all the settlers conquer them and they surrender."

The Bailey family fled Louisiana during the fighting of the 1990s,
as did most of their peers. "The war ran me from there," he says. "It
ran many people from there." With Sinoe in ruins and the nation's
economy in shambles, few had reason to return home when the fighting ceased. "Some came here, to Monrovia, some went to Ghana, some
to Nigeria," he says. "There are not many old people left in Sinoe." The
possibility exists, he adds, that I might actually find the people I am
looking for here in Monrovia. "Most of the people in Sinoe now, they
came there, they not born there. The majority of the Sinoe people now
are in Monrovia. There are no Rosses in Rossville. The old, old people—
they knew about Mississippi, but no one now."

Ever the optimist, Edward points out that had I been able to travel
to Greenville I might actually have missed the people I am looking
for—because they had fled to Monrovia.

There is little left of the Sinoe County that Reverend Bailey knew before 1994, he says. I ask him about the buildings, which I had wanted to see because they are said to resemble antebellum architecture in the American South. He confirms that most of the mansions were destroyed by rebels who saw in them the manifestation of the ancien régime. There are a few examples of settler architecture on the streets of Monrovia, he says, perhaps as many as survive in Greenville.

The buildings were apparently seen by many as an affront after the 1980 coup and during the civil wars of the 1990s. Monuments were bulldozed, historic buildings were looted and burned, and written and photographic archives were scattered to the winds. The destruction was wholesale, and devastating beyond Americo culture. Today there is no public library in Monrovia, and with so little surviving documentation within Liberia, and so few elderly people who can help fill in the blanks, the best sources of the nation's history are housed in libraries in the United States.

Later in the day, when Edward and I visit his mother, Abbie Jones, at her home in a rural community called Duport Road, she reiterates the reverend's assessment of the situation. Abbie, who is in her fifties, also left Louisiana during the fighting and settled outside Monrovia. She leans back in a chair beneath the shade of a massive plum tree, shakes her head and says, "I tell you! My people! Je–SUS! All of the old people, gone."

Edward explains: "Most of the old people, they starve during the war. In the early eighties Rossville, Louisiana, Lexington, Blountsville were all places to see. The old people were there. Now you have mostly the youth, born since the early seventies. They don't know. We did not have time to sit and talk to the old people, and now they are mostly gone."

The loss of the elders is much lamented, but for most people, making it through the day and maintaining some sense of normalcy are more pressing concerns. Neither Abbie, nor Edward, nor any of their family members can find jobs, and when I ask her about the bare utility poles leading past her house that have been shorn of their lines, she says that the electricity was cut during the war and never restored.

"They only have lights in parts of Monrovia and parts of Greenville," she says. "There is none in Louisiana."

She entertains no illusions about ever returning to her native Louisiana, but remembers the place fondly.

"It's just a small farming community, with wooden houses," she says. "No jobs. The women mostly just sit on the porches and enjoy the breeze. Sunday, go to church. All the men go deer hunting on Saturday."

"Deer hunting?" I ask.

She nods.

Suddenly we are back to strange juxtapositions. I tell her that deer hunting is popular in the American South, too, where hunters often mount the antlers of the biggest bucks on the wall.

"It's the same here," she says. "They hang the horns on the wall, something like a decoration."

Edward says that when he was young, he and his brothers often went on deer hunts, to help control the dogs.

"Most of the time they hunt around Rossville," he says. "It's up the river from where we live."

I ask if they know of any Rosses who still call Rossville home, but both shake their heads.

"There is not much there now," Edward says.

I ask if they still have family in Louisiana.

"Just a few," Abbie says. "Most of them are here. My family came from Louisiana, to Louisiana, but they leave during the fighting. One of my sisters went to the U.S. She is in Louisiana."

"Louisiana, in the U.S.?" I ask.

She nods. "I don't really know the name of the place. All I know is Louisiana."

Beyond her, a flock of white cattle egrets probes for insects in an open field. Edward notices me studying the birds and volunteers the name—"cow birds."

I tell him we have the same birds in Mississippi. I've been told they flew in from Africa in the eye of a hurricane, years ago.

"The same birds," he says, and smiles.

Beyond fading memories and crumbling facades, many cultural links remain between Liberia and the American South. The most pronounced, literally, is Liberian English, which has an antiquated sound and mixes pronunciations and expressions from the antebellum South with the cadence of traditional West African speech.

John Singler, who spent years studying this hybrid dialect in Sinoe

County, wrote that the language of Greenville reflects the greater contact of the original settlers with what he called "speakers of White Southern Vernacular." Greenville was settled primarily by more educated slaves, while upriver settlements such as Readsville were settled primarily by illiterate field workers. Paradoxically, Greenville's greater exposure to outside influences caused the city's residents to become more African in speech, while the upriver settlements "remain fundamentally North American," he wrote.

The slow erosion of homogenous Americo culture began, as most such disintegrations do, when the old people—in this case, the original settlers—began dying off. Some of the original settlers had continued to communicate with family members in the United States until the turn of the twentieth century, but in their wake the personal attachment began to fade. Incrementally, their culture became more mixed, and more African.

As Edward and I stroll through an outdoor market and pass a vendor selling dirt for human consumption, I mention that some African-Americans in the rural South have eaten dirt habitually for generations—not just any dirt, but dirt dug from favored sites—and that there has been speculation that the habit was brought to America from Africa.

"Sometimes it's hard to say where something comes from," he says. "You look to America and you see some things you recognize, but really it's hard to say: did the African take it from here to there, or did the settler bring it from there to here?" Or from here to there and back—and perhaps from here, back to there again?

Most Liberians of immigrant descent identify with African-Americans in the United States but consider themselves the reverse—American-Africans, he says. This is certainly true of Reverend Bailey, who was born and raised and has lived his entire life in Liberia, but is quick to point out that he's "originally from America" on both sides of his family.

"If you are an American-African, what happens if you emigrate to the U.S.?" I ask. "Are you an African-American-African, or an American-African-American?"

Edward laughs. "I guess in the U.S. I would just be African-American."

Having a connection with America is still considered an important edge, and it remains a source of pride for many despite the civil war,

Fernando Po, and the seeds of cultural integration that were planted in the 1950s and 1960s, when other African nations began overthrowing the rule of colonial powers. Although the 1980 coup was the crowning blow to Americo cultural dominance, neither side has presented a united cultural front in the years since. On the contrary, Liberia's contemporary elite consists of Taylor, his family, and a small group of friends and associates, while the average Liberian's lot is poor regardless of ancestral descent.

Still, old times here are not forgotten. One Liberian with whom I spoke, who is of indigenous descent, lashed out at the nation's flag, which vaguely resembles the American flag, with broad red and white stripes and a blue canton bearing a single star, saying it is a symbol of old Americo dominance. His offense mirrors the feelings of many black Mississippians over the state's official flag, which incorporates the banner of the Confederacy in its canton corner. One is a reminder of slavery, the other of the empowerment of freed slaves in Africa. Both are divisive.

Later in the day I meet with a teacher at the University of Liberia, Sleweon Nepe, who is originally from Sinoe County. Like so many others, he fled to Monrovia during the fighting. In Greenville, he says, memories of American culture once colored every aspect of life, and before the war the city held an Arrival Day celebration on Mississippi Street each July 9–10.

"There was a big dance, a formal ball," he says of the celebrations. "People give candy to the children. They cook food, drink beer. There was always a special program to tell friends about how the pioneers came, how they landed, how they were received by the local tribes. They wore the suits with the top hat and long tail coats. The women wore the long dress, white, like a hoop skirt. Some of them kept these clothes during the war, put them in plastic and buried them. The local people, they wore their local dress. Everyone participated. They allowed the militia to turn out in khaki for a big drill.

"In the 1920s and 1930s there was tension, but when Tubman took over in 1944 he brought all of these people together," he continues. "We all went to the same schools. There is the feeling that we are all Liberian. But even today the people look to America. The settler people, they know what state their ancestors immigrated from, and the indigenous people, they see that a connection with America is important. The Liberians showed other people in Africa that you could be independent—even South Africa. We showed you do not have to be a slave. We have a commonality, despite our differences. It all goes back to America, because America established this country, which is why America cannot allow everything to be in vain."

CHAPTER NINETEEN

EVERY NIGHT THE YOUNG men who work at St. Teresa's convent gather in the TV room to watch movies on the VCR. It is a real luxury for them, and they will watch anything that is available. When I return to the room I've taken at the convent, after a day spent trudging the streets in search of Rosses while trying to sort out real and perceived threats from the government, I see them gathered before the TV watching old American movies like *The Sound of Music*. Tonight, as I pass through the room, Abraham Johnny, who does the laundry, stands and greets me with the Liberian handshake. Abraham is a supremely happy man with a ready smile that makes his eyes squint. It is almost as if the structure of his face makes it difficult for him not to smile.

"Alan, you must come watch the movie with us," he says, and plops down in a round rattan chair.

"What's showing tonight?" I ask.

"It's called *Mississippi Burning*," he answers.

"Huh," I say, unsure what to think of this rather bizarre twist. "Well, you know, I'm from Mississippi," I remind him, and he beams and leaps to his feet to give me a high five.

All the other guys in the room do the same, and we go through the whole round of handshakes. This is a personal milestone: never before have I gotten high fives from a group of black guys after telling them I'm from Mississippi. They are amazed at their good fortune, to be watching a movie about America's Mississippi with someone who is from there. It is one of the perks of working at St. Teresa's convent that the staff occasionally has the opportunity to meet people from beyond Liberia, because in addition to operating a Catholic school, the convent has a dormitory used by visiting Catholic officials, international groups and—as is the case with me, who was brought here by Peter Toe—people who simply come with a recommendation and need a place to stay. So here is an opportunity for the workers gathered in the TV room to talk with someone who is actually from the place that the movie is about.

"It's actually a terrible movie," I say, which deflates things a bit. "The good people and the bad people are all white. The black people are portrayed just as victims." They wait for more. I sit down.

"Is the movie true?" asks Gargard Menyongar, the convent's resident artist and librarian.

"The story is true," I say. "It was bad in Mississippi at one time. But it's much more complicated than this movie makes it seem."

"Are these men actors or is this really happening?" Abraham asks, glancing back at the screen, where a Klansman is setting fire to a poor black man's barn.

"They're actors," I say. "But it's based on a true story."

Scenes flicker by, mostly of black people reacting helplessly to the assaults of bad whites while the good whites, actors Willem Dafoe and Gene Hackman, argue over how to save them. Abraham and Gargard are impressed when I tell them that the FBI car in which Dafoe and Hackman tool around town belonged to my sister, and was rented to the movie company.

"You have ridden in this car?" Gargard asks, motioning toward the old black Impala in which Dafoe and Hackman are now dramatically arguing.

I nod. My having ridden in the car in the movie delights them, but further confuses the issue of what is real and what is not.

When the movie again descends into violence, Abraham asks, "Alan, do I really want to watch this?"

"It's very violent," I say. "It's painful to watch. It was pretty rough in Mississippi back then."

They nod. I think: my God, you guys have seen a lot worse. Still, it is embarrassing to see whites attacking blacks on the screen, to hear them saying "nigger" this and "nigger" that.

I explain that the men were never convicted for the killings, in the 1960s, of the three civil rights workers who are the subject of the story, whose names were Goodman, Cheney, and Schwerner, but that the state is now preparing a case against the surviving suspects.

"Really? *Now?*" Gargard asks, pointing to the floor.

I nod.

He grins, gives me two thumbs up. "I love America," he says.

As it turns out, *Mississippi Burning* proves to be more or less a lame action movie for them. They show no reaction to any of the scenes except for those in which blacks gather in church to sing spirituals, at which point they all sing along. Eventually they get bored and one by one get up and leave. I head back to my room. The TV plays to the end of the movie, for no one.

Later a group staying at the convent as part of a UK-based human rights workshop takes over the sitting room, and I hear them laughing hysterically at *The Brady Bunch*. There is something unsettling about this, their laughing at a silly American sitcom from the 1970s as I sit on the edge of my bed before the oscillating fan, listening to the sound beyond my window of men chanting angrily within the walls of Monrovia Central Prison a block away, where the British film crew was held.

Each night I hear the chanting, the sound intermingling with African hymns being sung to the beat of a drum in a nearby church and the laughter and squeals of children playing in the darkness below. Sometimes I am unsure what I am hearing, how to interpret the sound. One morning I awake before dawn to hear a man singing and calling out in the distance, which sets the neighborhood dogs to howling. He sounds as if he is in the grips of an insane outburst, or perhaps he is preaching. It is pitch-black outside. Perhaps it is a call to prayer—I know that there is a mosque nearby.

Other times I hear a bell ringing in the wee hours, like a church bell. It rings and rings and rings—for what? Is it an alarm clock for people with no electricity? But it is too early, five A.M. I ask several people but no one knows. I ask a missionary volunteer from Massachusetts, Lucy McGovern, who is also staying at the convent, but she doesn't know.

"In the village where I live I often hear drums early in the morning, from village to village, and I wonder what message they're sending," she says. "But then I drift back to sleep and I always forget to ask anyone their meaning."

One night I hear a soccer game playing on boom boxes and transistor radios scattered through the darkness. Liberia is playing Ghana. A cheer erupts in the neighborhood, telling me that Liberia has scored. The sound is both joyful and unnerving.

As a white American, I bring my own prejudices. I often think, as I walk around Monrovia, that I would never be caught on a street like this in the United States. This night, hearing the cheering and the chanting of crowds gathering in the streets after the Lone Star victory, I think of the riots in Chicago after the Bulls won, and of fights at British soccer matches. But there is only joy. Cars honk, drums beat, people cheer. There is something indiscernible about all this, the cacophony of familiar and unfamiliar sounds, these messages that I do not understand, this overlay of joy upon an undercurrent of violence that seems pervasive yet does not crop up when you expect it. I am reminded of another law of the jungle: that when you're on a hunt, what you're looking for often appears from where you aren't looking.

Most nights at the convent I go down to the gate to hang out with the guards, two middle-aged men who invariably want to talk about the war that broke out on April 6, 1996. During the war, six of one of the guards' eight children starved to death. As I jot down notes, he asks, "You put our names in your book?"

"Do you want me to?" I ask.

"Noooo," he says.

"We have nothing to gain from that," the other guard says. The government does not like it when Liberians talk about the war, he adds.

This is not surprising, yet few of my conversations fail to touch upon the subject.

During the war, fighting between the forces of Doe, Johnson, and Taylor raged back and forth across the city from Capitol Hill to Mamba Point to Bushrod Island.

"They see you on the street, they quick, they cut you and eat you," one of the guards says. "They eat human beings. Terrible war. But it is not the fighting that kills the most people, it is the hunger. People eat the leaves on the trees, the flowers. One cup of rice costs one hundred and fifty dollars." I do the math: it amounts to less than $4 U.S. "A woman will sleep for a rebel for rice," he adds.

They recount the daring wartime exploits of Sister Barbara Brilliant, who once ran the convent and still works here. I had met Sister

Barbara, who is from Maine, when I arrived, and she had not been glad to make my acquaintance. She had listened as I explained the purpose of my trip, then said, "You are here at a very dangerous time for a journalist, particularly an American journalist. You know that. You came here knowing there is a U.S. travel advisory. You should not be here." That pretty much ended the conversation. I wanted to say, *Hey, even the drunk guy with the AK-47 at the checkpoint said, "Welcome."*

The guards laugh when I tell them how Sister Barbara received me. "You have to know about Sister Barbara," one says, then launches into a series of Sister Barbara stories that sound apocryphal, yet plausible.

According to his version, one morning during the war a hundred of General Butt Naked's troops arrived at the convent, naked, of course, and demanded that the archbishop be turned over to them. They were going to take him to the barracks, site of many recent executions.

"Sister Barbara comes out," he says, "and she have her gun. She tell them no one is going to the barracks, they will have to kill her first. So she have that gun, and she turn them away. She spend the rest of the day in her jacket, driving everybody from the archbishop on down to the embassy. She drive them to the embassy while the guns are shooting. That woman is a fighter. She is very brave. No one mess with her. When the Sisters are in Gardnersville, she want to go and rescue them. They don't want to leave, they think they are safe in Gardnersville. You cross the bridge you are killed. So the ambassador find out that Sister Barbara is going, and he park a vehicle across the convent gate, so she cannot go. He know she would never get there. She would be killed."

By then the nuns—among whom were five Americans from an order in Illinois—had already been murdered by the rebels.

"General Butt Naked is now a street preacher," he adds. "Someone told me he is in the States."

At this point, two pretty young girls who belong to staff members emerge from the convent door and sashay out to the gate, singing "Tomorrow" from the musical *Annie*. They are all dressed up, slowly waving their long scarves. When they reach us, they stop singing. They listen silently as we talk.

I ask the guard what happened at the convent during the fighting. He points to bullet holes in the convent wall, which is topped with shards of broken glass.

"The rebels are coming over the walls," he says. "The nuns have gone to the embassy. I am at my house. They take what they want and destroy everything else." UN Drive, he says, which leads from the convent to the American embassy, was littered with bodies.

I glance down at the two girls, who seem uninterested. They soon sashay off into the darkness.

During another of our meetings at the gate a guard's wife arrives, hoping to sell me a coconut. The tub of coconuts she balances on her head is very heavy but she walks confidently and purposefully, even gracefully, under the burden. The guards have to help lift the tub off her head to set it on the ground. She wears traditional African dress, which looks truly traditional—not superimposed, as it so often appears on more affluent women, who wear makeup, jewelry, fashionable handbags, and decorous, carefully coiffed dreadlocks. Her dress and bandana are shades of bright aqua and lime.

I buy one of the coconuts and she pulls out her machete and chops the skin away until there is a hole to the center, which is filled with milk. She hands me the coconut, motioning for me to drink. "Make small, small lips," she says.

The milk is sweet. She makes me drink it all, then smiles with satisfaction. She is a beautiful woman, her skin smooth and very dark, her cheekbones high. She and her husband have seven children, aged six to twenty-five.

Her husband tells me, "My gift to you will also be a gift for me. I will give you one of my seven children to take home with you as a servant!" He laughs.

I laugh, but it ends in a rather awkward *ha-ha*.

He later tells me that each morning his wife goes to the dock to buy coconuts for $2 Liberian apiece (which equals about five cents U.S.), then roams the streets selling them for $5 Liberian apiece (or about twelve or thirteen cents U.S.). She works as long as twelve hours a day, sometimes returning to the dock for more coconuts. If she sells her entire load, she may make a profit of $2.50 U.S.

Such small exchanges are what keep Liberians going. Monrovia is a city of a million people, give or take 100,000, depending upon the flow of refugees, and the whole place is a frenzied market with people rushing down crowded streets with wheelbarrow-loads of batteries and used shoes and dried fish and towels for sale, serenaded by the constant honking of cabs. At one point I see a woman dart across the street with a small refrigerator balanced on her head. I wonder where everyone is going. With unemployment so high and even those who have jobs often going months between paychecks, it seems that everyone has places to go and people to meet. Even more amazingly, they are almost all immaculately dressed. I stop by a laundry and find people making starch from scratch, from vegetable matter, and pressing clothes with coal-fired irons that are heated by a chamber filled with embers. Shoe-shine men do a brisk business along Broad Street, alongside the money changers and people selling used clothing, counterfeit watches, peanuts, transistor radios, and flashlights.

Most Liberians, I notice, are careful about their appearance, and are sticklers for shiny shoes—even tennis shoes are slathered with white polish. One Sunday morning, before I attend church with Edward Railey and his brothers, they take one look at my shoes and haul me down to Broad Street to have them shined. Somehow just keeping clean and pressed is enough to keep people getting up each day to wander the squalid streets, hoping something good will come along.

When I mention this obsession with neatness to a British woman I meet, she scoffs. "It's absurd the way they spend money on shoe shines and cheap jewelry that's just in bad taste to us, when they can't afford lunch," she says. "What's that about?"

"Self-esteem?" I suggest. "Pride?"

She rolls her eyes.

I am reminded of whites back home who joke about the stereotype of the shiny Cadillac parked before a dilapidated shack. From the vantage point of Monrovia, the stereotype looks different. I think: isn't that what land-poor white women did in the American South after the Civil War, when they dressed in their best clothes to receive company on the galleries of dilapidated mansions that they could no longer afford to maintain?

Lucy McGovern, who is visiting at the convent but lives at the Catholic mission in Maryland County, is not entirely enamored of Liberia, but says she is impressed by the resiliency and decorum she has observed here. She repeats the familiar horror stories—torturings, murders, robberies—but adds, "I'm amazed that the people can still laugh and talk like normal people at all, considering what they've been through."

I am also amazed by their knowledge of American politics. One night, the guards talk about the American presidential election, which they know all about, down to the cabinet appointees. When they pause to listen to the news of the sanctions debate on a transistor radio, I glance down at the pristine white tennis shoes one is wearing, and think: here is a man laughing and talking earnestly about politics, who keeps his shoes white while strolling through the muck of the streets of Monrovia, who watched six of his children starve to death five years ago. This resiliency, gentility, and unflagging joyfulness was never mentioned in anything I read about Liberia before coming here.

Most mornings I awake to the relentlessly cheerful sound of children in the courtyard of the convent assembling for school. They sing songs, including the Liberian National Anthem, say "The Lord's Prayer" and the Liberian Pledge of Allegiance, then shout, very loudly, when the headmaster arrives, "Good morning, how are you!"

"I'm well, thank you! How are you!" the headmaster calls out.

"Well! Thank you!" the children shout.

When I mention the Liberians' perfect manners to Brother Dennis Hever, who teaches at the convent, he smiles, then quickly brings me back to the opposing reality. He lives in the compound where the American nuns were murdered in 1992, and, "a few months ago the children were in our yard laughing and playing and suddenly gunfire erupted," he says. "Everything was perfectly normal and suddenly there was gunfire, and the children started screaming. Even when things are normal you're aware that anything can happen. So there was panic. It was a small incident between different security forces, but it set off this panic. Things can change very quickly."

Each morning when I emerge from the convent gate I am met by a group of men who spend the day there, first sitting in the morning shade of the convent wall, then moving to the shade of the wall on the opposite side of the street. I see groups like them gathered on street corners all over Monrovia, listening to the radio. It is a familiar urban scene, but for one important detail: they're not listening to rap or hip-hop music, as is so common in the United States, but to the world news.

This group calls me over each time I exit the gate and again when I return. They want to talk about anything, but particularly the contested American presidential election. One points out that America would condemn such a questionable election if it had been held in an

African nation. I can't argue with that, I say. They are also interested in my story and tell me they know a descendant of one the families I name who came from Prospect Hill. He lives nearby, in an empty walled compound. They promise to take me there.

The men always ask for cigarettes, never money, but one eventually asks, "Why is it America sends no money? No medication, no books, no food, no clothes? We look to America. Why they not help? Liberia is covered with the blood of Jesus!"

Another offers an answer. "They not help because if they send money, you just see the big car, and the big car run over the foot of a man like me."

I nod. I have seen the big cars, the air-conditioned Lexus and Mercedes SUVs speeding down the streets of Monrovia.

"Do you know what happens to a poor man if he gets sick?" another asks. "The hospital have close. So if you are a poor man, you get sick, you die."

At this point I see Edward approaching. He does not condone my being friendly with the malingerers outside the convent gate, because he knows they have an agenda and he is not sure what it is. I trust them, but I trust Edward more.

"Gotta go," I say. "I'll see you this evening."

Today Edward is taking me to J. J. Ross High School, whose director, Maurice M. G. V. Pelham, is a descendant of the man for whom the school was named.

When we arrive at the school I ask Maurice about J. J. Ross and he says, "He came from a place, a state, called Mississippi." I ask if he was not among the Georgian Rosses, because I have read that some of the Rosses from Sinoe County originated there, but he says, no, that J. J. Ross was from Mississippi, and that he settled in Mississippi in Africa and later in Greenville. Eventually he moved to Monrovia. The school is in Ross's former home, a sprawling, three-story structure hard by the sidewalk on Ashmun Street, with a large courtyard out back that is now home to several families of squatters. The school was founded by Ross's granddaughter, Louise Rogers, to educate orphans, says Maurice's sister, Kema Langama.

"For the needy and the less fortunate in society," adds another brother, Aaron Pelham. "But right now, nothing is doing. We used to have a family in France that gave money, but now, because of the war, we have nothing. So the school is private, which is to say that a small, but for many, unaffordable, tuition is charged."

J. J. Ross illustrates that not all of the slave immigrants sought to exploit the indigenous people. He served as a senator from Sinoe County and was later vice president of Liberia. Maurice does not know much about the family history, but when I show him a copy of an immigrant ship registry he points to a line identifying the passengers as slaves freed by the estate of Captain Ross and says, "I have heard this name mentioned."

Maurice allows that some Rosses "were not related at all," and that others among Sinoe's original immigrants were Africans recaptured from slave ships, who, he says, "did not make it to the plantation." Some of the latter also took the Ross name, perhaps as wards. J. J. Ross, he says, was primarily a trader and farmer of cocoa and coffee. The family was once prominent in Sinoe, but Maurice knows of no Rosses who still call the place home. He has visited Greenville only once, he says. "I went to bury. I remember the port there is named for Alfred Ross, who was also a vice president."

There are about 400 students at J. J. Ross High School, he says. The students wear uniforms of blue-and-white striped tops with navy pants or skirts. Their mascot is a type of raccoon, which is similar to the North American species except that it has spots. The school's motto is "Docility." Because Isaac Ross included in his will plans for the funding of an institution of learning in Liberia—an effort that was thwarted when the legal contest consumed much of the money in his estate, I tell Maurice that it seems appropriate that one of the Ross immigrants managed to do so. He agrees, but says the future is in doubt. He has entreated the government to provide some financial help, "but they say people don't have clothing or shelter, and they have to wait for education," he says. Charles Taylor's niece graduated from the school in 1999, and the president made a commencement speech, he adds.

"A lot of our students are self-supporting," says his sister Kema, the school's business manager. "They sell in the market to make money to go to school. Come, let me show you our library."

Down the hall we enter a dark, musty room where dust motes drift through sunlight falling from a single window. A few ruined books litter the floor, with perhaps a dozen more, all with broken spines, tilting on broken shelves. "This is all there is," she says, and waits for a reaction. "So you see, we need books."

Books, I have found, are in short supply all over. I met one man who was preparing a speech to a Baptist Bible seminar on the separation of church and state in the United States, using as his source a book published in 1950. The only accessible books I have come across are used Barbara Cartland romance novels for sale on the sidewalk.

Further down the hall, we peek into classrooms that resemble scenes from Walker Evans photos during the Depression. The rooms are starkly beautiful but almost devoid of teaching tools, with bare wooden floors, unfinished wooden desks, and old-fashioned blackboards.

"What we would most like to see happen is for the school to grow and reestablish the family's full might," Aaron says.

Kema nods. "We have been waiting for you to come along," she adds, with a wry smile. She says she has long held out hope that the school would receive some outside attention that would result in a charitable gift or sponsorship. It is a common kind of hope in Liberia. Before I leave she goes out onto the street to hire one of the itinerant photographers who always seem to be lurking about Monrovia, so that they might document my visit for posterity. She gives me a copy of a videotape of the 1999 graduation, when Taylor spoke, and says, "I beg you to remember us."

Later in the day I meet Maurice at the National Museum, a nearly empty, decaying husk of a building that once housed a massive collection chronicling one of the more interesting histories in Africa. After three separate lootings during the wars, the collection is down to only a few items, including the boot of warlord Roosevelt Johnson, which hangs from a nail in the wall. There are a few photos and letters, an American flag, and what the curator describes as "a traditional journalist's hat and vest"—an elaborate woven helmet decorated with seashells and a similar vest, which were worn by runners who delivered news between villages, chief to chief.

"The building was damaged by bullets and rocket fire," the curator tells me. "People come in and take things. Display bows were used for firewood. More than ninety-five percent of the collection was looted in 1980, 1990, 1996. We need donations of items, but people are slow to give."

"Not surprisingly," I say.

He looks at me curiously, nods, then introduces me to the museum director, Robert Cassell, who says he has heard about me from the Information Ministry. The two show me through an exhibit depicting UN efforts to repatriate Liberian refugees, who at one time represented about a third of the country's population. I say it's interesting that "repatriation" was also the term used for the American colonization effort in the nineteenth century, but they offer no reply.

The museum has a small collection of historic photographs that Maurice wants to help me go through, but the curator is not happy to hear this. Like so many people in positions of responsibility in Monrovia, the curator's demeanor can change abruptly from friendly to officious without warning, and Maurice's request to see the pictures, which does sound more like a demand, gets a decidedly cool reaction. The curator would rather have had more time to get the photos in order, he says, though in the end he agrees. He charges me $5 U.S. to look at the pictures, another $5 to photograph them.

Maurice goes through the photos, pointing out now-vanished mansions built by the freed slaves, which look like the antebellum homes of Mississippi—imposing frame buildings, most of Greek Revival architecture, with broad, columned verandas and shutters on the windows. Although many are sheathed in metal siding in a vain effort to forestall tropical rot, the houses are not the naive approximations I had expected. Most are finely executed. I don't know why this should come as a surprise, because even without access to architects, some of the immigrants were no doubt among the artisans who built the houses that have been so lovingly restored in Natchez, New Orleans, and Savannah. Maurice only comes across two photos of people whom he recognizes, both Rosses, one of whom poses demurely before a painted backdrop in a long, black hoopskirt.

After going through the photos, we stroll the nearly empty museum. Maurice turns to the curator and asks, "Why do you have the boot of Roosevelt Johnson?" Clearly, he is not a fan of Johnson's.

The curator bristles, and glares at him.

"It's a part of history," I offer.

The curator looks at me. "Exactly," he says, then turns his back to us.

Maurice and I head off to lunch. Walking down Broad Street we pass a garbage barrel emblazoned with the words KEEP OUR CITY CLEAN, which is overflowing with refuse. It seems such a futile effort, with litter everywhere, sewage flowing in the gutters, the air hazy around the clock with the pungent smoke from burning garbage dumps. A maddeningly loud electric generator belches black smoke from the Ministry of Finance building directly into the faces of passersby.

Men urinate on the streets, keeping their backs to the crowd, and here and there are signs painted on the walls of buildings admonishing PLEASE DON'T PEE PEE HERE or DON'T PEE HERE IF I CUT YOU. What is a person to do? I think. There are few bathrooms in Monrovia. There is no garbage pickup. Maurice has been drinking from a bottle of water, and when he finishes, throws the empty container to the ground.

We pass the ubiquitous shoe-shine men under their umbrellas, working away. We enter a walled compound at a corner where there is a small, air-conditioned restaurant, where Maurice's younger brother, Oso J. J. Ross Pelham, joins us. The younger Pelham has a brooding face that immediately erupts into a broad grin when the conversation touches upon the subject of America.

"You know," Maurice says, "the settlers, they had goals in life, and they worked. Joseph Ross made his mark. We're still trying to keep on."

"We are proud, but it is on our sleeves," Oso says. "Our pride will not be lifted until we regain our citizenship. We're American. We're not really Liberian. We're proud that J. J. Ross was vice president, proud of the school, but for us it is kind of hard to be proud. I don't want to move to the United States to stay. I would like to go there to complete my college education, because here I have no tools to work with. If the U.S. would grant me a visa, and I could complete my education, I could be everything my grandparents wanted. I want to study computer engineering. I want to gain knowledge. But for now I'm out of high school and can't go to college. I won't stay in America because I have to come back and make my country proud."

He says the farthest back his family can see is Mississippi. They do not know where their ancestors originated in Africa. "All we know is we went to America and we came here," Oso says. "When I was in high school, studying history, one day I realize: my great-grandfather is not from Africa! I wonder if that was where my vernacular, my dialect comes from. I wonder about Mississippi."

"Sometime we get sick of being here, ourselves," Maurice says. "The war. But we feel we have an obligation. A responsibility."

"The love of liberty brought us here," Oso says, quoting the Liberian national motto. "We fought for independence to prove we aren't outcasts. We can make something. That's why we're the oldest African nation.

"It's a funny thing, since the war we socialize more than before. We can play basketball at night. Play soccer. During the war the only place that was jammed was the club, the disco. A lot of people were scattered by the war. Liberians in Ghana, in our refugee camps. Our refugee camps make us proud—they say the camps don't look like refugees live there. So you know, whites are not the only creature of God. You guys mechanize things. . . ."

"And you have the facilities," Maurice interjects. "I feel I owe a loyalty to my family and to society," he adds. " 'What you're left, leave after you,' is the saying. I live for my family and society. I don't live for selfish gain. I live for the people. I can assist in life. People come and ask me to put their child in school, they can't pay, they come and ask and I accept. When it comes to hospitality, the Liberian people are good. We know how to treat people who come here. We make them feel they are a part of us. Ninety percent of what we are came from America. Someone like a Ross is always in a better position to help. Louise Ross worked at Firestone, reared a lot of orphan children, became a reverend mother. She founded King Peter's Orphanage Elementary School. In 1974 she founded J. J. Ross High School, so you could go on from there. They always felt we left America as a slave, we need to do something with ourselves in Africa. They had to do something on their own. We still consider ourselves Liberians, but we know where we come from."

Oso says he has a favor to ask, and already I know what it will be. He wants help getting a visa, and perhaps a scholarship to an American school. He is one of many bright, motivated young men, including Edward Railey and his brothers, whom I have met in Liberia who deserve a chance. I tell him I will see what I can do.

After lunch I return to the museum, where I meet Edward, who has been sitting with a relative who has malaria. On the way back to the

convent, we pass a group of children on Broad Street flying a kite fashioned from a newspaper. We pass a food vending van parked on the
street advertising "Jumbo is the ultamost good taste until you lick the
plate!" Every cab we see has a motto or name painted on the side: "Even
Jesus Wept," "Baby Dog," "Mother Knows Best," "No. 1 Gentleman,"
"Only God Knows," "Why Now?" and "No Situation Is Permanent."

We pass three children selling Cokes and candy bars from a
makeshift stand on the curb. The oldest child, a boy of seven or eight,
is playing a board game with his sister, who looks to be around six,
while a toddler sleeps on a towel nearby, protected from the sun by an
umbrella and from the pandemonium of the street by an ice-chest bar-
ricade. There are no adults around. Across the street, painted on a
wall, is the only graffiti I have seen in Monrovia. It reads, "Bad Boyz of
Mechlin St. Merry Christmas and Happy New Year 2001."

We pass a vendor selling cassettes, and, as always, it seems, Celine
Dion is blaring from a raspy speaker. I understand the affinity with
America, but the love of schmaltzy, hyperwhite pop music baffles me.

"What's the deal with Celine Dion?" I ask Edward. "We hear her
everywhere we go."

"You don't like her?" he asks.

"No," I answer, emphatically.

"What about Michael Bolton?" he asks.

"Actually, no," I say.

"I like them very much!" he says.

As we approach the convent, we come upon a friend of Edward's
whose name is Elvis Crusoe. We chat for a moment and then move on.
I tell Edward I feel the circle is complete.

"I've watched *Mississippi Burning* in Liberia, I've found descendants of the Rosses of Prospect Hill, and now I've met Elvis on the
street in Monrovia."

"And you have many days left!" he says, quite happily.

CHAPTER TWENTY

AN INCUBUS OF SMOKE from burning garbage slowly drifts over the wall of St. Teresa's, enveloping the garden where Benjamin Ross and I sit beneath a tree filled with pale pinkish orchids. I have asked several people what kind of tree this is but surprisingly, no one knows. It is something like a magnolia, very old, with roots that sprawl over the surface of the ground.

This garden is the closest thing to a sanctuary I have found in Monrovia, aside from the carefully manicured, fortified compound of the American embassy. It provides a welcome respite from the din of the streets, although there is no escaping the miasma that drifts and hovers over the city day and night. There is no garbage collection in Monrovia, so refuse piles up in every green space, including the cemeteries, until someone sets it on fire. The postcard view of the Atlantic from the city's highest hill, at Mamba Point, is spoiled by the sad specter of children picking through smoldering garbage beneath the swaying palms. Real estate like Mamba Point would be worth a fortune elsewhere, but its value has been subverted here, like so much of the country's real and potential wealth. Most of Mamba Point is a scenic dump, a wasteland with palms.

It is hard now to imagine Liberia as a promised land, yet that is how Benjamin Ross's ancestors saw it in 1849. Benjamin is the brother of the entrepreneur Nathan Ross Jr., whom I met at the Mamba Point Hotel, and we have come to this garden to talk about those ancestors, about his family history, which for all practical purposes began with their departure from Mississippi for Liberia, where crops grow year-round and the hills and streams are riddled with diamonds and gold.

One of Benjamin's ancestors, William Nathaniel Ross, left Prospect Hill with his family when he was a boy. The name of the plantation has been lost in the family's telling over the years, and likewise there is no account of the decade of litigation that preceded their immigration, but the link is there in the ship registry of immigrants from Prospect Hill. All anyone in his family knows is that a Mississippi slave owner named Isaac Ross paved the way for them to come to Liberia, and that, after an arduous ship passage from New Orleans, they arrived in 1849.

From that point the story becomes more real for Benjamin: the trials the family faced on the Liberian frontier, their rise to prominence over the decades, their political alliances and feuds, the outbreak of civil war, which occurred during his own lifetime and which, although it has officially ended, never seems to end. Somewhere along the way he happens upon an enchanted night, the most important moment in his personal history, when he meets the woman who is now his wife.

It is a tale of love in the ruins. It was during the war, early on, and Benjamin had bought an old taxi to shuttle people around Monrovia. "I was driving that evening and she hailed the taxi," he says. "She was the only passenger."

I know from experience what a rarity that is in Monrovia.

They were two strangers, alone, wending their way through the darkened streets of the war-torn city, through the throngs of people, serenaded by the incessant horns. Benjamin made small talk as he drove, sizing things up, getting up his nerve. She was very attractive.

"Finally I ask her if she is obligated to anyone," he recalls. "She said no. I ask for an invitation to visit her. She said no." When Benjamin put her out at her house, he made a mental note of the address.

"After a few months, I went to the house where I had left her," he says. "I thought maybe the big brother would give me a hard time, because she is younger than me, but he didn't."

Her name was Georgia Ezeagu, and she was then a student at Monrovia Business School. She had no money for the tuition to enroll in the University of Liberia, so Benjamin decided to help out.

"I sent her to the university," he says.

He pauses to brush a few ants from his shoulder that have dropped from the tree. People in Liberia are constantly brushing ants off their shoulders, and off mine, when we sit or stand beneath trees.

"So that is how it started," he says. "Now I am hoping to go to

America, where she is." Georgia Ross, who now lives in Philadelphia
with the hope that her husband and children will soon join her, will
laugh when I tell her, over the phone, after I return to the United
States, how her husband recalls their meeting.

In her version, "It started as a friendship. It was 1987. The war had
not started. We met through a friend of mine. He must have told me
he wanted a friendship, but I really didn't take to the relationship in
the beginning. Then I saw the way he was treating me. He was chasing
me wherever I go! I would be at my school activities and he would
show up. So in the end I give in. He became a part of me."

The remembered cab ride? "Oh, so many nights he picked me up
in the cab," she will say, with a sigh that is audible even over the phone.

The irony escapes neither Benjamin nor me, that his ancestors
risked their lives to emigrate from America to Liberia, and now he is
struggling to get back. But it is not about failure, he says. He is simply
responding to the situation at hand, just as they were. Liberia is his
home, but like most descendants of freed slaves here, he feels a very
real tie to America. If he is allowed to leave he hopes one day to
return, but for now he must do what is best for his family.

The couple's marriage, in 1993, took place during a break in the
fighting between factional groups in and around Monrovia. The year
before, Charles Taylor had launched his successful offensive to take
the city, and proclaimed himself Liberia's leader. When Interim President Amos Sawyer, representing the political party with which Georgia
Ross was aligned, resigned, no one could be said to have control of the
country. Reports by international refugee organizations and the United
Nations estimated that during the worst fighting more than 150,000
people had been killed and more than 700,000 forced to seek refuge in
the Ivory Coast, Guinea, Sierra Leone, Ghana, Gambia, and Mali.

Through it all, Benjamin and Georgia Ross remained in Monrovia,
where he worked as an administrator in a bank, and she worked for the
interim government, and later, the National Investment Commission.

"We went through a lot of things," Benjamin says. "Just in '99 my
wife and I decided that one person should go to the States. She's a lady,
so I said she should go ahead. It's faster for women to attain [immi-
grant] status. She left in September 1999 and she was granted citizenship. Now she has filed for me and the children. We sent all the
children to Ghana, to the resettlement. Everything is at a standstill. If

things work out well in Ghana, they'll leave and I will follow. Then after four or five years I will come back to see how the country is."

The couple's five children, aged fourteen to nineteen, are being supervised in a refugee camp by an aunt. "They went in 1999," Benjamin says. "The war was over," he adds, but they were in danger due to Georgia's association with Amos Sawyer's Liberian People's Party. "In 1993 the country was divided, with Taylor controlling one portion, Sawyer another. Our side was relatively calm because of the ECO-MOG intervention forces. It was right after a bad time. There was mass destruction during Octopus, in 1992. Then, we could move about. ECOMOG had things pretty calm." ECOMOG stands for the Economic Community of West African States Cease-fire Monitoring Group, which briefly maintained the peace in the region. Octopus is the name Liberians give to the particularly intense fighting that swept across Monrovia when the forces of Taylor and Johnson converged in October 1992, their tentacles reaching out from the various strongholds in and around Monrovia.

"I have not seen her since she left," he adds. "We talk twice a month over the phone and we have had three letters carried by people."

I had expected Benjamin Ross to be something of a maverick—an influential banker who had chosen to stick it out in Liberia. But he seems chastened, subdued, diffident, as if he has been forced to repress his self-assuredness. He chooses his words carefully. His clothes are nondescript, designed to say nothing: a short-sleeved white shirt, dark pants, dark shoes.

Yet his status is evident in subtle ways. On the day we first met and arranged for our talk in the convent garden, I had arrived at the Central Bank to find a boisterous crowd in the vestibule, calling out entreaties to two armed guards sitting at a desk with telephones. It was clear that no one was allowed to enter the bank without the permission of the guards, who grant it only upon the confirmation of someone inside. The crowd was excited because the Central Bank is where the money is. They sensed access. As soon as I walked through the door, one of the guards summoned me to the front of the line. Everyone noticed, of course, but no one seemed to mind. They were more curious than anything, as were the guards, who exchanged a glance when I asked for Benjamin Ross.

The guard made a phone call, spoke to someone, and soon Benjamin appeared and we retreated to a side room to talk. He seemed interested, if slightly mystified, by my explanation for why I had come to Liberia. He seemed aware of the guards' attention, and said he could not talk at the moment but suggested we meet a few days later, at the bank, and then move to the quiet courtyard at St. Teresa's convent. We shook hands—the more traditional handshake, I noticed, without the snap, and agreed on a time for me to come back.

Today, when I returned, Benjamin and I left the bank in his battered old Volvo, which is a luxury car by the standards of the average Liberian. As we pulled away, a wild-eyed beggar with a long beard approached the driver's window, talking excitedly. Benjamin gave him five Liberian dollars and the man responded with a crazy diatribe that I could not understand, but that made Benjamin smile. A policeman who observed the exchange laughed and waved, and I told myself that any Liberian who is able to give money to beggars is relatively fortunate, and recognizes it.

As we sit on a bench in the convent garden, he wants to hear what I know about the story of Prospect Hill. I give a thumbnail account, then ask if it is the same story he has heard. "Similar to what you told me. . . ." he says. "I believe there were three brothers, and one settled in Sinoe, one in Montserrado and one in Maryland. I came from the one in Montserrado."

He has not heard about the painful crucible that preceded their arrival. Perhaps the details were lost in the overpowering memory of the mayhem the family encountered once they arrived in Liberia.

Benjamin was born in Paynesville in 1944. His father, James Monroe Ross, was named after the American president from the time the colonization began. After his father died, he was reared and educated by his uncle, Nathan Ross Sr. The elder Ross, who was in the Liberian Congress, sought political asylum in the United States following the coup in 1980. "Our grandfather was William Nathaniel Ross," he says. "He was born in Caldwell, Montserrado County. Our great-grandfather, also William Nathaniel Ross, came over at age four. Our grandfather was a cousin of the late President William Tubman. He was a Methodist preacher and was in the Liberian army. Later he worked with the maritime bureau. I think he was the first Commander of Maritime Affairs in Liberia. Our grandfather used to fight with Tubman. He ran against the late Frank Tolbert, brother of the late president, in an election to be senator from Montserrado County. It was a close election, but because of the relationship they gave the position to Frank Tolbert. Our grandfather was outspoken, so the president was afraid of him. After that, the president found a job for him, the maritime job."

During his career as a Methodist minister, his grandfather erected three churches in Liberia, in Johnsonville, Paynesville, and New Georgia. "The Sinoe brother was John Ross," Benjamin says. "He lived on Mississippi Street. My grandfather's brother. The family was original to Sinoe. Some were traders, some were farmers. Our grandfather here farmed cattle and rubber. He established cocoa farms. The one in Maryland, he had a rubber plantation. It was large—if I'm not mistaken, about one thousand acres. Joshua was his name." Along with the plantations the family owned large, antebellum-style houses.

"Being from Mississippi meant something to them," he says. "Even the natives wished to be a part of that because they were privileged. Having an education helped a lot. They educated the natives, they shared what they had. Some of the natives took the Ross name. They took them into their house. It still happens, but not like before where you carry the children and they take your name."

It occurs to me, listening to him, that the Ross name has a strange currency, a strange fluidity. The white Ross clan originated in Scotland but emigrated to Ireland and then to the United States. From Isaac Ross the name was passed on to his slaves, who in turn passed it on to their wards in Liberia.

"I would be curious about the Rosses in the U.S., to get the family tree," he says. "Most of those who had traced the family tree here are gone. Most of the old people die." I offer to mail him copies of the records I have, but he points out that the postal system in Liberia is unreliable. "Maybe you will be able to mail it to me in the U.S.," he says, and smiles. "If my wife's request to bring the family is approved this year, I leave this year."

In the meantime, there is only the waiting. "Some days it's very difficult," he says. "Some days you can't afford a meal. We are working, I'm an administrator; I've been at the bank fourteen years, but some days you can't afford a meal." He is not complaining—he is simply describing the lay of the land.

❖   ❖   ❖

When Benjamin suggests that I talk with his uncle, Nathan Ross Sr., I tell him that we have already spoken, on the phone, before I came to Liberia. I had been referred to him by a woman I met at the meeting of Sinoe County expatriates in Atlanta. Nathan Ross Sr.'s account of the family history differs from Benjamin Ross's, possibly due to the replication of names, because there were at least two William Nathaniel Rosses, as there are two Nathan Cicero Rosses. During my research I also found a 1984 article in the Jackson, Mississippi, *Clarion-Ledger* about the immigrants from Prospect Hill, which noted that General William Nathaniel Ross, who died in 1969, was aide-de-camp to the president of Liberia and the son of William Nathaniel and Caroline Rebecca Hannah Ross of Cape Palmas, in Maryland County. He had moved to Monrovia with an uncle, Reverend W. N. Ross, in 1912, returning to Cape Palmas in 1929, where he worked at one of the Firestone plantations. This was apparently the man Benjamin Ross referred to as his grandfather, because he later became a Methodist minister. The article noted that he also rose to the rank of captain in the state militia, and in 1950 was commissioned an aide-de-camp to President Tubman. It seems possible that the Reverend W. N. Ross also had the same name.

Nathan Ross Sr. had said that the boy, William Nathaniel Ross, who immigrated from Mississippi, was his father. At the beginning of the call he had very politely told me that it was not a good time for him to talk because, "One of my sisters' sons is dead in Liberia," yet just as I was about to offer my condolences and say good-bye he added, "My father was a Ross. He was William. He was from Mississippi. He came in the 1800s. He was a freed slave." William Ross was four when the family immigrated in 1849 and fathered children into his old age, including Nathan Ross Sr. in 1916, he said. The odds seem impossibly long—that I should happen upon anyone today who is the son of a slave, much less one who immigrated from Prospect Hill to Liberia, but the math adds up.

Nathan Sr. said his father married his mother in 1913, when he was fairly old, "and I'm the offspring of them." Most of the Rosses, he said, settled in Rossville, north of Greenville, but many later left that part of Liberia in search of jobs. "Monrovia is more central. Some went to Cape Palmas in Maryland County. They landed in Sinoe and from Sinoe they found themselves in different places," he said.

Nathan Sr.'s immediate family moved to Monrovia, where he was elected to the Liberian Congress, which is patterned after the United States Congress. He was a member of Congress in 1980 when the coup took place, and, "After that, my children, who were in school here [in the United States], suggested my wife and I come over." This sounded like something of an understatement, and in fact his wife, Alice, later told me that following the coup he likely would have been executed.

When the 1980 coup came, his wife said, the couple was attending an international meeting of parliamentarians in Norway. "That's where we were when they killed the president, Tolbert," she said. Because her husband was in Congress and considered part of the Tolbert regime, it was unsafe to return. Some of his fellow congressional representatives did return and were killed.

"So we left all our things there. We left to go to a meeting and then we could not go back. They raided our house and took everything in the house. The house is still there. They shot at it and shot at it but they couldn't knock it down," she said, with some satisfaction. "My mother died during that tumult," she added, her voice growing quiet. "She was living in the house there with us. Some of our children were there and they had to run for their life. Luckily, my daughter was working for the American Cooperative School and they helped her to get to the United States, to Colorado, where she was given a job as a teacher. But my mother was wounded. She was paralyzed and they pushed her wheelchair down the steps. She died from the injuries. Our children took her to the hospital but she died, and they buried her before they left."

"It's difficult," she said, describing their inability to attend their nephew's funeral in Monrovia. "We're here, we're not working, we can't go there." The couple has been back only once since the coup, she said. "We left to go back and live and then decided they are fighting again and we have to get out again."

Nathan Sr. told me that he knows very little about his family's Mississippi connections in the United States. "One of the young men in World War II stopped at Roberts Field and he came to Monrovia and said he was a Ross from Mississippi, but we lost his address," he said, ruefully.

With the loss of the Mississippian's address, he added, the possibility of reestablishing an American connection dimmed. But when he emigrated to the United States he found that there were "quite a lot of Rosses, white and black. Once I met a man named Nathan Ross, who was white." He said he is still surprised by the number of American Rosses. "I look on the TV and there are Rosses. In Hollywood there are Rosses. Diana Ross—I've met her. Ross seems to be a very popular name on this side."

Alice told me the family still considers Liberia home, but that for her and her husband the prospects of returning are slim. She said her last visit to Liberia was in 1986. She went alone. "I told him, 'You stay. You were in the government. I can go.'"

She still has cousins in Liberia, and they are apparently among the more fortunate, since they have a telephone. "It's difficult to talk to them sometimes, though," she said. "Just recently we heard they were fighting again. It's a civil war. . . ." Her voice trailed off. Then she regrouped. "Both sides of our children are in the U.S. They are all married and have children. Our oldest boy, Nathan Jr., travels all the time. He goes to Liberia." This will turn out to be the same man whom I meet at the Mamba Point Hotel.

After talking with Nathan and Alice Ross, I checked the list of immigrants aboard the barque *Laura*, which sailed from New Orleans on January 29, 1849, for Liberia, and found William Ross, age four, the child of Frances Ross, who was also listed in the inventory of Ross's estate, age twelve in 1836 and valued at $500. William Ross was number sixty-nine among 141 Mississippi immigrants on board who had been emancipated by Isaac Ross's will. Also listed were William's siblings, Epsey, age nine, Sarah, age one, and their mother, Frances, whose age was listed, perhaps erroneously, as twenty-eight at the time.

Benjamin says he is mindful of the sacrifices made by so many to establish his family in Liberia, and of the irony of his attempting to reverse the course, as he now seeks to emigrate to the United States.

"I don't know what that makes me," he says. "I guess when I get to the U.S. I will be an African-American, but one day I hope to come back. This is my home. We in Liberia always like to identify with the black American. It's a prestige. It seems as though you are above the other Liberians just to be connected with America. I think the reason is poverty—it gives you hope of getting out of poverty. When your name is linked with some family in America, it gives you privilege. It gives you hope."

That hope, which once buoyed the family in Liberia, now beckons him to the United States.

Benjamin's family separation is only the most recent episode in a drama that is filled with bittersweet longing. Like their ancestors before them, he and Georgia faced significant obstacles from the start. There was the matter of their age difference—twenty-two years. There was the noteworthy difference in their ancestry—she is half Nigerian, half descendant of the Kpelle tribe, from near the Liberian border with Guinea, while his ancestors were among the ruling class of freed slaves. There was the war, which often pitted descendants of native tribes against the descendants of freed slaves. Now there is the aftermath of political instability and economic devastation, which has scattered the family to three countries.

Today, he says, the Ross family's numerous homes are mostly gone.

"In Sinoe the family house was frame, with plank floors and pillars, two-story," he recalls. "In Paynesville the house was three stories. They're both gone now. All of them are gone. The war, in 1990, took them down. The soldiers sprinkled gasoline inside them and burned them." The monument erected to the freed slaves on Johnstone Street in Greenville was razed by supporters of the coup who believed there were diamonds and gold in the foundation.

"Only the vaults in the cemetery, they don't bother," he says. "There is nothing left, really. Just vast land. Nothing."

CHAPTER TWENTY-ONE

EDWARD RAILEY WAS A small boy in 1990 when his family's Louisiana home was nearly destroyed by the war. The family repaired the house only to see the fighting return, and this time they were forced to scatter, which was a serious trauma for him at such a young age. He fled Louisiana on foot with a local Methodist official and two other boys, walking for two days.

"We walked by the beach from Sinoe to the Cesta River so the soldiers, the fighters—who were mostly sixteen- or seventeen-year-old kids—would not find us," he says. "If they found us they would make us fight. They make everyone fight, boys and girls."

His group managed to elude the rebels, then crossed the Cesta River on a bridge the soldiers had built and found a man to drive them to Monrovia, where Edward had heard that his mother had taken refuge. As it turned out, many had fled the city as well, trying to escape the fighting that was sweeping the country. No place was safe.

"No one was hardly living in Monrovia then, we were hearing," he recalls. "We did not know what we would find. But I found most of my relatives, and then I went to find my mom."

He found her living on the outskirts of Monrovia, in Duport Road. He found his brothers, Kaiser and Augustus, and his sister Princess. There was a joyful, if tenuous, reunion. Duport Road became their adopted home. Then the fighting came to Duport Road.

"This area was very heated during the war," he says as we walk the path to his mother's house. "Many die." The community is not far from the highway he followed from Sinoe to Monrovia in 1992. "The war introduced the road," he points out. "They made the way easier." The soldiers and rebels had needed better routes to maneuver through the bush, and once they were built, such roads offered the refugees more and quicker avenues of escape.

Despite the fragmentation of his family's life in Liberia, Edward says his life is not all bad. He has known worse, just as he has known much better. As we talk about his family history, I picture the sort of dotted lines that might be used to trace an explorer's voyage around the globe. But the point of origin, like the final destination, is unclear. In Atlantic, to the United States, where he wants to go to school to study theology. From that point it would backtrack to Monrovia, where his dream is to return and help resurrect his country from its ongoing despair.

The aftermath of the war is what compels him to try to leave. He spends his days honing dreams of escape, which are as pervasive in Liberia as the stories of dispersal that brought the original immigrants here. Dreams are contemplated during quiet times, and despite all of their troubles and the threat of violence, that is how most Liberians view the current period. Many, including Edward, recall walking a hundred miles or more to flee the fighting, thinking only of survival.

Duport Road is a half-hour drive from Monrovia, but the trip requires three changes of cabs, which makes for an adventure since the old yellow Nissans often break down and no cab driver in Liberia considers his car full until there are seven passengers aboard. Many of the cabs have cracked and even shattered windshields, which provide a disquieting vantage point from which to view the passing scenery. On the way to Duport Road, we pass an old, tidewater-style house, long unpainted, with a swept dirt yard, which looks as if it has been lifted from a scene in the Carolinas in the 1930s. We pass a monument inscribed with the words, EVEN WARS HAVE LIMITS. Scattered along the road are the bare chassis of cars, stripped of everything that can be removed. We dodge gaping holes in the pavement where sewer grates have been scavenged for cooking grills. We stop to pick up a bewildered-looking old woman in a country dress who approaches the cab and scans the door, trying to figure out how to open it. When she gets in, she slams the door on her foot, and Kaiser Railey leans over to tell me, "The car is a new thing for her. The war force many people from their homes in the bush and they have no way to get back." The old woman watches the road ahead tentatively.

When we get to Duport Road, we take a red-dirt footpath to Abbie Jones's home, past a crudely built open-air market, a soccer field, and a scattering of houses in groves of palms surrounded by fallow fields. There are no vegetable gardens behind the country houses here, as there are in the American South, which seems odd. When I mention this, Edward says that people buy produce from farmers who live farther out in the countryside.

Abbie lives in a small duplex with no electricity or running water, both of which it had before the war. When we arrive she is busy preparing a ceremonial meal for me, the out-of-town guest. Most everyone is here—Edward, Kaiser, their brothers Augustus and Prince, their sister, Princess, and two wards named Amie and Samtoinette, who everyone tells me are like a brother and sister to them. Another sister, Joetta Railey, and several uncles and aunts live in Monrovia. The "Old Ma," as they call their grandmother, Nora Jones, lives in nearby Barnersville in her son Boy Jones's home. The father and grandfathers are dead. Edward is the one who helps care for his niece who has malaria and helps arrange the funerals of two aunts who die during my stay in Monrovia.

Seeing them gathered together, I am amazed at how upbeat everyone appears. They are a happy family despite their circumstances, and glad to be together. We sit for hours outside, greeting passersby who follow the footpath that crosses Jones's yard. There is a cool breeze under the palms, but step into the sun, and it is like moving close to a fire. The wards and Princess wash and starch clothes in buckets as we listen to news of the sanctions debate on the radio, and later, to a soccer game, which is the passion of seemingly every boy and man in Liberia. Sitting here, watching the chickens search for bugs beneath the palms, listening to the soccer game, it is easy to forget what the family has been through, and what they are still going through. Stories of unimaginable sadness and horror come up in conversation, sometimes at strategic points, but they only accentuate the joy and determination that people like the Raileys and the Joneses project. It is important to everyone, even strangers, for visitors to have a positive experience in Liberia, particularly because so many come, as I came, expecting the worst. Princess Railey had earlier questioned me about my opinions of various Liberian foods and today, as she goes into her mother's house to help prepare the meal, says, "I have not forget the plantains," and smiles.

Jones has prepared a dish called foo-foo, which is a patty of ground cassava root eaten with a stew of meat and greens. Foo-foo takes days to prepare. First you grind the cassava root, then mix it with water and place it in a container to sit for a day or longer. Finally, it is cooked in something like a Dutch oven over a fire. Preparing comparatively elaborate meals is the done thing when visitors are in town, and it is not negotiable.

When we later visit Joetta Railey's house in Monrovia, she insists that I sit down at a tiny, rickety table and eat the meal that she has prepared. She sends her daughter out onto the street to buy Cokes.

Joetta lives in a crude shelter perched at the end of an alley strewn with rubble overlooking Providence Island, where the freed slaves landed in the nineteenth century. Hers is a community of hapless souls, with low expectations, where street vendors' racks lean against the walls of their dark houses. She has two tiny rooms, no water or electricity, and a single, shuttered window without glass. She has a thin foam pad for a bed. Her clothes hang from nails in the wall. There is an old dresser with a broken mirror.

Joetta looks as if she might once have been attractive but she is worn down now. Her eyes are watery. She has a cold, and smokes. Still, what she has she will share.

"You will always be welcome here," she says. "If you ever need a place to go, you can come here. If there is trouble, you can come here. If you find yourself on the street at night with no place to go, you can stay here." Then she adds, "I am over the family, and I have nothing. Anything would help."

I realize then that her meal has a hidden cost, which is the exception to the rule. She wants money, which will anger her brothers when they later find out. Joetta takes me outside to ask, and I never mention it to the brothers, but somehow they figure it out on their own. The brothers are, if nothing else, aware. They want to know how much she asked for, and it becomes apparent that a family meeting will soon follow.

"This makes me very angry," Edward tells me after he finds out. "You are our guest, she should not ask for money. We have seen how you volunteer money, without being asked."

There is so little that someone in Edward's position can control. Like anyone would, he clings to what he can.

Joetta's ragtag house in Monrovia is a stark departure from the home Nora Jones shares with her son in Barnersville, on the outskirts of the city. Nora is the true matriarch of the family, and her home is immaculate. Flowers bloom in beds scattered throughout the swept-dirt yard. She greets us at the door, resplendent in a purple and green plaid dress, green beads, a silver bracelet, and tinted glasses. Inside, the walls are painted vivid pastel green and the floor is gleaming, faux-marble tile. White ladder-back chairs are perfectly arranged around a coffee table, and sunlight filters through a skylight above.

Nora is a quilter from Louisiana, although, she says, "People don't buy the quilts now." When I ask why, she replies, "No money, my dear."

"I was born in Lexington," she says. "My mother was from Louisiana. Her grandfather was a Walker." When I tell her that the Walkers were among the group who immigrated from Prospect Hill, she nods. "These are the people you are looking for?" she asks.

Some of them, I say. I have a list of the Walkers who immigrated, and it seems likely that her ancestors were among them, but there are no written records and she does not have names of her own.

"I don't know much about where they came from," she says. "Most of the people have left Sinoe. Sometimes people talk about going back, but not many do because they don't know what the future holds. Still, you know, there's no place like home."

She pulls out her only remaining quilt, which has an appliqué of a basket overflowing with red and green flowers, surrounded by borders of yellow, green, and red interspersed with flowering vines. There are two large, red patches where she has repaired tears in the fabric.

She lost most of her quilts during the fighting, she says. "They put a rocket on my house during the war—I was in the Ivory Coast at the time—and the roof fell. This is the only quilt I could find."

She says she remembers when people grew cotton in Louisiana because she used it in her quilts. The practice of quilting, too, was brought to Liberia by the immigrants from America.

Such remnants are among the few that people have managed to preserve during their forced wanderings. The disruption of family life and everything it encompasses has been total for many. I notice a very beautiful little girl, Joyce, who lives with Nora, and when I ask whose child she is, she answers, "My son, he found her." The family will rear her as one of their own, christen her, and see that she is educated. Wherever Jones's family lives will be her home.

For people like the Joneses, the Raileys, and the Rosses, home is literally where the heart is, and seldom more. Physical buildings collapse or are destroyed and are left behind. People take with them the familiar customs and whatever else they can, but their history is a series of encampments of varying duration—the slave cabins of the American South, the frame houses of Sinoe County, whatever accommodations they may find in Monrovia now, perhaps an apartment in America somewhere down the line. The quest for home started when the first of their family members were dragged from their huts somewhere in Africa and shipped off to America as slaves.

This is not to say that they do not firmly identify with their communities. Nora's family, after all, lived in Sinoe County for 150 years. The only constants now, though, are their family ties and certain aspects of their culture, the most lasting of which has proved to be the church.

For slaves in the old American South, religion provided the greatest source of hope and the only outlet for their longing for freedom that was generally sanctioned by their masters. The colony of Liberia was seen as an opportunity to spread Christianity to Africa. As a result, churches are found everywhere in Liberia, and aside from the single, aberrant massacre of hundreds of refugees in a Lutheran church in Monrovia in 1990, most have been immune to the fighting. The predominant religions are Methodist, Episcopalian, and Catholic, although there are also places of worship for the Muslim, Lutheran, and Baptist denominations, as well as for native faiths. Revival meetings are popular, often held under tents at night. Along one rural road I saw a sign pointing to the mission of a group that called itself the Explosive Messengers of Christ. When I asked my student-activist friend the most important legacy of colonization, he said, without hesitation, "The church."

The Joneses and Raileys are active in the Methodist church, and on my first Sunday in Liberia, the brothers took me to services at S.T. Nagbe United Methodist Church in Monrovia. The service was familiar but with an occasional exotic twist. There was a lot of music, the songs ranging from soft, reverent lullabies to a rousing "Holy, holy, holy" with drums, to what sounded like slave spirituals, to something like trance music that went on and on with an off-tempo clap. I noticed that there were holes in the stained-glass windows, which Kaiser Railey later told me came from stray bullets. Ceiling fans stirred the muggy air as the preacher, who once lived in America, delivered a poignant, inspiring sermon. At one point the visitors were asked to speak into a portable microphone and tell where they were from, and each announcement drew thunderous applause. The response I got was similar to those given to the other visitors, but I felt the spotlight when the minister made the requisite plea for money and mentioned— pointedly, it seemed to me—that because America is unimaginably rich, Americans with money could do a lot for a church in Liberia. Afterward the plate was passed, twice.

The service was long, and after a couple of hours Kaiser Railey and I took our leave during a prayer. As we slipped out, a man leaned into the aisle and quietly asked for my address and phone number.

Kaiser often accompanies Edward and me on our forays around Monrovia, and we have developed a rapport. I ask how he spends an average day, because he is unemployed, has no job prospects, and cannot afford to go to college now. He has a room in a relative's house but does not spend much time there, he says.

"I can't work, I can't go to school," he says. "The time is wasting out. I don't stay in my room because I think about this. So I walk."

Kaiser's abiding passion is for soccer. Aside from the church, it is his greatest source of joy, and it is uncompromised. Although church is important to him, he refuses to take communion because, he says, "I see people taking communion and then they go back to living their life just like before. I do not take communion until my life is right."

Soccer is another story. I have come at a fortuitous time, during the playoffs leading up to the Africa Cup. After several languorous hours in Duport Road, the brothers and I head back to Monrovia to watch the Nigeria-Ghana soccer match on television, which is particularly important because Liberia will play Nigeria next, and both teams are in the running for the cup. The beauty of soccer is that you can play it anywhere—I see boys playing on the beach, in empty lots, in the streets. When the country's team is elevated in international status, it puts every Liberian on the map. Everyone feels a rare national pride.

On the main dirt route through Duport Road, we catch a cab to the highway, where we board another cab back to Monrovia. As we pass the president's second home, which is known as the Number Two executive mansion, a band is playing on the road shoulder with a sign wishing the president a happy birthday. Tomorrow Charles Taylor will be fifty-three. There are sandbag bunkers on the roof of the mansion, as there are on the roofs of the buildings at the American embassy. In Monrovia, we take another cab to a neighborhood that looks rundown even by Liberian standards, where a house similar to Jefferson Davis's Brierfield plantation home, but smaller, stands at the end of the street. Inside a small building, through a curtained door, men are watching the soccer match for $25 Liberian, about sixty cents U.S.

Kaiser looks inside, tells me to check it out. Behind the curtain, perhaps thirty men are crowded into a tiny room, sitting in straight-back chairs, watching the fuzzy picture on an old black-and-white TV. It is stiflingly hot and stuffy.

"It's very crowded," I say, doubtfully.

Kaiser looks at Edward.

"Why don't y'all watch it, and I'll go find something to eat?" I say.

They think about this. They would forgo the match if that was what I wanted, but I insist that they watch the game, so Kaiser walks me back to the junction to catch a cab to the convent, where I follow the action by the sound of cheering in the neighborhood outside my window each time Liberia scores. The scene is repeated a few days later when Liberia beats Nigeria and the cheering erupts again, accompanied by a serenade of horns in the streets.

The next day the Railey brothers and I discuss the match at a bar called the Rivoli, which is their favorite place to stop because it is normally beyond their reach—a place right on Broad Street that sells Guinness beer, which is expensive to them but remarkably cheap to me. Whenever there is a break in my appointed rounds—which normally drag us along the streets of Monrovia all day long—the brothers sense an opening and I know that the path will soon lead us back to the Rivoli. The bar is above a rundown theater that shows Indian movies, Rambo-style action flicks, and films that were never released in the United States, and each time we come Augustus makes a point of saying that his birthday is approaching and that the best gift he can imagine would be to have enough money to spend an entire day at the movies. I take the hint.

From the balcony of the Rivoli we watch the man with the badly broken leg, whose name is Sheriff, as he attempts to navigate the traffic on one crutch. I feel bad when I find that I ignored him as we were coming up the stairs. "Hey, chief," he had said, and I pretended not to hear even though he was only a few feet away. I had not recognized him.

When we get to our table Edward says, "Did you know that was your friend who you gave the money to?"

I shake my head. I had seen someone out of the corner of my eye, but had heard what sounded like a sales pitch in his voice, and so ignored him. It was an American moment for me. I was at a low ebb, one of many during my stay in Monrovia, when I grow weary of the constant attention of people on the street. It is something no one in Liberia apparently feels, or if they do, it does not show. Sometimes I can't endure any more heartfelt attention, any more plaintive calls from strangers, any more solicitous, hopeful stares from people wanting to meet me, to get my name, my phone number, my address, thinking maybe I can get them out of this mess. How can I help everyone find a home? The push and pull of conflicting forces that characterizes everything about life in Liberia affects me, too. I vacillate between wanting to help and wanting to be left alone. There is so much need. Unable to escape their notice, I am often overcome with a desire to go home.

My interaction with people on the street occasionally draws unwelcome attention to the Raileys, as when Kaiser and I are walking to their sister's house and speak to a man in passing, and he responds by berating Kaiser. "Why does the white man speak to me and you don't?" he shouts as we head down the street.

When I ask the brothers what most people think when they see us walking down the street together, Augustus Railey says, "They think you are from the U.S. . . ."

"And they think we are trying to get money from you," Kaiser adds.

On another occasion, when Kaiser and Edward are waiting for me outside the American embassy, they overhear one of the guards say to another, "I've been seeing these guys going up and down the street with that white man."

At times I tire of all this recognition and seek refuge at the convent, but it is only a matter of time before the attention follows me there. People find out where I am staying and a few convince the guards to let them through the gate, find my room, knock on the door, and introduce themselves to me and tell me their lament. Eventually people within the convent begin to fill me in on their travails. Someone knocks on my door. I don't answer. I hear someone say, "Mr. Alan, Mr. Alan." Then I hear him say to someone, "I am looking for the white man, Mr. Alan." I go to the door. He wants to give me his résumé. He wants me to give it to someone, anyone, maybe a member of Congress, maybe they will hire him as a security guard at the embassy. When I realize I can no longer even retreat to my room, I am briefly overcome with a need to escape. I want out.

Then I realize: this is how many Liberians feel every day—trapped. How could they leave me alone?

Lucy McGovern, the missionary volunteer from Massachusetts, told me that she reaches this point of saturation now and then. "Sometimes I hear the knock on the door and I don't answer," she said. "I never thought it could feel so good not to answer a knock at the door. I ask myself, What would Jesus do? He wouldn't hide. But he's God, and I'm a human being. I have limits. And I know that Jesus came empty-handed. He didn't come to bring them money. I have come empty-handed, but they don't believe that. I have given them my life but they want money. Even the UN has gotten tired of Liberia not being able to help itself."

Lucy is here to help but feels frustrated, taken advantage of, and seems to grow more so during the time I am here, in part because her closest friend, another American missionary volunteer, has given up and headed home. There is also the matter of a severe and inexplicable breakout on her face, a rash that people have been telling her often besets visitors to Liberia and will go away, but which is, in fact, getting worse. It is not just her soul that is reeling right now. Her face is changing.

I can relate to Lucy's confusion. Sheriff, the man with the swollen, broken leg, experiences the full range of my waffling. Yesterday I chatted amiably with him on the street and gave him money, and today I act like I don't know him.

"You know, I feel bad that I snubbed Sheriff," I tell the Raileys. "I feel like the guy in the Bible who crosses the street to avoid the beggar."

"It's okay," Edward says. "You made him happy that you gave him some money. He thinks maybe you don't hear him this time."

Edward is perennially upbeat. His face seems always to be verging on a smile, though sometimes, in between smiles, his brow is noticeably, deeply furrowed.

The friendliness of everyone around me can be infectious, and I welcome the overtures of strangers, which bewilders Edward because he knows that once I start handing out money there will be no end to it. Every introduction wends its way hopefully toward a transaction, and once someone finds out that you have given away money, they naturally want in on the action. I forget that I am often the lone, comparatively wealthy American on the streets of Monrovia, a city of a million people. As I waited for Edward on the street in front of the National Museum, I was actually surprised that he managed to spot me and wave from two blocks away—forgetting the obvious, that mine was the only white face in a very large crowd. I was reminded when I glanced back toward the street and noticed that the cabs were slowing down and people were staring at me as they passed, as if I was a traveling exhibit at the museum. In a city where cab drivers have been known to go out of their way to pass through the one functioning traffic light, it is impossible to discount the novelty of a white man loitering on the street, particularly because I have more money in my belt than most people here will see in a lifetime. I am a flash of hope in their world that will fly away in a few brief days.

Among the Liberians who have jobs, few make more than $20 to $25 U.S. per month, if they get paid at all. Most are hopelessly unemployed and have been for some time. People need money for everything: amputees need crutches and wheelchairs, students need tuition, schools need books, sick people need medication, almost everyone needs food, and hundreds of thousands need simple protection from the elements. Homelessness is not a condition of people on the fringes here—it affects a significant part of the population. The one need that cuts through every sector of Liberian society is for help in leaving the country. For all their resiliency, and despite long-standing disputes between the descendants of freed slaves and indigenous tribes, the majority of Liberians need what America has to offer. They are not alone, of course. The world is full of people who share that need. The biggest difference is that Liberia and the United States have significant family ties.

Before I came to Liberia, I read an article in the Baltimore *Sun* concerning the possible deportation of approximately 10,000 Liberian refugees in the United States whose special political refugee status was about to expire. The article quoted Danlette Norris, president of the Liberian Community Association of Rhode Island, who said of her homeland, "The whole region is in chaos. Sending us back is like sending us back to a death trap. We consider America our mother country." This view of Liberia, as a satellite of America, is not limited to refugees or to people who want to emigrate.

J. Paye Legay, at the Ministry of Information, said he has no desire to emigrate, but still believes that America should have a greater role in supporting the country. It is a recurring theme in all our conversations. I ran into him on the street outside the convent after he had dropped his car off at a garage, and as we talked a large slab of concrete broke from one of the ruined buildings across the street and crashed to the ground. Luckily, no one was standing nearby. Watching the dust billow into the street, he said, "You see? You see how much needs to be done?"

In his mind, Liberia is the Liberian's rightful home, not America. This is true whether your family once lived in America or has been in Africa all along. But he asserts that America has influenced Liberia's history in profound ways, and has a responsibility to ensure that the country survives.

It is hard to argue with him. The expectation pervades Liberian culture, which is why I—as an American—attract so many entreaties. Faced with such an onslaught of need, sooner or later I have to tune it out, until someone comes along and says, with a broad smile, "Hello! How are you today?" and I get pulled back in. Sometimes these encounters reinforce my feeling of separateness, but more often they obliterate it. The approach is almost always gentle, which is why I have no qualms about walking streets that I would not venture down in the United States. For whatever reason, and despite the transience, the overwhelming need, and the constant undercurrent of fear, I feel strangely at home here. If nothing else, everyone I meet is intent on making me feel at home. As we walked through a crowded market one morning, Edward and I came upon a friend of his who asked if anyone had bothered me on the street. "Has anyone humiliated you? Anyone?" he asked. I shook my head. "See?" he said, smiling. "Liberians are not all bad."

Later, one of the guards at the convent told me that I could move freely through Monrovia because no one wanted to see harm come to me. "Liberia is not a bad place, not completely bad," the guard said. "You, a white man, could walk all the way across Monrovia at night and no one bother you. Only when the heat is on, then you have trouble."

Edward says much the same thing, although he does not agree with the notion that I would be safe alone at night. He says that making sure I am comfortable is everyone's concern, and although the cynic in me thinks that there is often a thinly veiled agenda—that there is some benign duplicity at work—most of the time the interest I encounter seems genuine. If anyone were to bother me on the street, Edward says, others would rush to my defense, but he makes clear that I am not to be out after 9:30 P.M., because there are no lights and thieves and prostitutes take over the streets. He is alarmed when I tell him that the men who hang out by the convent wall in the morning have asked me to meet them there one night.

"No," he says, flatly. "They may be okay, but maybe later this month they be talking about armed robbery, because they hungry. So promise me you will not go out the gate alone at night."

I acquiesce, thinking that before I came here I could not have imagined needing such advice. I had expected the worst. I had envisioned Liberia as a place where nothing is sacred, where people roam the countryside and the battle-scarred city streets without regard to laws, where only a few stalwart souls, including the residents of old Mississippi in Africa, struggle to remain rooted and civil in a world that is disintegrating around them. I had imagined that Mississippi in Africa, Sinoe County, would be my refuge. My idea of Liberia was carefully researched and constructed, and all wrong. There is no safe harbor, but there is the kindness of strangers. You may be uprooted, but if you can survive the tumult there will always be someone to take you in.

I read nothing of this aspect of Liberian life before coming here. Instead I came across endless accounts of the war's atrocities and its aftermath of despair, and numerous bold-faced warnings for anyone crazy enough to consider traveling to a place that epitomizes chaos and the dark end of the civilized world. Even seemingly objective accounts were unwavering: according to the most recent U.S. State Department travel advisory, "Monrovia's crime rate is high. Theft and assault are major problems and occur more frequently after dark. Foreigners, including U.S. citizens, have been targets of street crime and robbery. Residential armed break-ins are common. The police are ill-equipped and largely incapable of providing effective protection. Hospital and medical facilities are poorly equipped and incapable of providing basic services."

Reading this, I had pictured a place that was like a sprawling, crime-ridden housing project in America, where there is little regard for life, where even crossing the street poses a considerable risk. What I found instead is a place where soldiers sometimes commit acts of unspeakable violence, where the government is astoundingly corrupt, where atrocities are a part of the backdrop of daily life, but where most people are remarkably friendly and crime is typically the petty kind. Coming from a place where people are held up at gunpoint before scores of witnesses in broad daylight, where drive-by shootings are common, where robbers follow elderly people home from grocery stores and pistol-whip them or shoot them in their driveways for their money, the pickpockets and prostitutes of Monrovia seem almost quaint. It is the monster lurking beneath—the threat of renewed civil war, and the menace of the government—that makes you wonder how useful warmth and generosity will be in the end. No doubt that is why so many want to leave.

I try to remain mindful of my safety on the streets. I heed Edward's advice because I have a lot to lose. I let the Raileys make all of my transactions for me, including changing money. They are my go-betweens. I let Edward order another round of Guinness at the Rivoli.

When we first met, Edward and I knew nothing of each other. We had only John Singler, who had taught his mother in school, in common. John's name comes up in conversation often because Edward and his family have all benefited from his kindness and consider him family. John taught in Sinoe County in 1969 and 1970, lived there again in the 1980s, and considers Liberia his home away from home.

Edward is shocked when I tell him that John and I have at this point never met, that we communicate over the Internet and have spoken only by phone. This sort of friendship is unimaginable in Liberia, where despite the dispersals, relationships are almost always built upon physical presence. Our visits to the homes of Edward's family members, which are scattered around Monrovia and in communities in the nearby countryside, are rarely scheduled. We just show up and are welcomed. If someone is not home, we come back later. Although there are always long lines at the handful of Internet cafés that first opened here in October 2000, the average Liberian's daily life is a world away from virtual friendships, cell phones, and e-mail. This is not to say that finding someone is always easy. You just head out and hope for the best. From what I can tell, no one ever gives up on finding someone. Liberians, of necessity, are tenacious.

As we have traipsed around Monrovia and the surrounding countryside, Edward and I have become friends. He has let me into his life, and has probed every resource at his disposal to help find leads for me in my research, while keeping my personal safety a paramount concern. My search for the descendants of Prospect Hill intrigues him in part because he knows little about his own family history other than that they lived in Louisiana. Beyond that, the past is as hazy as the future. But as we sit at the Rivoli bar, it dawns on me: I know where his family is originally from. In my zeal to find the Rosses, it had slipped my mind before I had left the United States, John had told me that the Raileys were emancipated from the same region of Mississippi as Prospect Hill.

"Railey is an old Mississippi name," he said, referring to Mississippi in Africa. "They were there by the 1843 census. They were freed by James Railey, who was the brother-in-law of James Green." Green was the Mississippi planter for whom Greenville, Liberia, was named. James Railey was also a member of the Mississippi colonization society, and his home, Oakland Plantation, is now a bed-and-breakfast on the Natchez African-American historical tour.

Railey beams when I tell him the news.

"So!" he says. "When I come to America, the first place I go is Mississippi!"

Kaiser and Augustus raise their bottles of Guinness. Everyone clinks.

"Well, I'd love that," I say. "I'd love to take you there." But I offer a disclaimer, that Mississippi is very poor—the poorest state in the

United States, and that Jefferson County is among the poorest counties.

Their smiles fade. They look incredulous. Sudden dreams dissipate into the filthy air.

"But why?" Kaiser asks.

For a moment I am stumped. Poverty is such a given in Mississippi today, I have never been asked to account for it. "I guess because most poor people in the U.S. are black," I say (although I later realize this is not actually the case), "and Jefferson County is the blackest county in the country." It is an insufficient answer, and the brothers aren't satisfied. "Maybe because the whole economy was built on slavery, and it never really recovered," I add, realizing that this, too, is an incomplete explanation.

Edward stares at me. Kaiser glances down toward Broad Street, thinking it over. Augustus picks at the label on his bottle of Guinness. Mariah Carey whines, loudly, over the tattered speakers.

Then Edward grins. "Well," he says, "when we come to Mississippi, we go to a similar place like this and have a beer. We will do that!" He has no intentions of letting history, politics, or poverty—here or there—bridle his hopes.

Kaiser is circumspect. "When people we know go to the U.S., they are working within three or four months," he says, flatly. "So if they are not working they must be lazy." In other words, we are not talking about people like him.

I shrug.

"Well, Alan, now that we know about our family, you should find out about your own family here," Edward says. "You should find out about Huffman Station."

A friend of his whom we had met on the street had told us that there is a community called Huffman Station in Cape Palmas, in Maryland County. "There is also a Huffman River," he said. "There are many Huffmans right here in Monrovia."

My first thought, upon hearing this, was to check the phone book, until I realized that I have seen no phone books in Monrovia. I don't know much about the Huffman history, other than that they were mostly small farmers and not, as far as I know, slave owners. My mother's family, the Ainsworths, had slaves, but I have not come across their name here.

"Are you sure it isn't Hoffman Station?" I ask. "I've read about an Episcopal missionary from the U.S. who came to Liberia whose name was Hoffman."

"No, it is Huffman. H-U," Edward says, and laughs. "It's funny that you come to Liberia, you are doing this other family, these other families, and now you find out your family is here also."

"Well, it would be funny," I say, "but I don't really know if they're family."

"But, they are here!" he says. "The Huffmans are here, in Maryland County! Before it's over, we find out that we ourselves are related." He smiles at the idea of Liberian Huffmans and Raileys intermingling, then glances at his watch. "But now we should go."

It is time to head down to Broad Street to join the crowds for the Lone Stars' triumphant return, which is scheduled for today. Although it was also scheduled for yesterday, Edward is confident that the team will arrive this time, so we pay our tab and head out. We go only a short distance before we hear the roar of a crowd at the far end of Broad Street, coming down the hill toward us. For a moment I revert to American mode, and mindful of an escape route, steer us to the side of the street toward the convent. The roar of the crowd is unnerving. It grows louder. We hear people cheering and chanting. I see thousands of people running toward us.

"The team is coming!" Edward cries.

We take a position in the median, then climb atop a monument painted red, white, and blue, along with a group of other men. People are rushing toward Broad Street along all the side streets. The crowd quickly fills the street, jostling the women peddlers, who reach up with one hand to steady the loads on their heads. Suddenly the thronging mass pushes through, in front of, around, and behind an open car bearing several jubilant athletes who stand up in the back. One, Salinsa Debbah, stands above the rest, shirtless, his muscled arms pumping the air victoriously. A few people grab my sleeve and exclaim, "He's the star of our national team!"

Everyone cheers as the team speeds past, and the crowd surges after the car down Broad Street. Some people disappear down the side streets hoping to catch the team on their return, the next street over. As we climb down from the monument I realize how absurd it was for me to have been worried. Did I really think that anyone would concern themselves with me when Salinsa Debbah was coming through? It was a beautiful, awesome spectacle, and it felt good to see this outburst of joy along such godforsaken streets.

The memory lingers for several days after, so when I move from the convent back to the Mamba Point for my last three nights in Monrovia, I invite the Raileys to my room to watch soccer on TV. They are giddy with excitement: soccer games on a color TV in a private, air-conditioned room! Kaiser, in particular, frequently bursts into hysterical laughter for no apparent reason. They forget everything else—their troubles in Liberia, their fractured home, their yearning for America. They chatter away, paying me no mind. Kaiser ends up spending the night, watching one soccer game after another until he falls asleep atop the sheets with the remote control in his hand.

CHAPTER TWENTY-TWO

ONE OF THE GUARDS stops me as I am leaving the convent to tell me he has a message for me from the American embassy. Someone had attempted to deliver the message to my room, but I did not answer the knock at the door, he says. The message is from Sarah Morrison at the U.S. Information Service, asking me to come to her office.

It has been more than a week since I have been called to the embassy compound, but I have been half-expecting to hear from them each day, because the UN sanctions vote seems imminent. I ask the guard to tell Edward, when he arrives, to meet me at the embassy compound, then hurry off down UN Drive, wondering what news Sarah has for me.

As the date of my departure from Liberia approaches, I have grown increasingly apprehensive about the government. When I stopped by the Liberian Ministry of Information one afternoon for an unplanned meeting, hoping simply to gauge J. Paye Legay's attitude, he had told me a few more parables, then described a particular landscape scene along the beach near Roberts Field. The scene was inconsequential but what struck me was his comment, "You will see what I am describing, assuming you are on that plane when it leaves on Monday."

"Assuming?" The word bounced around my head as I lay in bed that night. When I asked Edward what he thought the comment meant, he said it was a standard disclaimer, that he might as easily have said, "God willing." But I am not so sure. It did not help that as I was leaving the Ministry, J. Paye had said, "I'll see you on Monday," although we had not planned to meet.

Throughout my time in Liberia, I have been concerned that the government would detain me. I have made many friends in Monrovia—history professors, school officials, student activists, ministers, even a human rights worker from the United Kingdom. I would like to think that they would rush to my defense if I were accused of spying, though I am unsure whether it would matter in the short run. My greatest concern is that my notes, which I carry in my money belt, will be confiscated.

As I walk toward the embassy, I am startled by a truck loaded with soldiers in fatigues and red berets that screeches to a halt beside me. The soldiers, all carrying automatic weapons, leap from the truck, blocking my path. It is the moment I have been dreading. As I stand frozen in the middle of the street, I watch the driver back the truck onto a lot where people are washing cars. They have stopped to have their truck washed. I realize then that the Taylor government's paranoia is infectious, and it has infected me.

When I arrive at the embassy compound, it turns out that Sarah just wants to show me photos of Greenville that she took a year before, because I will not be able to go there myself. I look through the photos, which are mostly crowd scenes against a backdrop of plain buildings. I thank her, then return to the gate to wait for Edward. I am growing weary of wondering, of not knowing if my imagination is running away with me or if the threats are real.

A cluster of shops in an alley near the embassy represents the closest thing Monrovia has to a tourist market, and I decide to browse their wares for a few souvenirs. I cannot imagine what sort of souvenirs would be appropriate reminders of this trip, but it seems I should buy something. I had noticed one shop selling old tribal masks, which struck me as curious because there were no such masks in the National Museum. I decided that I might buy a few of them and perhaps donate one to the museum. The lack of tribal masks at the museum is an obvious shortfall, and I decide that if a tourist can take home such relics of Liberian history as souvenirs, the museum collection should have at least one of its own.

When Edward arrives, we enter the shops, which causes quite a commotion, because tourists are so rare. The shops sell mostly paintings, carvings, and fabric. Some of it is pretty nice, but the hawkers are relentless. There are probably twenty vendors and I am the only customer, and no doubt the first in many days. I don't have room to carry much of anything in my bags, and the truth is, I feel guilty spending money on any sort of indulgence in a place where there is so much deprivation, particularly in front of Edward. Still, I have to get something for the folks back home. All that really catches my eye are the masks.

I have seen a few African dance masks in shops in the United States, all reproductions with exaggerated features, carved in ebony. These are the real thing. They are very old and worn. Coming from a variety of tribes—there are sixteen or seventeen distinct ethnic groups in Liberia—the masks are remarkably varied. Some are stylized and unadorned, others have beards fashioned of burnt reeds and long mustaches of black animal hair. Some depict a hybrid creature, part human, part bird. The going rate is $50 U.S., an exorbitant amount of money here, but as the only customer, I know I am in a good position to bargain. I don't have to have a mask. I offer $50 for two and the guy immediately says yes, which means I have overbid. I pick out two, then make the same transaction in another shop. I now have four masks—one for myself, one each for friends back home, and one for the museum.

It occurs to me that the masks may actually have been housed in the museum at one time, before the lootings, but my decision to donate is not entirely philanthropic. It seems prudent, and in any event I will need a letter from the museum authorizing me to take antiquities from the country. A donation would dovetail nicely into my personal PR campaign and no doubt make friends in the museum. I decide the largest and most elaborate mask will go to the museum.

Robert Cassell, the museum director, who was so somber when we first met, is clearly stunned when I tell him what I propose to do. "I must go and get someone from LCN," he says, referring to the Liberian Communications Network, the government-run print and radio media.

"That's not really necessary," I say.

"No," he says, already on his way out the door. "*It is necessary.*" He says this very sternly, almost as a reprimand.

In a few moments he returns with a slightly confused reporter carrying a tape recorder. I realize, listening to the director explain what I am doing, that he has in mind to showcase the mask as a gift from an American benefactor—for that is how I am to be portrayed, which points out the need for funding for the museum. His spin is that my gift of the mask proves that the museum has international importance, which strikes me as a bit pathetic, though if my casual donation draws attention to the museum's needs, I am happy to accommodate him.

The reporter asks how I embarked upon "this cultural exchange program," and I tell him it would be overstating the case to call it that, because I simply wanted a mask for myself and decided it would be appropriate to give one to the museum. I recount the sad story of the museum lootings and point out that it will be a monumental effort to rebuild the collections, but that you have to start somewhere. Then he asks me about my book, which the director has mentioned. Although I had started out my trip trying to maintain a low profile as a journalist, I soon realized that this was going to be futile. At this point, I figure, I have nothing to lose. If people all over Monrovia hear of my book in the context of my donation, I will have greatly expanded my retinue of protective friends. I tell him the story of the slave immigrants from Prospect Hill.

He nods. "It is an interesting story," he says.

And it's true! I want to proclaim, from every boom box and transistor radio in town. But I merely agree.

The reporter turns to the museum director, who reiterates the importance of the museum's collections in chronicling the history of Liberia. He then gives me my letter, and we say our good-byes.

I miss the interview on the radio, and never manage to find the newspaper in which it runs, but a few days later when I stop by the Information Ministry on my way out of town, it is obvious that J. Paye Legay has heard about it. He is full of warmth and praise. He smiles, gives me the Liberian handshake, and is pleased to see that I have finally mastered it.

He chats amiably about relations between our countries and says he has decided that there are two reasons why the United States does not support Liberia: "The United States helped Taylor remove Doe so he could do their bidding, and then he refused. Also, Liberians in the U.S. try to paint the country in a bad light, so they will be allowed to stay in the U.S." Then the smile returns to his face. "I hope you got the information you came for," he says.

It seems that if he did not before, he now believes that I came to Liberia for the reasons I gave him. The irony, of course, is that I could probably travel to Sinoe County with the government's blessings now, when it is too late. Then again, maybe not—and it's a moot point any-way, because I found descendants of Prospect Hill here in Monrovia.

After the meeting at the Ministry, I stop by to see Sarah Morrison, who says she has been asking around and has found that the story of the masks has tipped the scales in my favor. The Liberian journalists and others with whom she has spoken have told her that the government accepts my reasons for being here.

"There's no reason to expect a problem at the airport," she says, but just in case, she gives me the name of a man who works for the embassy as an expediter there. "If there's a problem, he will see you," she says. "Just tell him that you are here as my guest."

As the day of my departure approaches, I begin to feel a sort of vicarious desperation regarding the Railey brothers. The one unifying factor among the majority of Liberians I meet, of whatever ethnic or economic background, is their desire to emigrate. U.S. visas are extremely hard to come by, even with a recommendation from an American citizen, because so few Liberians who leave want to return home. Single young men like the Railey brothers have it the hardest, because they have no vested interest in going back.

The only way they can reach the United States, even as students, would be to find someone who will sign an affidavit stating their will-ingness to support them financially while they are in college, and to have a college that is willing to take them. This is a challenge for many reasons, not the least of which is the difficulty communicating with people in the United States. I certainly am in no position to do so. Without the ability to communicate with others, how can they find such a school? How can they find a benefactor? How can they effect the paperwork? How can they get inside the embassy compound, and once there, manage more than a terse dismissal from Abbie Wheeler or one of her employees?

None of this seems to diminish anyone's hope. Whether they want to emigrate or are resigned to stay, hope is all that most Liberians have, and they nurture it. When I mention to one of the guards at St. Teresa's that almost everyone I meet wants to emigrate to the United States, he nods, then says, in a tone that sounds as if he is trying to con-vince himself, "In some ways it is better here. If I'm American, I walk down the street I get arrested or a gangster take my money and kill me. So I hope things will get better for us here."

"Maybe I can't go," says a second guard. "But I have hope, because God is here."

Sister Scholastica Swen, an administrator and cook at St. Teresa's, tells me that she has high hopes for just about everything—for the convent school, for the souls of Liberia, for the future of her country, and for a better life in the United States. Swen spreads hope in her wake as she shuffles from the kitchen to the dining room to the offices of the convent. She is self-confident, pragmatic, and kindhearted, and can turn a couple of fish into a feast. On one of many nights when I am at the gate talking with the guards, she comes strolling through the compound singing in a beautiful voice, and lingers with us for a while. She tells me that her father is from Sinoe, her mother from Maryland.

Then she puts the question to me: "So tell me, how do you find Liberia?"

Many people have asked me this, and I always give the same answer. "I love Liberia," I say.

She smiles, but it is an ironic smile. "You love Liberia, and we're all fighting to get out," she says, and laughs.

"Well, let me qualify that," I say. "I love the people of Liberia."

She nods.

"I love their warmth, and their resilience," I add.

She nods again, claps her hands, then strolls off into the darkness, singing. Clearly love of Liberia is one thing, staying there another.

The student activist who met me at the airport when I arrived, and again a few times at St. Teresa's convent, tells me he also intends to leave Liberia if he can, at least for a while. He wants to better himself, to expand his network of connections. It is not that he cannot endure Liberia, because endurance is his countrymen's strong suit, he says, and he, if anyone, should know. Although he never volunteers the information to me, John Singler had told me the young man's painful story, while cautioning me not to name him for fear of government reprisal.

The young man has long been involved in politics as a student at the University of Liberia. During the Doe regime, he was suspected of being involved in an explosion on campus, and so fled to Freetown, Sierra Leone. While in Freetown, he was imprisoned with a group of other Liberian students and, as John said, "The government forgot about them, literally. And of forty-seven LU students, only six lived.

He was one of them. He came back to Liberia and was hospitalized. It was '92, Octopus was going on, they were fighting in Monrovia. One day he was napping and a stray bullet hit him. Knowing all that, it's hard to believe how sweet he is."

I have to agree, yet as sweet as he is, the student activist shows no fear. When I tell him that I was concerned that the government might arrest me, perhaps even as I am attempting to depart the airport, he says, "Not in my Liberia."

The student activist is now a member of an international student organization and has participated in several conferences outside Liberia. In June 2000 he was invited to a UN conference in New York, but the U.S. government would not grant him a visa due to the supposition that he would not return home after the event was over. He has since been invited to an international student conference in Norway, based on an essay he submitted, but is having trouble raising the money to go. He is a brilliant, controlled, and determined man, and wants to help improve Liberia, and so would never leave without planning to come back. He represents the potential for Liberia, waiting in the wings, and not all that quietly, either.

When I broach the subject of Liberian emigration with Brother Dennis Hever, who lives in the Catholic compound in Gardnersville and teaches at St. Teresa's, he says the Marist brothers in the United States recently asked him to come home. "There is a feeling that something is going to happen," he says. At the Gardnersville compound, he reminds me that five American nuns were murdered there by rebels during the worst of the fighting, but says that he had decided to stay because he has a group of young men who depend on him.

Brother Dennis invites me to the compound for Sunday lunch, and later to a nearby beach controlled by another American religious group. We are accompanied by several young men who work at the compound. Because the undertow is so fierce along Liberia's coast, we spend most of the afternoon sitting in chest-deep water in a tidal pool, tilting to and fro with the shifting currents, watching guys playing soccer on the beach, and, at one point, a bare-breasted woman running through the surf with a monkey on her shoulder. Two bright, motivated, and frustrated guys sit with me for a while in the tidal pool and tell me their stories. One had a promising career as a soccer player and even had a chance to go to the United States to play, before the war.

He had a friend, Mike Burkely, from Boston, who was with the Peace Corps, who was trying to work it all out. "Then the war came. I had to flee from village to village," he says. "I would have been forced to fight. They force everyone to fight. I lost all my documents, all my addresses, all my contacts, my sources. Everything. It was 1996. Now, nothing is doing."

Both young men reiterate the difficulty of getting visas and say that what they most need right now is a radio so they can hear news from the world outside. "I once had my own radio but it spoiled," the soccer player says. "I think, maybe if we listen to the radio long enough we will hear about a scholarship." He asks if I would try to find his Boston friend, and when I agree he hugs me twice, then shakes my hand four times.

Another young man tells me that if he manages to get to the United States he will eventually return to Liberia, although he knows that most who emigrate never do. He knows a woman who studied abroad to be an obstetrician gynecologist, but just as she was making plans to return, the John F. Kennedy hospital in Monrovia—the only public hospital in the country—closed, leaving her plans in limbo. Many people go to the United States and get an education with the intention of coming back to make a contribution to Liberia, but, "What do you do?" he asks. "There is nothing to do. You're making fifty-thousand dollars a year in the U.S., and there is no job for you here. Those people you see on the street changing money, a lot of them have a B.A. There's nothing. Liberia has so much—iron ore, diamond, they have just discover oil! We have the largest rubber plantation in the world and people are driving around on worn-out tires, and the tires are imported. Why?"

These are very personal problems for everyone, including Edward Railey and his brothers, all of whom are in their early twenties, motivated and frustrated. Their lives are ahead of them, they are ready to begin living them, but they have nothing to do, and there is no sign that things will change for them in Liberia. The Raileys have family in America, but there is not much they can do to help. Augustus Railey wants to go to study business management. Kaiser Railey wants to study computer science. Edward is interested in theology. We go through all of this again in the hours leading up to my departure. I will find out if there is any possibility that they can get an invitation to go to school, if there are scholarships, what must be done to acquire the necessary visas. I am not optimistic, but they are. They are determined to go to Mississippi, in America.

On my last day in Liberia, the brothers leave me at the Mamba Point for a while as I pack my bags, then return with a parting gift, an African shirt they want me to wear. We stroll the streets of Monrovia, me in my incongruous shirt, imagining a future meeting in Mississippi, and then suddenly it is time to go. We return to the Mamba Point, get my bags, and wait for the car that Edward has arranged for the drive. There is some confusion because he has impressed a cousin to provide her car, and she and two friends, as well as Princess Railey, want to join us. It becomes clear that someone is going to be left behind. The brothers decide that it will be Augustus, the youngest, and he watches sadly as we drive away. Augustus, more than his brothers, has a look of almost desperate hunger on his face, and it is excruciating to leave him behind. He will follow us in a cab, Edward says, but I do not see him again.

There are eight of us in the car, wending our way through the streets of Monrovia, past the comparatively modern sports complex, past Sky High Jewelry—not the best advertising, I think—past the military barracks where so many executions occurred after the 1980 coups, and the two executive mansions, through the gates to the city. Outside Monrovia is a landscape of old Africa—mud and thatch huts, palm groves in broad, swampy fields, women carrying firewood in stacks on their heads. I take photos freely along the way, because no one is around. I am still not convinced that I won't be hassled at the airport, but I tell myself that I have built my case.

When we arrive at the airport, I get out of the car and the student activist puts his hand on my shoulder and says, rather urgently, "Put the camera in the bag." Then I hear him say, "He is not taking photos of the airport. It's all right. He has not taken photos of the airport."

I do not look up. I stuff the camera in the bag. From the corner of my eye, I see a guard walking away.

We wait for a while in the parking lot of the ruined Roberts Field Hotel, making small talk. No one likes good-byes. Then the time comes and I head out, promising to do what I can. As I walk toward the airport, I am more curious than nervous about whether I will be hassled inside.

As it turns out, there is only one small problem. One of the men at the baggage search is concerned about my tribal masks—not because he cares about them, apparently, but because they represent an abnormality, which means: an opportunity. I show him the letter from the museum, but he is unimpressed. He must show the letter to his superior. This takes a long time. He returns, still skeptical. I suspect that he wants a bribe, that he expects me to get impatient, to take the hint, and slip him some money to expedite things. He tells me to step out of line while the issue is resolved, because I am causing a bottleneck, but I hold my ground. Before coming to Liberia I had been told repeatedly that I would have to bribe everyone, yet I have bribed no one and I don't intend to start now. I have the letter.

People are getting restless behind me, waiting to have their luggage searched, and eventually the guy gets irritated, stuffs the masks into my bag, and tells me to move along. The airline check-in comes off without a hitch, as does the payment of the special airport tax, which leaves only Immigration. The same man who checked me through Immigration upon arrival checks me through for departure, and he is extremely friendly. He remembers me. Things are going well. Then, as I am waiting in line to board the plane, convinced that I am home free, that no one is going to confiscate my notes, I hear a man's voice call my name.

I turn to see a uniformed man. Everyone else who is in line or waiting in the departure lounge turns to watch. Then I recognize the man from Immigration. He is smiling, and beckons me to step out of line. He wants my name and address, a contact in the United States, and asks if I will mail a letter for him when I get home. He is grateful for whatever help I can provide, and says that if I or anyone I know needs assurance that they will be allowed to pass through Liberian Immigration in the future without a hassle, I should let him know. I take the letter, we shake hands—a truncated version of the Liberian handshake—and I follow my fellow passengers out onto the tarmac.

The jet's cabin lights glimmer in the darkness. I smell the smoke of fires in the bush. I follow the missionaries, the women in African dress toting empty bags, the Eastern European businessmen talking conspiratorially among themselves, onto the plane. I take my seat next to a

British woman who has lived in Monrovia for three years, and it soon becomes evident that the experience has embittered her.

When I tell her that I will miss my friends in Liberia, she says, "You think you have friends here, but no one is your friend. They just want your money. If they find out they aren't going to get money they're no longer your friend. The white person always gets better treatment and always pays more."

She is particularly angry, she says, because someone in Immigration told her that when she returns, she must bring him a basketball if she does not want to be hassled.

She goes on like this until I say, "You must really hate the place."

"I do," she says.

"Then why do you stay?"

"I fell in love," she says, "and my boyfriend won't leave. He's in mining. But really, the place is hopeless, and you can't blame them all for wanting out. If I could, I'd leave and never look back."

I think of Kaiser Railey telling me that if he were able to emigrate, he would not be one of those Liberians who decide not to come back. He said he does not understand why his relatives in the United States can't or won't help him. "I want to go to the U.S. for a lot of reasons," he said. "But one of them is, I want to see if I will go there and then forget. I want to see if I am the kind of person who will forget the people back home."

As the plane takes off I glance back at the darkened airport and think of the Railey brothers turning back toward Monrovia. When I set out for Liberia, the last thing I expected was to try to help people like them, descendants of Mississippi immigrants, to essentially reverse the last 165 years. Although Liberia is the only home they have ever known, I feel like I am abandoning them.

Part III

COMMON GROUND

CHAPTER TWENTY-THREE

IT IS A BRIGHT spring morning in McComb, Mississippi, when I arrive at James Belton's house to find him sorting through stacks of papers at his kitchen table, piecing together the riddle of his family's tumultuous past.

James represents an unexpected windfall—a crucial source who appeared after I thought my research was finished. He is an inquisitive man with a quietly keen mind. A retired schoolteacher who now works as a federal housing inspector in McComb, he has spent the past several years researching his family history, which stretches back to South Carolina and encompasses the saga of Prospect Hill. Like Youjay Innis and Artemus Gaye, the two Liberians who were tracing the lineage of their ancestor, Prince Ibrahima, James is on the same path I am on— but he and I are going in the same direction.

Earlier in the week, before Ann Brown called to forward me James's name and number, I had pretty much resigned myself to the fact that some of the blanks in the story of Prospect Hill would never be filled. I still did not know for sure what Isaac Ross's motives were for seeking to repatriate his slaves, I had found no corroboration of the slave uprising, and I had not spoken with anyone who was knowledgeable about the slaves who chose to remain behind. But when I phoned James to arrange a meeting, I felt renewed hope that I would find some answers.

As we begin our conversation, James explains that he has no particular genealogical mission other than documenting what he has been told. He has done his homework, has thought things through, and before our meeting is over, the story of Prospect Hill presents itself in an entirely new light.

"I just know what I was told by my father, what was passed on by my grandfather and great-grandfather from my great-great-grandmother, Mariah Belton," he begins, then drops the first of many bombshells: "My father told me I had two great-uncles who were part of the uprising at Prospect Hill—Wade and Edmond Belton."

Just like that, a major line of demarcation between the black and white versions of the story vanishes.

In fact, James says, his father believed that Edmond Belton was one of the masterminds of the uprising. "Dad said he was a high-tempered fella," he explains.

The back story begins in Camden, South Carolina, where his ancestors were originally enslaved. There, before emigrating to Mississippi, Isaac Ross came into possession of the Belton slaves from relatives who, in some ways, set a precedent for the terms of his own will. According to James, the chief directive of those slaveholding relations was that the slaves be kept together because they were kin to each other as well as to them, the slaveholders. The slaveholders sought to remove them from the Camden area, he says, because the influential families found the combination of geographic and familial proximity discomfiting. He shows me copies of some of the Belton slaveholders' wills, which, as he puts it, "indicate that these people were not to be sold, in no uncertain terms, and that they were to receive the best of care."

After receiving the Belton slaves, Isaac Ross, whose sister-in-law was Mary Allison Belton (who is also buried at the cemetery at Prospect Hill), took them with his own slaves to the Mississippi Territory. "Most of the slaves he brought with him to Mississippi were mulattoes," James says. Among them was Mariah Belton, who lived first at Prospect Hill, and then at Rosswood, where she remained enslaved after choosing not to emigrate to Liberia. She was listed in the Rosswood Plantation inventory in the 1850s, valued at $400. "She got her freedom after the Civil War, and ended up in the community of Union Church, when the government gave them the 'forty acres and a mule,'" he says.

The core of the Belton family account of the uprising is almost identical to the slaveholders' version, although its prologue and denouement are very different. "The house was burned by the slaves in retaliation against Isaac Ross Wade, who contested the will," James says. "Eventually the courts ruled in favor of the will. But before that happened, there was the uprising. During the uprising, the white family's after-dinner coffee was drugged and the house set afire, but without the intended result—eliminating Isaac Ross Wade. I wish it could have been resolved in a better way. When you have to resort to—I guess you could call it violence, to burning the house that the slaves themselves had built, when the little girl lost her life, that's sad. I don't like that page of the story. Everything else, though, I'm proud of it. I don't think it was their intent to get the children. Why would anyone let the children drink the coffee? They thought if they could just get rid of Isaac Wade, they could go to Liberia and have a better life."

Edmond and Wade Belton, he says, subsequently fled Prospect Hill to avoid the lynchings. "Obviously, they didn't want their identity known," he says. "From what I was told, Edmond was last seen crossing the Mississippi River on a ferry from Rodney."

No one knew what became of Edmond or Wade Belton until the early 1990s, when James became intrigued with the story and traveled to Converse, Louisiana, across the river from Rodney, and found the descendants of Edmond Belton. "Then, I found out that Wade had gone to It, Mississippi, in Copiah County," which is east of Prospect Hill. There, again, he found Belton descendants, he says.

How did Edmond and Wade escape, and avoid recapture as fugitive slaves? Did they manage to pass for white, or were they simply assimilated into another community of slaves? Belton considers the questions.

"Them being mulattoes, they might have just blended in," he says. "But I am almost positive that they got help in escaping. I don't think they could've done it alone. It had to have been more or less people who were connected with the colonization movement, but I have to admit that I was small when my daddy was telling me all of this. He was proud of the story, and he loved to tell it to us children at night. He was a sharecropper and we didn't have a radio."

James says that as an adult, he noticed in his travels that there were enclaves of Beltons in other Southern states, and wondered what their connection might be. He suspected that they were all related to the South Carolina Beltons, but when he found the connection with the

Beltons in Louisiana and in Copiah County, he knew he was onto something. That was what set the genealogical hook.

I have no doubt now about the veracity of the story of the uprising, but it still seems incredible that so many slaves would agree to embark upon an endeavor that was clearly doomed to fail. Even had they killed Wade, how could they have expected to get out alive?

"From all indications," Belton says, "from listening to what my father told me, the slaves were coached by members of the American colonization society to get rid of Isaac Ross Wade." Such encouragement may have instilled more confidence, he says. More importantly, the slaves were desperate. They believed they had an opportunity for a better life, and this was their last shot at claiming it. If they had lost the fight to emigrate, they would have become common slaves, which was something they had heretofore never been.

"Isaac Ross was a unique fella during that time," James says, in typical understatement. "He went along with slavery but his slaves were not slaves in the traditional sense. I doubt seriously if you would find anything written about the slaves before 1870, when blacks were first included in the census. But from word-of-mouth, folklore, what was passed down from generation to generation, it is apparent they were not like other slaves. I was told, you know, that some of those Beltons actually attended Oakland College. They were not free, per se, but they were educated."

Before the Civil War, Oakland College was a private school for planters' sons, and Isaac Ross sat on its board. Today it is Alcorn State University, which was founded in 1871 as the first land-grant college for blacks in the United States.

Most historical accounts note that many Prospect Hill slaves were taught to read and write, and that they all enjoyed relative freedom within the confines of the plantation. Ross never sold any slaves, and it appears that he kept them sequestered from the slaves on neighboring plantations. When Isaac Ross Wade took over as master of the plantation, however, they were treated like any other group of slaves, James says. "By the time of the burning of the house, from what I gather, all of the slaves but a few were extremely bitter. Isaac Ross had treated them like relatives, and the truth is, a lot of them were relatives. The Belton ladies who worked around Prospect Hill were very light—you couldn't hardly tell 'em from white ladies, my father said. But after

Isaac Wade contested the will, they weren't getting the treatment they had gotten during Ross's lifetime, and resentment just built up. That was how they came to set fire to the house."

Why did any of the slaves choose to remain behind when the majority emigrated to Liberia? James has a ready answer. A few were not given the option of being repatriated, he says, "most likely because they were just bad apples, like you have in any community."

The others, he says, may have been wary of traveling to a distant, unknown land. But Mariah was different. Belton believes she chose to remain behind because her two sons, Wade and Edmond, had fled Prospect Hill to escape being lynched in the aftermath of the uprising, and she perhaps knew their whereabouts.

"It may have been the grief she was keeping within over what had happened," he says. "She knew her sons did not go to Liberia, and perhaps she thought, 'For me to ever see my sons again, I have to stay in the area.' So she was sold to Walter Wade and transferred to Rosswood with her son, William. He was my great-grandfather." He digs through the stack of papers on his kitchen table and pulls out a photo of the young man, which looks to have been taken around the 1850s, with an inscription that identifies him as a carriage driver.

Given the bitterness that led to the uprising, why did the letters from the Liberian immigrants express such affection for Isaac Ross Wade and his wife? "It's possible that was in their best interest, to do that," he says. In other words, they had nothing to gain from distancing themselves from Wade once they had immigrated to Liberia. It is also likely, he says, that many of the slaves did not support the violence.

James still has a lot of questions, but most of them concern the genealogical riddle. He has organized the documents pertaining to his family and Prospect Hill on a CD-ROM, complete with images of the portraits of Isaac Ross and his wife, and of tombstones in the graveyard, and he plans to give a presentation on the subject at the next Belton family reunion. Since 1984 the Beltons have held reunions, often several times a year, at various locations. Last year the event drew more than 4,000 people, he says. "I had to get my facts in order," he says of his Prospect Hill presentation. "I don't like to lose history, and the first time I mentioned all this at the Belton reunion, the whole place went quiet. People's mouths dropped. They said, 'A white man did that before the Civil War—in Mississippi?' They didn't believe me.

One fella who did believe the story said, 'Man, you need to get in touch with Spike Lee. It'd make a great movie.'

"There's a lot about our history people don't realize," he says. "Like that a lot of blacks in the South owned slaves." In his view, the story is complicated, and it is shared. "Some of the white Rosses have helped me put a lot of information together, and the white Beltons, too," he adds.

When I mention what so many have said about the story not being simply black and white, he smiles. He says there are a lot of gradations between any two extremes, and cites as an example the quasi-ward system that he remembers as a child, which was similar to that which exists in Liberia today.

"It was basically the same way here," he says. "It wasn't like slavery, but I grew up with a stepbrother and -sister, who Dad took in and raised 'em, and they worked for the family. They were like family, and they were less fortunate, and they worked for us. I see a lot of that—people who are less fortunate, maybe because they're darker skinned, and they weren't given the same opportunity.

"It's a funny thing, I was playing gin rummy with my daughter not long ago, and I don't know why she asked me this but she said, 'Dad, what do you like about yourself?' I thought about it and I said, 'Well . . . everything!' And she said, 'There's nothing you don't like about yourself?' and I said, 'There is one thing: my complexion.' My wife looked up and said, 'What're you talking about?' I said, 'It's always kinda bothered me that sometimes there might be several of us applying for a job or something, and maybe some of them were more qualified than me, but I got it because I'm lighter skinned.' That's happened a lot in my life. I feel I'd have been a stronger person if I was darker and had to work harder. I feel bad that I was given preference over darker people—even by blacks—because of my complexion. If we look at ourselves and get a true picture—you can see, even back in slavery, people just . . . how did you put it? They use the tools at their disposal to make the best of the situation. And sometimes they just go too far."

CHAPTER TWENTY-FOUR

ENOCH ROSS IS A high school basketball player in Walla Walla, Washington. He was a founder of an African-American church in Connecticut. He participated in Iowa's constitutional convention in 1844. An Internet search for "Enoch Ross" produces nearly one hundred hits, but none of the incarnations fits the parameters of the story of Prospect Hill. It is still unclear what became of the remaining key player in the story—Isaac Ross's mysteriously treated manservant.

Court documents show that Enoch and his family were freed two decades before the Civil War and allowed to emigrate to a free state in the North. Beyond that the trail is cold. It is not even certain that his surname was Ross, though I work under that assumption because I have nothing else to go on.

Some of the Enoch Rosses I find are white and some are black. In another time and place, which is where Enoch eventually found himself, he could have been either. Perhaps he passed for white, or he might just as easily have been among the African-Americans who fled white mobs in Cincinnati to Canada in the 1840s. His descendants could be writing letters to the editor of a local newspaper arguing for slave reparations, or they could be living in a midwestern suburb with a black-faced lawn jockey by the front door. They could be anywhere in between.

Thinking about Enoch as a white man *and* as a black man is a reassuring exercise. It would be simpler for blacks if all their problems could be blamed on white people, and for whites if all their problems could be blamed on blacks, just as it would be simpler for those of settler descent in Liberia if they could blame the tribes for all their troubles, and vice versa. But there are always people with whom one has a kinship among the other groups. There are always connections. The trouble starts when people choose to ignore their affinities, to see others as intrinsically different—as more prone to exploit the weak, perhaps, or to resort to violence. For whatever reasons, people all over the world expend a lot of energy searching for, and then fighting over, common ground. All of this clamoring has taken its toll on Mississippi, but the effects are far more pronounced in Liberia, a place the South begot.

It is the failed connections that my friend Scottie Harmon mentions when he tries to summarize the legacy of Prospect Hill and Mississippi in Africa. "So, they brought them over here from Africa, then they went back to Africa, and now they're trying to come back here," Scottie says. "It sounds like, whatever it is they're looking for, they keep just barely missing it." Another friend reached an even more disheartening conclusion: "So, basically," he said, "the whole colonization experiment was a failure."

For some reason these observations surprised me. I know that many who hear the story will inevitably draw similar conclusions because they seem to be pure and simple truths. Liberia is undeniably a mess. My friend Paul de Pasquale even suggested, half tongue-in-cheek, that the title of this book should be *Mississippi: Role Model for Disaster*. Yet the truth, as Oscar Wilde noted, is rarely pure, and never simple. No one I spoke with who is knowledgeable about Liberia sees the country as a failure. They are saddened or even embarrassed by events of the last two decades, but see the turmoil as similar to periods of unrest in other nations' histories. When I asked John Singler if he considers the colonization a failure, he said, America "basically dumped people there without the tools they needed, so how could it succeed? Yet some of them did succeed. The war really devastated Liberia's self-esteem. They ask, 'What have we done to bring this onto ourselves?' Nora Jones asked me, in 1994, 'What did we do to God?' The U.S. government made a mockery of democracy when they certified Doe's election, knowing it was fraudulent. Reagan sent five-hundred million dollars to the Doe regime. Now the U.S. is looking for reasons to turn their back."

With so many Liberians trying to use their American connections to make their way to the United States, it is tempting to think that the descendants of the slaves who remained at Prospect Hill are better off today than those whose ancestors remained in or emigrated to Liberia. The unintended benefits of American slavery were the subject of an essay written by Booker T. Washington back in 1932, in his book *Selected Speeches*. "Think about it," Washington wrote, "we went into slavery pagans, we came out Christians. We went into slavery pieces of property; we came out American citizens. We went into slavery with chains clanking about our wrists; we came out with the American ballot in our hands. . . . Notwithstanding the cruelty and moral wrong of slavery, we are in a stronger and more hopeful condition, materially, intellectually, morally and religiously, than is true of an equal number of black people in any other portion of the globe."

The idea is contentious, to say the least—particularly in the context of the debate over slave reparations. It is also countered by the desires of people such as Georgia Ross to return to Liberia if the current problems can be solved. Georgia, whose husband Benjamin waits in Monrovia while she works to bring him and their children to Philadelphia, does not believe Liberia is a failure. "It's a temporary situation," she says. "Most would go back if the situation improves." She hopes that her family will eventually be able to return to a Liberia at peace. "As I speak to you on this phone, I would go home," she says. "Nothing is like a home. Things get better in Liberia, I'd be the first to go. People who have been here twenty years, they have a small apartment, they are not able to pay their bills."

She misses the Liberia that existed before the turmoil, and prays that it will return. "I miss the way you always have some help in everything you do, unlike here where you do everything for yourself," she says. "People help each other in Liberia, they care about each other. Generally, it's love. We still have some good things that we cherish. The little we have we try to share. Liberia was formed on Christian principles, and the concern, the care, the love—that is what I miss. Here, you can't afford to call people sometimes. They say they are busy, they can't talk. That never happens in Liberia."

Still, she adds, "I do love America. There is equality here. You can't really be cheated. It's not the same in Liberia. You never get anything if you're not part of the government there, now. Education won't get that for you. If you go to the university in America you are able to get a job. It's not the same in Liberia."

Talking about the current situation is difficult, she says. "I just spoke to my children in Ghana. I talk to them every other week. The situation there is deplorable. I try not to discuss it because it brings depression on me. I just ask God to take care of them."

Before the war, Georgia says, "Liberia had been a peaceful country. It's hard to predict trouble, to predict war. We didn't think about it. The people are now suffering. The tribe-settler problem is still there, but you don't see it as much because we have a recognized government on the ground. When the war struck they used that opportunity to get even, to pay back."

Alton Johnson, who immigrated from Liberia to the United States in 1985 and now teaches at Mississippi's Alcorn State University, sees connections between the respective places everywhere he goes, but they're mostly academic for him now, because he sees himself as an American. Alton lives in Natchez, a city known for its elaborate, columned mansions—emblems of the culture and power of slaveholders. When he first arrived, he says, "I was impressed that there were so many skilled woodworkers and carpenters. I was told it was because of slavery, that the masters had their slaves trained to build the mansions." The architecture was also familiar to him. "Every time I pass these houses," he says, "I think they look like the houses back home."

Though he is descended from Liberia's indigenous groups, Alton's father was a ward of a family of slave descendants and ultimately took their name, which gave him access to both cultures. Returning to the source of one of those cultures has further broadened his view.

"Folks who were descendants of slaves, their forefathers, they help the master in the house, they cook for him, they wash his clothes, they take out the chamber bucket," he says, describing the lives of house slaves in antebellum Mississippi. "This is the same lifestyle back home [in Liberia]. They learn that way of life, so they treated the indigenous people that way. So there was a rift. It was the same arrangement like here in slavery days, but not with bad intentions. That was the only way of life they knew here. The indigenous sons and daughters were interested in getting an education, so people like my father lived with the people like the Johnsons, took their name and went to school."

He notes that Mississippi and Liberia have gotten their share of bad publicity, much of it deserved, but says he does not believe Liberians are more violent than people elsewhere, or that Mississippians are more racist. On the contrary, he says, "Liberians are very hospitable. You're riding a bus, you give a lady your seat. You don't do that here. People in the South are generally hospitable compared to people in the North—here in the South everybody speaks. Maybe it's just a little shake of the head, but they do it. They say 'sir' and 'ma'am.' You don't do that a lot in the North. In Liberia it's a different type of hospitality. People take you into their home, they give you something to eat. They share what they have."

Likewise, he says, he has never personally encountered racism in Mississippi "as such." The reason, he says, is "if it occurs, I ignore it. I think Mississippi gets a bad rap a lot. I've encountered that in Alabama, you see it in Arkansas. If you go to Maryland you see a lot more. I have not heard about the Ku Klux Klan marching in Mississippi, but I've seen them march in Arkansas. Their headquarters is in Missouri. Louisiana to me is scarier than Mississippi, but because Mississippi was the last state in the union to undo the racism it has a bad rap.

"The racism that I see here is different, it's more subtle. My son and your daughter go to the same school as the white kids, and every little village you go to in Mississippi you see one white house, one black house, all in the same place, which you don't see everywhere in America. We can go to the same school, we can have a fish fry together, but we can't go dancing together. Racism is not blunt like it used to be. It gets into academia—we will do work together as professionals, you praise me, but if I want a job in your department you don't want me. I don't let it bother me because I know people want their kind. It's human nature. Once you get an education nobody can take that away from you, you don't have to prove anything to anybody, and one day people will forget. I've had people who apologize to me. They're old, they realize what happened here was bad. So I just live my life."

Though he is now a U.S. citizen, Alton says he does not encourage Liberians to try to immigrate to the United States, particularly if they have no means of support. Neither does he plan to return to Liberia. For him that connection has been broken.

"If a person like me went back they'd say I was taking their job," he says. "When I was leaving Liberia fifteen years ago, the guys carrying weapons of destruction were boys of five or ten; now they are older and I'm a threat to their society. I don't really think a lot about that country now. I don't go to places I'm not invited. I may go there in the

long run, but I will have to work for an international organization—the
USDA [U.S. Department of Agriculture] or something. I'm not going
to go there as a Liberian."

As we discuss the historical ties between Liberia and the American
South, he mentions the Mississippi state flag, which has brought so
many old prejudices to the fore, and I tell him about the similar controversy brewing in Liberia over its national flag, which some of ethnic
descent want to change. Even Liberia's motto, "The love of liberty
brought us here" is considered an affront by some of native descent.

"I don't see any problem with the flag over there," he says. "That's
how it was, how the country was established, period. I've heard about
the motto, and some people say it would be better if they changed it
to, 'The love of liberty brought us together.' I have no problem with
that. But changing the flag itself—are we going to go back and redo independence? There are eleven stripes for the eleven signers of the
Declaration of Independence, there is the lone star on a dark background representing the only republic, the first republic, in the dark
continent of Africa. If you look at what's happening here, one of the
things that made the Mississippi flag look bad is people using it for
something different, using it for a sign of hate. That's what they've
been doing with the rebel flag. People have abused the flag, using it to
show hatred. It is heritage, and people should keep that. It should be
remembered and put in a very good place. Life goes on. It's time to
start improving relationships."

Many hoped the vote on changing the state flag would present
an opportunity to put Mississippi's divisive history behind, but the
prospects of that happening looked slim even before the votes
were tallied. Prior to the special election, every other editorial in *The
Clarion-Ledger*, it seemed, was written by a sixth-generation Mississippian descended from someone who fought in the Civil War.
Surprisingly, many supported changing the flag, as a gesture of reconciliation, but more expressed their conviction that it was time to stop
giving in to the demands of blacks.

On the other end of the spectrum was Kenneth Stokes, a Jackson
city council member who was vehement in his opposition to the existing flag, and publicly vented his anger after other council members
proposed an ordinance regulating the naming of streets and bridges in
Jackson. Stokes said the ordinance effort was racist, since he had ear-

lier named three bridges for black ministers, and warned that if the regulation was put in place he would research every street name in the capital and, "If any end up after slave owners, we might have to change those names." Notably, the city of Jackson was itself named after a slave owner, President Andrew Jackson, who was in office when the state joined the Union. In fact, the vast majority of American presidents prior to the Civil War owned slaves.

There is certainly no shortage of wedges to drive between people. Some of the pro-flag editorialists fretted that if the flag was changed there would be no end to the cleansing—that place names would indeed be changed and that the ubiquitous statues of Confederate soldiers on the state's courthouse squares would inevitably be removed. In one letter to *The Clarion-Ledger*, a man wrote, "How far do you go to appease a group that suddenly decided that our heritage offends them? You think destroying the flag will stop their ruthless attack on us?"

For supporters of the flag, the effort to change it was rooted in expediency or a desire for retribution. But for those who fought tooth and nail for racial equality, the flag represented a blatant reminder that in some people's minds black Mississippians are still to be treated, essentially, as uninvited guests in their own home.

On April 17, 2001, statewide voters opted to keep the existing banner, Confederate emblem and all. Jefferson and Claiborne counties were among only four which voted overwhelmingly to replace it. The day of the vote the national media swarmed over Jackson in search of sound bites representing the extremes, and in one curious aside, a group of reporters and cameramen crowded around a black man who sat on a bench at a bus stop, draped with a rebel flag. Meanwhile, white children waved from the backs of pickups decorated with state and Confederate flags as they rolled past the capitol. I found myself wishing that blacks would start waving the Confederate flag themselves, so that they could co-opt the symbol and make the whole thing just go away. But that would be a bold maneuver, and in truth I am not sure that everyone wants this issue to go away.

If there were not ample evidence in the historical record, Mississippi's contemporary life is filled with reminders that slavery and its aftermath were devastating, and that the wounds have been slow to heal. The toxic residue includes widespread poverty, political divisiveness, and crime. Mississippi is today the poorest state in the nation, and Jackson, the capital, with a population of less than 200,000, was listed in the top ten highest-crime cities in the United States in 2002. In such an unstable environment, it is possible to forget about race, but not for long. The same is true for the settler-tribe division in Liberia. Both places are struggling to extricate themselves from the legacy of conflict that drove the story of Prospect Hill, and unfortunately nothing can ameliorate the evil of slavery and oppression, which started all the trouble in both places. Such longstanding conflicts are rarely resolved. Both historical and contemporary news accounts make clear that even if the source of trouble goes away on its own, memory lingers and by nature tends to preserve and even magnify the thing that gave it life.

Two weeks after I left Monrovia, the situation in Liberia began to deteriorate. First, four Liberian journalists were arrested and charged with espionage. Their crime: publishing an article critical of the Taylor regime's spending policies.

The Liberian government simultaneously shut down Monrovia's four independent newspapers, allegedly for delinquent taxes. *The Perspective*, the Liberian expatriate periodical, reported that the arrests followed the publication of an article in *The News*, a Monrovia newspaper, titled "U.S. $50,000 Spent on Helicopters," which challenged government spending on repairs to helicopters and an additional $23,000 U.S. on Christmas cards and souvenirs. The article noted that the expenditures were made at a time when the John F. Kennedy hospital had been forced to close due to lack of funds, and alleged that the arrests and shutdowns were designed to repress the independent media in Liberia.

"The prevalent view expressed is that in the midst of the discussion of sanctions and scrutiny, the Liberian Government is paranoid about views emanating out of the country that could challenge its propaganda campaign," *The Perspective* asserted.

The arrests disproved my theory that journalists would likely be immune from government harassment while the sanctions were pending. To make matters worse, the journalists faced the possibility of execution under Liberian law.

Two weeks later, the United Nations imposed partial economic sanctions on Liberia. The UN Security Council voted unanimously for a resolution which reimposed an arms embargo first used during Liberia's civil war. In May 2001 the council also imposed a diamond embargo and travel ban on top Liberian officials after concluding that the government was still backing the rebels of Sierra Leone's Revolutionary United Front, who had violated a peace deal and reignited that country's nine-year conflict in May 2000 by taking 500 UN peacekeepers hostage. Liberian timber exports, the subject of increasing concern by international environmental groups, which were also linked with the arms trade, were exempted from the trade ban at the insistence of France, a major importer of the commodity.

The Washington Post foreign service reported that Taylor had expanded his timber harvests into the virgin forests of Sapo National Park, and had received several million dollars from the Oriental Timber Company, based in Hong Kong, which, according to UN reports, he had used to buy weapons. "Sources with direct knowledge of Taylor's arms shipments, whose information was confirmed by intelligence sources in West Africa, said most weapons were coming to Liberia by sea, primarily in logging ships, because such shipments are much more difficult to monitor and detect than air shipments," the newspaper reported. According to internal OTC documents obtained by the newspaper, ships chartered by the company had on three occasions in the fall of 2001 delivered weapons to Taylor at the Liberian port of Buchanan, including 7,000 boxes of ammunition for AK-47 assault rifles, 5,000 rocket-propelled grenades, 300 howitzer shells, and tons of other equipment. An additional thirty tons of weapons reportedly arrived in mid-January 2002.

When I e-mailed Sarah Morrison at the U.S. Information Service to ask about the sanctions and the journalists' arrests, she wrote back to say that the guards at the Monrovia prison "call me by name these days, I've been there so often." Reactions to the sanctions were mixed, she wrote, but most people considered them fairly tame and assumed Taylor would manage to work around them. "The arrest of the journalists as the vote was imminent shows he really doesn't care," she wrote. "There are many angry people out there, and the numbers are growing. . . ."

Several international Liberian groups, including the West African Journalists Association, the Writers in Prison Committee of International PEN, and Reporters Sans Frontieres, called for the journalists' release, but there seemed to be less international outrage than there had been over the arrest of the British film crew in August 2000. The American media paid scant notice to the story.

The journalists' arrests prompted students and faculty at the University of Liberia to organize a rally to raise money for their legal fees, and the government responded by storming the campus with police on March 21, 2001. The police allegedly flogged numerous participants and arrested others, and some students claimed that several female students had been raped by security forces after the rally. The University Student Union reported that fifteen students were detained at the executive mansion and feared dead, according to an article by the Panafrican News Agency, though *The Perspective* later reported the students had fled to a refugee camp in Ghana. The Panafrican agency reported that James Verdier, director of the Monrovia-based Catholic Justice and Peace Commission, claimed to have had his life threatened for offering free legal services to the jailed journalists. The article noted that Verdier's predecessor had fled Liberia following a similar death threat.

In late March 2001 the journalists were finally released, after issuing apologies for the offending story, but a few days later, Milton Teahjay, former deputy information minister and Taylor's personal media consultant, disappeared. Teahjay had been outspoken in his opposition to the logging of old growth forests in Sinoe County, and was presumed to have been executed, according to *The Perspective*, which noted that he had been "sacked for 'acts inimical to the security of the State,' and arrested while trying to leave the country." The Liberian government originally confirmed Teahjay's arrest, then changed its story and denied that he was being held. The pro-government newspaper the *Monrovia Guardian* claimed that Teahjay was actually in hiding at the U.S. embassy, although Sarah Morrison told the newspaper the claim was "unfortunate and certainly not true."

Subsequent developments underscored the deteriorating situation that summer. On June 17, a U.S. diplomat, Sgt. James Michael Newton, was shot after refusing to stop at a checkpoint on the outskirts of Monrovia. Newton, the assistant military attaché at the U.S. embassy, was evacuated to the Ivory Coast for treatment of his wounds. During the same period, a ship of Liberian refugees was reported to be wandering the coast of West Africa while its captain searched for a country that would allow him to dock. The ship, with about 170 passengers, most of whom were children, had been turned away from numerous ports due to rumors that it was a slave transport. As with so much of the news out of Liberia, the details of the situation were difficult to discern.

In June 2002 another Liberian journalist, Hassan Bility, editor of Monrovia's *The Analyst* newspaper, was arrested and charged with collaborating with the rebel group Liberians United for Reconciliation and Democracy (LURD). Taylor claimed that Bility was an illegal combatant, and said he would not turn him over to the country's civil courts but would try him before a military tribunal. According to the international Committee to Protect Journalists, Taylor's government had ransacked the offices of *The Analyst* in April 2002 and closed it down on two occasions.

Meanwhile, the BBC News reported that fighting in northern Liberia had sent tens of thousands of civilians fleeing from the area, and that the conflict had moved to within 200 kilometers of Monrovia. Foreign aid workers, according to the article, "said Liberia was now facing a new and highly volatile situation."

The Liberian government responded to the bad news by imposing new restrictions on foreign journalists and diplomats, prohibiting them from traveling outside the city limits of Monrovia and from moving about the city after 8:30 P.M. Journalists were also required to give seventy-two-hour notice before arriving in the country, and a twenty-four-hour waiting period was imposed before accreditation could be granted. According to a Ministry of Information news release, "These guidelines are intended to minimize the impact of anti-government propaganda that is currently being orchestrated by a select number of foreign journalists and news organizations." The release referred to a recent *Newsweek* magazine article which portrayed President Taylor in a negative light.

I became increasingly anxious as I read of these developments, wondering if any of my Liberian friends had been caught up in them. I realized that I had managed to slip in and out of Liberia during a brief period of relative calm, and my own good fortune only emphasized the need to help the Railey brothers get out.

✳   ✳   ✳

Soon after the government takeover of the university campus, I get a phone call from Edward. His voice sounds urgent. He wants to know if I've had any luck finding a way for him and his brothers to immigrate to the United States.

Unfortunately, I have not. U.S. Immigration officials are clearly not inclined to grant visas to young men who have no obvious reason to go home, and none of the universities I check with offer scholarships for anyone other than U.S. citizens. The Methodist church offers a small stipend for international theology students, but the cap of $1,000 per year is far too little to satisfy Immigration's demands for proof of financial support. I have sent letters of invitation to Edward through the U.S. consulate in Monrovia, and have asked my congressional delegation to intervene, to no avail. An aide to U.S. senator Thad Cochran seemed sympathetic, but said it was not possible for the senator to influence the visa process, and insisted that the denial of Edward's visa had had nothing to do with his being African. My congressional representative, U.S. representative Bennie Thompson, did not return my phone calls. So I do not have good news for Edward. But I am glad to know he and his family are safe. I also get a call from John Singler, who tells me that he has heard from the student activist who acted as my fixer in Liberia and that he is safe as well.

Around the same time, I start getting numerous poignant letters and collect phone calls from other people whom I had met in Liberia, asking for money or help in immigrating to the United States. I now understand why I was warned not to give out my phone number in Liberia. I refuse the calls.

The Railey brothers call now and then to check on my progress with the immigration effort, and I am torn between wanting to give them hope and not wanting to set them up for disappointment. Like millions of refugees across the world, they yearn for what America has, and while it is easy to become enervated by so much global suffering, and to turn away, it is not so easy when you know the sufferers, their history, and their faces. I find myself wondering how their lives might have been had their ancestors not been freed, had they not chosen the dangerous path to freedom when it was first made available to them. But all I can really do for them is wire money for emergencies, which always seem to be developing.

Their calls become more frequent as the situation in Liberia worsens. On September 11, 2001, they call to see if I have lost anyone in the terrorist attacks, and Edward, for the first time, sounds despondent. He knows that his chances of getting a visa have evaporated for now, particularly after the allegations surface that the Liberian gold trade—in which American televangelist Pat Robertson is involved—and the illicit diamond trade are helping fund the al Qaeda terrorist network.

More driven than ever to raise the money which alone might improve his chances of escape, or, at least, of enduring increasingly unstable circumstances, Edward calls to ask me to wire him money so that he might travel into the bush to buy gold at the mines near the border with Guinea, to resell at a profit in Monrovia.

"It is very bad now," he says, not knowing that it will soon get much worse.

The gold idea proves worse than fruitless. On his trip to the mines Edward is caught in the fighting and forced to flee into the bush and hide for three weeks, during which he contracts malaria. The next call I get is from Kaiser, asking for money to pay for Edward's hospitalization and recovery. Edward has been lucky to be admitted to the Catholic clinic, but he still has to pay before receiving treatment.

The brothers call a few times after that, to tell me that Edward is recovering, to wish me Happy New Year, to send greetings from their mother, "the Old Ma," and their sister, Princess. But the next time Kaiser calls, I hear only muffled voices speaking in the background. I say hello several times, get no reply, and hang up. He does not call back.

A few days later comes bad news over the wire about the fighting between LURD and the president's security forces. Taylor has declared a state of emergency and begun forcibly rounding up young men and boys from churches and the few still-functioning schools, taking them to detention centers to prepare them to fight. There is a terrifying precedent for the practice: the roundups during the civil war of Taylor's notorious "small boys unit"—some as young as elementary school age, whose parents had been killed by the fighting, who were drugged and armed with automatic weapons to fight for the rebels.

When LURD fighters come to within twenty-five miles of Monrovia, the United Nations begins evacuating nonessential personnel, and people begin fleeing into and out of the capital. Some observers claim Taylor is staging the fight to draw international sympathy—raising alarums and excursions, in effect, to prompt the United Nations to lift the sanctions imposed upon Liberia. Whether Taylor is posturing is immaterial to the Raileys. What matters is that the atmosphere is again turning lethal.

"The Old Ma wants us to leave and go to Ghana, to the refugee camp," Kaiser says during his next call. "They are hunting people here left and right, especially young boys. We are mostly staying indoors. The Old Ma wants us to go, but it is costly. We've been thinking of you a whole lot."

I have no doubt about that. I realize that from the Raileys' perspective, I am no longer just reporting on the story, I am a part of it.

The brothers are now determined to flee, to become refugees. I wire them money for passports, but they also need money to make the overland trek to the refugee camps in Ghana, to buy food, bribe soldiers, pay for rides, do whatever is necessary to increase a refugee's odds. It is endless. A few days later, as they are preparing to go, Augustus calls to again express his hope that by becoming refugees they will be admitted to the United States. "We pray to be there for the launching of your book," he says, echoing the brothers' familiar refrain.

I imagine many reasons for their anticipation over the publication of this book—that it might bring them attention, good or bad, or that I might grow richer than they imagined me to already be, and feel inclined to share the wealth.

After Augustus calls I do not hear from the brothers for several days. All I know is that they are planning to strike out for Ghana. I e-mail their aunt, Annie Demen, who has a job at the United Nations in Monrovia, but she replies, "I have not heard from my nephews for some time now. Yes, it is true that young men are being picked up to fight, and some times relatives have to pay large sum of money before they are released. I will try to find them over the week end by God's grace as we are living on a day by day basis in Liberia now." In the next e-mail, she says she has still not located them.

A week passes, and finally the brothers reach me on an Internet phone. All I can hear are a few syllables now and then, but they manage to give me a number at a nearby house before the line goes dead. When I phone the house they are all there, and take turns talking. There is good and bad news: On the way to Ghana, Edward came down with typhoid, which he had also likely contracted while hiding in the bush. He became extremely ill, and his brothers had taken him to a Liberian National Red Cross clinic, where he was treated. By the time he was well enough to travel again, the fighting between LURD and Taylor's security forces had ended.

On the phone, Edward sounds like a very tired, old man.

"It's unfortunate the sickness will not leave me alone," he says, but adds that the medication seems to be working. Referring to the fighting, he says, "Things have subsided. It's some, but small. So we shall see. We are walking freely now in Monrovia."

I ask what he plans to do next. He thinks for a moment. "For most people leaving now, they are going to a church conference," he says. "They get an invitation from a church in America. I hope to get such an invitation, because everybody at the clinic is dying of typhoid. We pray that we will be together like we were before, in Liberia."

Sounding winded, he puts Kaiser on the line, who again asks when the book will be published. "We pray one of us will be there," he says.

The now-familiar ritual becomes more frequent in the coming months: the phone ringing at three A.M., the operator asking if I will accept a collect call from Kaiser in Liberia, his voice saying, "So, Alan, how is life? We pray that you are keeping well." No matter how much I remind them, the Raileys almost never take into account the six-hour time difference between Liberia and Mississippi, because if they find themselves near a phone they feel compelled to call. Sometimes when they reach me they come close to reproaching me for not being home to receive earlier calls. At my urging they eventually set up a free e-mail account, and although Monrovia's few Internet cafés are crowded and plagued by technical problems, this at least proves a more reliable method of communication, for a while. Usually their messages include further requests for money. Sometimes I hold back, as when Princess asks for money for a new dress to wear at her coronation as queen of her Methodist church conference. I do not have the means to fulfill every need of an extended family living in a destitute country. But my resolve never lasts long. In a subsequent e-mail Edward informs me that the consulate at the American embassy has been closed, and weary Liberians seeking visas to the United States now have to travel to Abidjan, in the Ivory Coast, to apply and, in all likelihood, be rejected.

In August, Edward writes, "Please be inform that things are not fine with us." Because of the recent serious illnesses of his mother and

Prince, the family has used up their cash reserves and without another infusion, will in a matter of days be evicted from the house that provided their final sanctuary during the war.

Meanwhile, the Ivory Coast, where he had been directed to apply again for his visa, is erupting in civil war.

There seems to be no real hope of improvement in the coming months, and for whatever reason the Raileys cease using their e-mail account. Their calls become more frequent, and more persistent. When the phone rings in the wee hours I know it is them. If I do not answer, they call again a few minutes later. Sometimes I am curt, asking why they do not e-mail me instead. They do not know what to make of my behavior. Once, when Edward calls, collect, and wakes me, he says he's been robbed, and has a number for me to avoid the high collect call charge. I say, "No, Edward, you must e-mail me. The money can be put to better use than long-distance charges. There's only so much of it, anyway. I'll wire some money, but e-mail me."

"Okay, I do that when I leave here," he says. "Good-bye."

I feel sorry immediately, because he sounds chastened by my impatience. I get no e-mail from him.

In April 2003 Artemus Gaye—one of the descendants of Prince Ibrahima—organized a small "freedom festival" in Natchez to commemorate the 175th anniversary of Ibrahima's release from slavery and emigration to Liberia. The Associated Press reported that a group of academics, together with descendants of Ibrahima, his master, and his liberators, gathered in Natchez to reenact the tale. The city government embraced the occasion by placing a portrait of the prince on the cover of a tourist brochure promoting African-American heritage sites.

Barry Boubacar, a Guinea native and visiting professor of African Studies at New York University, told the AP that hearing Ibrahima's story strengthened the connection in his own mind between American slavery and African history. "It's always been considered a separate history," Boubacar said. "It's one history."

This was a comparatively minor news event in the context of all that has happened and continues to happen in the interwoven histories of Mississippi and Liberia, yet it seemed to hint at a telling shift in public perception. There is a lot of give-and-take in those histories, a lot of back and forth, just as there are innumerable crosscurrents and conflicting personal and political views and motivations. But there is no denying that they are connected.

But as Artemus was staging his festival in Natchez, Liberia once again began degenerating into civil war. Complicating matters this time were reports that al Qaeda has capitalized upon the nation's economic anarchy to fund its global terrorist efforts—a detail often overlooked in media editorials that cautioned against any U.S. intervention in Liberia's strife.

As early as November 2001, *The Washington Post's* Douglas Farah reported on a European military intelligence investigation which claimed that the Taylor government had recently hosted senior al Qaeda operatives who oversaw a \$20 million Liberian diamond-buying spree and briefly cornered the market on the precious stones. The proceeds of the diamond sale were said to have been earmarked to buy assault rifles, ammunition, rocket-propelled grenades, and missiles from the Nicaraguan army for use by Liberian forces. Then, in December 2002, Farah reported that Taylor, who denies any involvement with al Qaeda, allegedly received one million U.S. dollars for assisting the operatives, some of whom had hidden out at a Liberian military camp for two months following the September 11 attacks in New York City and Washington, D.C.

The diamond-buying operation was said to have been a response to U.S. efforts to freeze al Qaeda assets after the attacks, and the *Post* reported that three of the senior operatives who were said to have supervised the deal—Abdullah Ahmed Abdullah, Ahmed Khalfan Ghailani, and Fazul Abdullah Mohammed—were on the FBI's most-wanted list for their role in al Qaeda attacks on U.S. embassies in Tanzania and Kenya. Abdullah was also believed to be al Qaeda's chief financial officer. The article noted that in the months following the September 11 attacks, the Pentagon had prepared a Special Forces team in neighboring Guinea to catch two of the men while they were in Liberia, but that logistical problems had prevented the mission from being carried out.

Equally alarming was a revelation in another *Post* article that U.S. intelligence sources were concerned that al Qaeda might be planning to undertake terrorist attacks at sea using mother ships flying so-called "flags of convenience," which offer registration under hidden ownership. Notably, Liberia is one of the leading suppliers of flags of convenience in the world.

Taylor has become an international pariah for his role in Liberia's turmoil and for the destabilization of West Africa, but as the *Post* reports indicate, there is an even broader context to the threat his government poses. Al Qaeda's involvement illustrates the danger of allowing the kind of turmoil that has gripped Liberia to go unchecked. In the absence of a workable connection with the United States, Taylor has begun forging dangerous alliances elsewhere.

Among the people who were allegedly involved in the al Qaeda scheme were Lebanese diamond merchants, Israeli and Russian arms dealers, Libyan security forces, and Senegalese and South African mercenaries. Their activities reportedly have included visits or communications with contacts in Afghanistan, Bulgaria, Belgium, Burkina Faso, Iran, Iraq, the Ivory Coast, Nicaragua, Panama, Pakistan, and Sierra Leone. David Crane, the American prosecutor for the special court, told Farah in June 2002 that Taylor "is not just a regional troublemaker; he is a player in the world of terror and what he does affects lives in the United States and Europe."

Following an expansion of the United Nation's economic sanctions against Liberia, in May 2003, Taylor was said to be increasingly desperate for money and arms to fight rebel insurgencies near the country's borders with Guinea and the Ivory Coast. The head of Sierra Leone's international war crimes tribunal meanwhile hinted that Taylor might be indicted for his role in that country's civil war in the 1990s, and specifically for his alleged involvement in the assassination of a fugitive from the UN-backed court. In an article in the Monrovia *News*, Liberian senator Thomas Nah Nimely responded by saying that any effort to arrest Taylor by the special court would result in a "full scale regional war." On May 22 the U.S. State Department advised Americans in Liberia to leave.

Farah wrote that the situation within Liberia had become so dire that it was unclear if Taylor's ouster would even help. According to intelligence sources Farah cited, the rebel force Liberians United for Reconciliation and Democracy, fighting near the Guinean border, were "a motley assortment of some of the worst elements who fought in Liberia's civil war both for and against Taylor." The rebels, he added, "have offered no program for governance, no ideology and no political vision beyond getting rid of Taylor," and were said to be "as likely to prey on the civilian population as Taylor's notorious government forces."

After another front broke out in eastern Liberia in April, relief organizations designated eleven of the nation's fifteen counties war zones. In May, attacks upon aid workers halted the delivery of food and other humanitarian assistance to hundreds of thousands of refugees, according to an article in *The New York Times*. "Over the last two months, armed groups have attacked these camps at the most opportune times—the very days on which the United Nations and private groups deliver aid," the newspaper reported. On such days, armed groups looted sacks of rice, flour, and other essentials, stole cell phones and trucks, forced aid workers to act as beasts of burden, and set fire to refugee huts—sometimes with people inside. "You falling down, you keep going, you hear bullets raining," one aid worker was quoted saying, after he had been forced to carry sacks of supplies on his head during a six-day journey through the bush. "They talk about killing you like it was nothing."

By then more than 300,000 Liberians had fled the country and 2.7 million had been displaced.

In May the worst of the fighting was centered around Greenville, the seat of old Mississippi in Africa, which had also been ravaged during the civil war of the 1990s. A group called the Movement for Democracy in Liberia had seized the city and its port, and all shipping had ceased after a Liberian navy gunboat began shelling the rebel positions. About fifty of Taylor's troops had fled the MODEL rebels by reportedly commandeering a Croatian ship in nearby Harper, which they had sailed to Monrovia with an estimated 1,000 refugees aboard. At a May 16 press conference in New York, a UN official told reporters that unless the situation stabilized, the fighting would soon engulf Monrovia, where an estimated 500,000 refugees were squatting in shantytowns on the outskirts of the city.

These were certainly alarming developments, with the potential to grow much worse, and I found myself wondering about Peter Roberts Toe, who had met me at the Monrovia airport, had looked after me for several days in the city, and was to have hosted me at his home in Greenville. Among the people I met while researching this story, none was more generous or determined than Peter. If he sought to dominate anything, it was adversity—the seemingly endless series of events which had threatened to undo not just him but his family and a widening circle of dependent friends. He was one of the few Liberians I met who never mentioned a desire to emigrate to the United States, and I felt a strong personal connection. He gave the continuing story of Mississippi in Africa a clear and personal focus.

In late May I received word from Peter via a mutual friend's e-mail account.

"The ongoing rebel war in Liberia has forced us to escape from Greenville for safety," he wrote. "My family and I are presently squatting in Monrovia—the only relatively safe place in Liberia. News reaching us from Greenville indicates that my house is burnt down to ashes.

"I am presently efforting to erect a structure to accommodate my family, which includes my wife and a dozen children (my natural children and others I have adopted). I am desperately in need of assistance presently. I would very highly appreciate any assistance you could render in this respect."

He signed the message, "Hopefully, Peter Robert Toe."

I got no immediate response to my e-mail reply, which was not unusual considering Peter's circumstances. Though he was clearly desperate for money, getting to an Internet café would be a challenge, and no doubt responding to e-mails is far down the list of priorities for someone who has a dozen people dependent upon them for survival.

After a few days I call our mutual friend John Singler and ask if he knows how to get in touch with Peter. He says Peter now has a cell phone, surprisingly, though the service is unreliable, and that he seems to be holding up well, even if his continuing travails are beginning to take their toll. He gives me Peter's number, and after several tries, I get him on the phone. He sounds more cheerful than I expect, and far more than I would, were I in his shoes.

"Hello, Alan, how are you?" he says. "I pray you're keeping well."

"Everything's fine here," I say. "I'm glad to hear you're safe."

"Yes, yes," he says.

The connection is bad, and it is difficult to understand some of what he says, but he manages to tell me that the Raileys and our friend the student activist are okay. I then ask about the situation in Greenville.

"The rebels are just killing people, burning down the houses," he says. "But I made it here with all my children. Everybody's here." The family is squatting in an area known as New Kru Town, he says, and he needs money for materials to erect a temporary shelter.

Then the phone goes dead. It takes several tries to get through again, so we cut to the chase. We make arrangements for a money transfer through Western Union. He promises to keep in touch, and then he's gone.

I phone Western Union. The operator takes the necessary information, then says I am required to give Peter a security code, and to pose a question for him to answer in order to claim the cash. These are safeguards, she says, to ensure that he is the rightful recipient.

For some reason I am stumped. What sort of question? It is a simple task, but so many questions are bouncing around in my head that I can't think of a logical one to pose. *Why is this happening? When will it end?*

"I'm thinking," I tell the operator. "For some reason I can't think of a good question."

"It just needs to be a simple question," she says, "like, 'Where is the sender from?'"

"Okay," I say. "'Where is the sender from?'"

I call Peter back, give him the code and the question. When I say, "The answer is—" he starts to laugh.

"The answer," he says, "is *'Mississippi'*!"

"Right," I say. We both laugh this time. It is obvious, of course. Mississippi is where I am from. It is where Peter is from. If there could be only one word for us to communicate between our respective worlds, to link us together, we both know what it would be. It would be "Mississippi."

It is the word that links our parallel universes, that connects a maverick veteran of the American Revolution to thousands of nameless refugees now fleeing their homes in Liberia. It forms the common ground between a retired schoolteacher in McComb and one very determined Monrovia banker who yearns for a better life, half a world away.

AFTERWORD

IN JUNE 2003 the fighting between LURD rebels and Charles Taylor's forces swept into Monrovia, killing hundreds of civilians and endangering an estimated 97,000 refugees huddled around the city, including 18,000 living in one high school without electricity or running water.

French military helicopters and a French warship had earlier evacuated about 500 trapped foreign nationals, including many Americans and Red Cross and UN staff. Soon England, France, UN Secretary-General Kofi Annan, and several African heads of state called on President Bush to deploy American troops as part of a proposed peacekeeping force in Liberia. Cameroon's UN ambassador, Martin Chungong Ayafor, said America should intervene in Liberia because, "It's their baby, and they have a responsibility there."

During the worst of the fighting, U.S. embassy officials opened the gates to a residential compound to allow thousands of Liberians to reach shelter from the shells, bullets, and rockets that were crisscrossing the city. Hours later, artillery rounds fell within the compound, killing at least nine and injuring eighty.

Journalist Sebastian Junger, who was in Monrovia researching an article for *Vanity Fair*, was at the compound when the refugees flooded in and the artillery rounds began to fall, and later said he believed the rounds came from Taylor's forces and were aimed at the refugees. He and photographer Teun Voeten soon found themselves helping carry the injured to a clinic operated by the international group Doctors Without Borders.

Sebastian also encountered a shootout between police and Taylor's forces over "looting rights" to one sector of town. He said that because the forces have not been paid in two years, looting was considered an acceptable form of reimbursement for their services. Even the refugees' shantytowns were looted, though there was next to nothing there to steal. I received word from John Singler that the National Museum had not been looted this time around, although the building supplies Peter Toe had bought to build his shelter were.

Pro-American sentiment was evident in the streets of the city, from civilians who begged for U.S. intervention and from soldiers who wore do-rags fashioned out of American flags or who dressed in a style reminiscent of U.S. Marines. But Sebastian reported encountering anti-American feelings as well, both from crowds angry that the United States had not come to Liberia's aid and from pro-Taylor forces. After being accused of spying, Sebastian and Teun left Monrovia for the airport aboard an armed diplomatic convoy escorted by local militia that had been hired by the American embassy, but which still was harassed at numerous armed checkpoints along the way. At one point, he said, soldiers thrust bayonets through the open windows of the vehicles and demanded to know if anyone inside was American. He wisely kept his mouth shut.

By that point, with the capital surrounded by rebel forces, and with a war crimes indictment hanging over his head, Taylor found himself backed into a corner. He began making offers in order to save himself, most of which he reneged upon. He agreed to a cease-fire, then backtracked; he offered to step down, then said he would do so only if the UN war crimes indictment was scrapped.

On July 4, 2003, President Bush acknowledged that America has a "unique history" with Liberia, and national security advisor Condoleezza Rice noted the terrorist attacks of September 11, 2001, had shown that "failed states" can spawn "so much instability that you start to see greater sources of terrorism." But Bush insisted that U.S. forces would enter the fray only if Charles Taylor resigned, and Taylor insisted that he would resign only after U.S. peacekeeping forces were in place. Cholera and starvation meanwhile spread through the refugee quarters.

Bush subsequently embarked on a visit to several African nations (not including Liberia) that was originally planned as a feel-good media event, but which was dominated by international calls for U.S. intervention in Liberia. When a small contingent of U.S. military experts arrived in Monrovia on July 8 to determine the lay of the land, thousands of starving refugees who were packed into the city's soccer stadium began singing hymns, waving American flags, and chanting "USA, USA." Within a month, Taylor had accepted an offer of sanctuary in Nigeria and was gone. The next chapter in Liberia's history had begun.

* * *

AT THE TIME of this writing, more than a year after Charles Taylor's flight from Liberia, a tenuous peace holds—the result of the combined efforts of African peacekeeping organizations; the UN; and the determined, war-weary Liberian people. Even after fleeing the country for Nigeria, Taylor continued to exert a destabilizing influence over West Africa, according to the presidents of Guinea and the Ivory Coast, who in May 2004 called on a special UN-backed war-crimes court in neighboring Sierra Leone to proceed with his prosecution. Although Taylor had been indicted by the tribunal for providing Sierra Leone rebels with arms in exchange for diamonds, he had so far refused to leave Nigeria and the Nigerian government had made no move to hand him over. The stalemate prompted Liberia's Catholic archbishop, Michael Francis, to call for the creation of a separate war-crimes tribunal in Liberia. The consensus seemed to be that as long as Taylor was waiting in the wings, peace would be a tentative state in West Africa.

The Raileys and Reverend Bailey struggle to get back on their feet, and Peter Toe, who returned to Greenville to find that his home had not been burned as had been previously reported, has resumed his medical practice. The student activist is helping organize a new national political movement. J. J. Ross High School has reopened its doors, as has the National Museum, whose small collection was preserved by a single man who kept the artifacts and paintings in a room across the street—at great risk to himself—as bombs fell on the area and the building itself was looted for the sixth or seventh time.

On the other side of the Atlantic, the only living link to the immigrants from Prospect Hill, Nathan Ross Sr., died. No one in his family has been able to tell me whether Benjamin Ross made the crossing from Liberia to the United States, and his wife Georgia's phone has been disconnected. As Mississippi continues to grapple with its own difficult history, the story of Liberia's tumult, along with its sidebars linking it to the United States, have quickly slipped from the front pages. A year later, from the American vantage point, it is almost as if it never happened at all.

Bolton, Mississippi
August 2004

AUTHOR'S NOTE

DURING MY RESEARCH INTO the story of the two Mississippis, I worked under the assumption that if I read everything I could find, listened to what everyone had to say, and saw as much as possible with my own eyes, the true story of Prospect Hill and Mississppi in Africa would eventually make itself known. Each time I thought it had, someone new sprang forth with new information that cast much of what I had previously heard into doubt. In some cases, firm conclusions proved elusive, because history is malleable, and it is still unfolding. But more information is better than less. The fact that there are conflicting versions does not alone make the story less true or whole.

Considering that the story of Prospect Hill and Mississippi in Africa unfolds against a backdrop that includes slavery, oppression, and war, it is not surprising that accounts and perspectives differ. What is surprising is how much goodwill can be found amid all the suffering—often, from unexpected sources. Isaac Ross was the most obvious benefactor, yet there is no discounting the monetary aid that Isaac Ross Wade sent to Liberia for a time, even after having fought tooth and nail against the freedom of the Prospect Hill emigrants, nor of the freed slaves and their descendants taking in less fortunate tribal family members out of a desire to help rather than exploit, such as J. J. Ross, who founded the school in Monrovia. Sometimes the generosity comes from people who might not seem to have much to share, such as Nathan Ross Sr., whose own life story begins with his father's enslavement, and who saw his power evaporate after the Liberian coups in 1980, yet managed to create a better life for his children in

the United States while continuing to provide financial support to
needy relatives back home.

Other connections are more difficult to reconcile, because even
generosity can be rooted in self-interest, and this is also a story about
the desire for control, and the quest for dominance—whether as a
means of survival or exploitation or out of necessity. Sometimes, it may
be a combination of all three. The desire to dominate was there among
slaveholders, among soldiers in both countries' civil wars, and among
slaves in the two Mississippis. It is there today among people in both
places who struggle against overwhelming odds. Dominance may
sometimes be the only alternative to being dominated, but it is dominance just the same.

The most dominant figure of the story was Isaac Ross, who helped
defeat the British as a captain in the revolutionary army, ruled over a
fiefdom of his own creation, controlled the fates of hundreds of slaves,
then triumphed, from the grave, over a legal and judicial system in
antebellum Mississippi that was at times overtly hostile to his aims.
Ross's success placed him at the forefront of those who contributed to
a broader legacy that still reverberates, in both Mississippis, and likely
will for years to come.

History is written according to the perspectives in vogue at a given
time, and during my research I found that even official documents
were sometimes erroneous or misleading. I figure my own account is
just the latest iteration, but I have tried my best to be objective and
fair, and to clearly frame my own subjectivity when I suspected it was
coming into play. A bona fide historian would have approached this
story differently than I have, partly because I was interested not only in
historical facts but in how the story was transformed by different narrators. As a result, when the record conflicted with or seemed irrelevant to the people I interviewed, I gave them leeway.

Those people included anyone I could find who knew about
Liberia or Prospect Hill or who was related to the Ross family, but
because African-American genealogy is so poorly documented, I
sometimes had to take leaps of faith—assuming, for instance, that a
black family with the surname Ross from the Prospect Hill area was
related to the story. My rationale was that a person who was descended
from slaves from the Prospect Hill area and who was related to the
Rosses could shed light on the story even if their own family line was

not clearly documented. Likewise, I did not question the provenance of certain Rosses who figured prominently in Liberian history, some of whom originated from Prospect Hill and others of whom immigrated from Georgia. There are only a handful of historians to document the nation's history, and while I drew much from them, in cases where family accounts and their research were in conflict, I let the families have their say.

In some cases the subjectivity of people I interviewed is not plainly evident, and there are no doubt mistakes that might need to be corrected—if only the information were available to correct them or to even prove that they are mistakes. I have been tolerant, perhaps to a fault, of variant spellings, genealogical hiccups, grammatical errors, and other irregularities from my sources, and I have preserved these variations. Even simple spelling errors can have a profound effect upon such a long, contentious and unevenly documented story as this one, but I have not attempted to correct them except when they were significant and obvious. I have let stand, undisturbed, certain disparities in the written record as well, such as the interchangeable use of the names Russ and Ross, and Read and Reed. Who can say, from this distance, in a world where a person might be documented just once in their entire lifetime in a single newspaper, and have their name misspelled, that one name might not be meant to represent another? In my account of the marriages of certain Ross relations who were said to be of mixed racial ancestry, it would have been useful to know whether "Randall" is interchangeable with "Randell" or "Randle," but I could not clarify these variations with any certainty.

I have quoted at length from the written record that I uncovered because in some cases this book may be the only publication of these facts. Whatever the outcome of Liberia's current tumult, history will be deprived of many of the details of how it all came to be, because the majority of the nation's historical records have been destroyed during the course of its conflicts. The outlook is only slightly better for many of the historical records in Jefferson County. A great many documents from Prospect Hill and the antebellum era are preserved at the Mississippi Department of Archives and History and in other public and private collections, but those that have managed to survive at the county courthouse are far from secure. County officials across the state have asked the Mississippi legislature for permission to destroy records that are taking up precious room, and regardless of whether they are granted their request, many irreplaceable documents that shed light on Prospect Hill and other stories that have yet to be told are moldering in tattered boxes and in some cases being surreptitiously hauled away. Those records are not always infallible, but they were crucial to the telling of this story, because they are often the most reliable source amid so many conflicting accounts. As an anonymous Liberian immigrant quoted on Joseph Tellewoyan's website said, when offering advice to others seeking to immigrate to the United States, "Remember: In America, if it is not written, it was never done." The written record is paramount—it was both the reason the Liberian journalists were arrested and the reason they were later released, because otherwise the government faced no accountability for its actions against them.

Finally, I have chosen not to provide the reader with certain tools typically offered in historical accounts—photographs, footnotes, indices, genealogical tables, and the obtrusive *sic.* I wanted the story to speak for itself as much as possible. I have mentioned the locations of unpublished manuscripts only when it seems germane, or when it is a prerequisite for their use (as with Thomas Johnson's memoir, *Twenty-Eight Years a Slave*, which is housed at the University of North Carolina at Chapel Hill). Again, my rationale is that this book is not a history, per se. It is an account of a story that gallops unpredictably and sometimes unaccountably across history, which is never cut-and-dried.

When Thomas Wade, the son of Isaac Ross Wade, was telling the story of Prospect Hill in the early twentieth century, he simplified it. When descendants repeat it today, they choose their own focus. I have sought to fill in the blanks, to point out significant discrepancies, to suggest other possibilities, to advance the story and draw from more varied stories, but it is still a process of winnowing. There is no doubt that I have left things out, misunderstood others, and imposed my own vantage point.

The history of the American South did not once have much room for details that we find particularly interesting today, such as intimate relationships between slave owners and slaves, the fact that Confederate soldiers deserted the cause by the thousands toward the end of the Civil War, that immigrants rioted over being drafted into the Union army in New York, that some African-Americans owned slaves, or that a traveler through the antebellum South might encounter "white" slaves, slaves on shopping sprees, or slaves along the road, at large without permission. Likewise, in revising history, we may steer away from essential truths that have been subverted in the past, in reaction to them. In the end we have only the story's pieces, and we pick among them.

We still have much to learn about the story of Isaac Ross, the slaves of Prospect Hill, and their legacies in Mississippi and Liberia today. As the story continues to unfold on both sides of the Atlantic, I hope that its essential truth will become clearer, and not lost to the vagaries of time.

SOURCES

The paper trail that forms the basis for this book ran from the haphazard files of the Jefferson County courthouse to a variety of state and national archives and Internet sites. Some of those sources are easily reviewed, such as those in the Library of Congress and the Mississippi Department of Archives and History, where a great deal of information is available in relevant subject files. Unfortunately, some are not so easily reviewed, if they can be reviewed at all. The Liberian national archives has been destroyed, and the most crucial documents relating to the litigation of Isaac Ross's will languish in the Jefferson County courthouse, where a prospective researcher must sort through boxes of incomplete documents in no particular order without the benefit of indexes. The following are among the more easily accessible sources:

Mississippi and the United States

Becoming Southern: The Evolution of a Way of Life, Warren County and Vicksburg, Mississippi, 1770–1860, by Christopher Morris, Oxford University Press, 1995.

Before Freedom, When I Just Can Remember, edited by Belinda Hurmence, John F. Blair Publishing, 1989.

"Claiming Place: Bi-Racial American Portraits," *Frontline* report memo, 1996.

Clarion-Ledger, The, November 18, 1984; February 1, March 17, 2001.

"Dear Master": Letters from a Slave Family, edited by Randall M. Miller, University of Georgia Press, 1978.

Emergence of the Cotton Kingdom in the Old Southwest, The, by John Hebron Moore, Louisiana State University Press, 1988.

Fayette Chronicle, The, October 3, 1913.

Journal of Mississippi History, Vol. IX, 1947, publication of Mississippi Historical Society, article by Thomas Wade.

Journal of Mississippi History, fall 2002, publication of Mississippi Historical Society, article by Rebecca Dresser.

Judicial Cases Concerning American Slavery, by Helen T. Catterall, Washington, 1926–37, William S. Hein & Co., 1998.

Library of Congress, WPA slave narratives and African-American Mosaic Exhibit.

Natchez Democrat, The, March 29, April 6, 2003.

Natchez on the Mississippi, by Harnett Kane, Random House, 1947; 1998.

Prince Among Slaves: The True Story of an African Sold into Slavery in the American South, by Terry Alford, Oxford University Press, 1977.

Record of the Descendants of Isaac Ross and Jean Brown, A, by Annie Mims Wright, Press of Consumers Stationery & Printing Co., 1921.

Reveille, The, August 21, 1902.

Selected Speeches, by Booker T. Washington, Doubleday, Doran & Co., 1932.

Slavery in Mississippi, by Charles Sydnor, Peter Smith Publishing, 1933.

Slavery Remembered, by Paul Escott, University of North Carolina Press, 1979.

Slaves of Liberty: Freedom in Amite County, Mississippi, 1820–1868, The, by Dale Edwyna Smith, Garland Publishing, 1999.

South-West by a Yankee, The, by Joseph Holt Ingraham, Harper, 1835.

Twenty-Eight Years a Slave, by Thomas Johnson, housed at the University of North Carolina at Chapel Hill.

Liberia

Abolitionists Abroad: American Blacks and the Making of Modern West Africa, by Lamin Sanneh, Harvard University Press, 1999.

African-American Diaspora: Who Were the Dispersed? The, by John Singler, unpublished.

Africana.com (undated).

Africanpubs.com (undated).

allAfrica.com, May 7, May 12, May 13, 2003.

American Colonization Society publications, including *Emigration to Liberia,* New York Colonization Society report, 1848, and *The African Repository and Colonial Journal,* February 1848.

Guardian, The, December 30, 2002.

Land and People of Liberia, The, by Mary Louise Clifford, Lippincott, 1971.

Liberian Dreams: Back-to-Africa Narratives from the 1850s, by William Jeremiah Moses, Pennsylvania State University Press, 1998.

New York Times, The, 1852, day unknown; October 22, 1992; February 4, 1998; May 15, 2003.

Panafrican News Agency, March 27, 2001, report.

Perspective, The, online periodical, spring 2000; fall 2000; spring 2001.

Roll of Emigrants to the Colony of Liberia Sent by the American colonization society from 1820 to 1843, The, housed at the University of Wisconsin.

Settlers in Sinoe County, Liberia, by Jo Mary Sullivan, Boston University Graduate School, 1978.

Washington Post, The, June 4, December 29, December 30, December 31, 2002; May 15, 2003.

ACKNOWLEDGMENTS

When I showed up at the Jefferson County Chancery Clerk's office in 2000, searching for records of the Prospect Hill litigation, I was blissfully ignorant of what I was getting into. It did not take long to realize that even the most rudimentary research was going to be difficult, and that I would need the help of others—a lot of others. Nekisha Ellis, in the clerk's office, quickly rose to the occasion, and introduced me to Ann Brown, the local genealogist who proved indispensable in helping locate people who could shed light on the story.

From there the list of people who were willing and able to help continued to grow. Among the more important were the two people who first told me the story, Tinker Miller and his mother, Gwen Shipp. When it became apparent that the most dramatic consequences of what happened at Prospect Hill were still unfolding in Liberia, my friends Lee and Dick Harding and Libby and Paul Hartfield overcame their reservations about my personal safety to give me the encouragement I needed to go. John Singler responded to one of my Internet postings and set about making the trip possible and ultimately productive, and helped me with contacts and background on Liberia. Sebastian Junger, who has covered more than his share of stories in dangerous places, offered valuable nuts-and-bolts advice that for all practical purposes enabled me to go, and later helped make this book possible by introducing me to my literary agents, Stuart Krichevsky, who saw merit in the book, and point person Patty Moosbrugger, who hit the ground running once the manuscript was in her hands, coached me on how to make it better, and sold my editor, Brendan Cahill, on the idea. I am indebted to Brendan, in turn, for making the book much better than it would have been without his involvement, which is everything you can hope for from an editor, and to his boss, my publisher, William Shinker, for sharing our enthusiasm. I met all of them through Sebastian, though at the time I first contacted him, we had never met. Sebastian has been highly successful as a journalist, but he has never forgotten why he became one or how important this kind of help can be.

Countless other sources helped me along the way, beginning with reporter Butch John, who referred me to Maureen Sieh, a Liberian living in the United States, who in turn led me to journalist Kenneth Best, who made his own recommendations. Ray Wright led me to Turner Ross, Nekisha led me to Butch Nichols, who introduced me to her aunt, Delores Ross Smith, who sent me to see Ruth O'Neal. The list goes on and on. The book benefited from the help of so many who responded to my Internet postings or recommended useful websites, including Ed Adams and Tewroh-Wehtoe Sungbeh, the latter of whom told me about the meeting of the Sinoe County Association of the Americas, where I met Evans Yancy and several other members who suggested people to talk with, including Janice Sherman and Jameille Nelson Ross, who then referred me to Nathan Ross Sr. At the U.S. State Department's Liberia Desk, John Olson put me in touch with people at the embassy in Monrovia and kept me abreast of breaking news as I prepared for my trip, while Associated Press correspondent Alex Zavis offered much-needed advice on travel there.

I am grateful to those who encouraged me and/or fretted over me while I was gone: my parents, A. D. and Inez Huffman, and the rest of my family, Judy and John Seymour, Pam and Buzz Shoemaker, Michelle and Devin Basham, and Erin and Bryan Anderson, as well as my friends the Hardings (and Lee, especially, for saving my eyesight by helping to transcribe nineteenth-century documents), the Hartfields, Andy and Jimmye Sweat, Josh Zimmer, Paul de Pasquale, Scottie Harmon, Neil and Catherine Payne, Robbyn Footlick and Robert Drury, Michael Rejebian and Cyrille Robic, who put me up in London and baby-sat me in the days before I left for Liberia.

I am indebted to countless Liberians, including those who not only ensured that my trip was safe but that it was productive and otherwise rewarding: the Raileys, my fixer in Monrovia (who, alas, must remain unnamed), the Joneses, Peter Toe, Charlie Kollie (to whom I was referred by Thomas Banks, owner of West African Safaris, who also helped with the logistics of the trip), the staff of St. Teresa's convent (especially Sister Scholastica Swen and Brother Dennis Hever), Drs. Joseph Guannu and Sleweon Nepe at the University of Liberia, and the staffs of J. J. Ross High School and the American embassy (especially Sarah Morrison).

I am equally grateful to everyone who was willing to sit down and talk with me about their lives and family history: the Raileys, the Joneses, the people at J. J. Ross, Rev. Charleston Bailey, Youjay Innis, Alton Johnson, Laverne McPhate, Tinker Miller, Hobbs Freeman, Butch Nichols, Benjamin and Georgia Ross, Nathan Sr. and Alice Ross, Nathan Ross Jr., Susie

Ross, Turner Ross, Delores Ross, and Robert Wade. Those toward the end of that list are the reason I chose to identify people in the book by their given name, rather than their surname, because in a story that follows several families so closely for so many generations, it was just too confusing otherwise.

I am also grateful to John McCarter for his efforts to preserve Prospect Hill and for indulging my interest in the cemetery and grounds, to Paul V. Ott for helping me track down and interpret old legal documents (which makes him *solely* responsible if there are errors), and to Judy Long, who tried.

Finally, I am thankful to James Belton, a very important and generous man, in my book, for bringing it all together in the end.

INDEX

Alan Huffman is the author of the photoessay book *Ten Point: Deer Camp in the Mississippi Delta,* and he has written for numerous newspapers and magazines, including the *Los Angeles Times, The Atlanta Journal-Constitution, The Clarion-Ledger, Smithsonian, Outside, The Oxford American,* and *National Wildlife*. He lives in Bolton, Mississippi.